On the Same Page

with

God

Embracing the Power of Praying Scripture

Jenn Soehnlin

On the Same Page with God
Embracing the Power of Praying Scripture

Copyright © 2024 Jenn Soehnlin

ISBN - Paperback: 979-8-9908941-0-5
ISBN - eBook: 979-8-9908941-1-2

For permission requests, write to the author at jenn.soehnlin@gmail.com or visit the author's website at https://www.embracing.life

Cover design by aksaramantra with assets designed by Freepik

Interior formatting by Autograph Publishing

"In *On the Same Page with God*, Jenn Soehnlin is a trusted mentor and authentic friend who guides us on the life-changing journey of praying Scripture over our circumstances. As we follow Jenn's lead to practice the sacred art of aligning our prayers with the heart of God, we will witness the transformative power of prayer when God's Word comes alive and plays out in tangible ways. This is a needed resource every Christian should have!"

   Becky Beresford, Speaker, Coach, and Author of *She Believed HE Could, So She Did.*

"This book is an excellent resource for those who want to pray God's Word back to Him, full of practical advice from the heart of a woman who's seeking Him earnestly. It's as if you're learning from a friend, and your prayer life will be better for it."

   Traci Rhoades, author of *Not All Who Wander (Spiritually) Are Lost* and *Shaky Ground: What to Do After the Bottom Drops Out*

"Jenn has lovingly guided us back to Jesus's feet, where we can cast our cares and embrace the yoke being easy and the burden being light. These prayers are heartfelt and spirit-led. This is a must-have resource for every person of faith."

   Laura Gethers, owner of Love Harder Marriage Coaching and author of *Pray Hard. Love Harder*

"Jenn delicately and honestly creates the perfect space for spiritual growth and transformation. She connects the practice of prayer to a love for Scripture, uncovering an intimate journey for readers. Jenn provides profound insights with authenticity and grace, making her book an ideal companion for anyone seeking to enrich their spiritual life and form a deep relationship with God."

   Mary Rooney Armand, creator of ButterflyLiving and author of *Identity* and *Life Changing Stories*

Table of Contents

Introduction

I've experienced firsthand how praying Scripture can transform your prayer life and your faith. Learning to pray Scripture is a beautiful journey of growing deeper in your prayer life, aligning your heart with the heart of God, and knowing that you are fighting for the things that matter to you and to God with both of the spiritual weapons we have been provided–prayer and His Word–combined together. Each time we read and pray Scripture, we are reminding ourselves of God's character, His promises, and His will. We find ourselves getting our hearts aligned with God, getting on the same page with God both literally and figuratively. And that is powerful and transformational indeed.

I wouldn't say I'm an expert on praying Scripture, but I've learned a lot about prayer and praying Scripture through personal experience, through reading books, and through reading the Bible, so you'll find a combination of all three in every chapter of this book. Sprinkled throughout the pages of this book, I'll also share several prayer practices that I hope will help you grow in your practice of praying Scripture. Some of these practices may resonate with you and others will not. We are all on a journey of discovering how to grow in our prayer life, and it will look different for each of us. We are each "fearfully and wonderfully made" (see Psalm 139:14), and that includes how we find ourselves best connecting with and worshiping our majestic Creator and our loving Heavenly Father.

At the end of each chapter, you'll find several Scripture-based prayers, which are meant to be a springboard to help you incorporate God's Word into your prayers. The Holy Spirit may bring other Scriptures to mind, or perhaps you already have several Scriptures you love to pray for each of these topics.

Unless indicated otherwise, the verses listed throughout this book are from the New International Version (NIV). I highly recommend you read the verses in the Scripture prayers at the end of each chapter in your own Bible. You may also want to read the verses before and after the Scripture listed to see it in its full context and see how that shapes your prayers as you pray a particular Scripture.

I encourage you to focus on each Scripture prayer, rather than reading through them all at once. Maybe pray one or two a day and meditate on them, or write out the Scripture in a journal, and then write out a prayer incorporating the Scripture. Make the Scriptures personal to the person or situation you are praying for. Insert names and pronouns and specific prayer requests related to the verse. The Word is alive and active (Hebrews 4:12), and you can enter into partnership with His Word by making it personal to your situation.

If a verse really resonates with you, I encourage you to memorize it, if you haven't already. Write out the verse(s) you want to memorize, place it where you will see it, and read and recite it throughout the day until it sinks deep into your heart and mind. The more of God's Word you have memorized, the more it will work its way into your heart and your prayers.

At the end of this book, you'll find a list of discussion questions to help you reflect on and apply the content in each chapter. If you're leading a small group, these questions could help guide your group discussions.

Thank you for joining me on this journey of embracing the power and practice of praying Scripture together. May this book and the practice of praying Scripture bless your prayer life and your faith abundantly.

Part 1

The Practice of Praying Scripture

Chapter 1

The Power of Praying Scripture

Have faith in God. I tell you the truth, you can say to this mountain,
"May you be lifted up and thrown into the sea," and it will happen.

–Mark 11:22-23 NLT

I discovered the power of praying Scripture one Tuesday night at a women's Bible study during one of the hardest seasons of my life. The Bible study itself wasn't about praying Scripture. To be honest, I don't even remember which Bible study we were going through at the time, though I do remember after our discussion, our leader asked for prayer requests like usual.

My mind swirled with the overwhelming flood of doubts, anxieties, and challenges I was experiencing at the time. I had so many prayer requests, I didn't even know where to start, so I usually kept my requests to myself or kept them at surface level. I was tired of praying for mountains to move and watching nothing happen. I was tired of feeling like God was silent and far away when I needed Him the most. But hope fanned afresh in my hurting heart–maybe He would answer the prayers of the ladies in my Bible study group.

And so before I even knew what I was doing, I shared everything that had been weighing on my soul and my mind for the last few years. The multiple diagnoses of both my sons. The challenges of meeting all their extra needs. The never-ending appointments to help them learn to do what came effortlessly to most children. My wrestling with why a good God would create and give me two children with special needs. Me questioning if the reason God wasn't answering my desperate prayers was because I lacked a strong-enough faith.

After it all came spilling out, I stared down at my hands clasped tightly in my lap, ashamed of the struggles I had dared to speak aloud. I feared their reaction to my vulnerability, and yet yearned for God to move through one of these women.

I will never forget what happened next. Without anyone saying a word, each woman abandoned her chair and Bible study materials, and they all gathered around me. Each of them laid a hand on me, and they took turns praying over me.

Warm, salty tears spilled down my cheeks and splattered onto my jeans as I listened to the prayers of these women. I honestly don't remember a single specific prayer that was prayed over me that night, but what stands out so clearly to me is that every single woman incorporated Scripture into her prayer.

They each took a turn boldly declaring the Word of God over me–my anxiety, my doubts, my faith, my struggles, my children, and my marriage. Scriptures they had memorized–and perhaps even clung to in their own moments of need–were infused into their prayers and claimed over me and my faith and my family.

Cocooned by the hands, love, and prayers of these women, I felt my storm of anxieties and doubts dissipate. As the women finished their prayers and I joined them in their final "Amen," I realized my weeping had changed from tears of grief and shame to those of joy, hope, thankfulness, and freedom.

I felt the power and peace and love of God in that moment. I experienced the power of praying Scripture. And I wanted to experience that power, peace, and love for the rest of my life.

How Prayer Can Get Us "On the Same Page" with God

Jesus promises in John 15:7 that "if you remain in me and my words remain in you, ask whatever you wish, and it will be done for you." Psalm 37:4 tells us to "take delight in the LORD, and he will give you the desires of your heart." Sometimes we take those verses too literally, believing that God is similar to our personal genie, granting us whatever we ask. However, what these verses indicate is that as we remain in God–through prayer, reading His Word, and delighting in His presence–we'll find our desires aligning with His desires and our will with His will.

Jodie Berndt says in her book *Praying the Scriptures for Your Life* that Jesus' promise in John 15:7 indicates that "the Bible–God's Word–actually creates our desires. The more we dig into Scripture, letting the words we read penetrate our thoughts and shape our perspective, the more our longings will start to reflect what God already wants to do."[1]

Praying Scripture is powerful because in the Bible God has given us the words that He wants us to know, believe, claim, and pray. We tend to pray for the things we want to see happen, but praying Scripture will help align our desires with what God wants to see happen. And when our desires are aligned, that's when we're most likely to see God move powerfully in our prayers and in our hearts.

My desire was that God would miraculously heal my children. I clung to the Bible story of the man born blind who was healed by Jesus "so that the works of God might be displayed in him" (John 9:3b). I imagined how much glory God would receive if we could tell our friends and our church members the testimony of my children experiencing miraculous healing. But through the practice of praying Scripture, God helped me lay down my own desires for my children and instead start praying for His will for them. God had other plans in mind so that His work would be displayed in my life and my sons' lives. It wasn't my boys' healing that would bring God glory, it was my own.

Instead of healing my boys, God began teaching me a lot about faith and prayer and parenting my neurodiverse children. He helped me to see that my children weren't broken or in need of healing but that they were "fearfully and wonderfully made" (see Psalm 139:14) and had so much to offer the world around them. He taught me a lot about His will and His goodness, about the power of praying Scripture, about community, and so much more. If God had simply healed my boys and answered all my prayers, I wouldn't be writing this book, nor would I have written my first book for Christian mothers who have a child with special needs.[2] Instead, when I surrendered to His words and His will and His plan, I was able to experience what God says in Jeremiah 33:3: "Call to me and I will answer you and tell you great and unsearchable things you do not know."

When describing our journey of learning to pray, Richard J. Foster writes, "In the beginning we are indeed the subject and the center of our prayers. But in God's time and in God's way a Copernican revolution takes place in our heart. Slowly, almost imperceptibly, there is a shift in our center of gravity. We pass from thinking of God as part of our life to the realization that we are part of his life. Wondrously and mysteriously God moves from the periphery of our prayer experience to the center. A conversion of the heart takes place, a transformation of the spirit."[3]

The phrase or concept of being "on the same page" with someone is to have the same understanding about a particular topic or to be in complete agreement with someone else. Getting on the same page means that as you communicate with each other, your perspectives, understanding, and your hearts are coming into alignment with each other. This can be a messy yet beautiful process. When we pray God's Word, we are expressing that we understand and agree with God's words in the Bible–His literal words spelled out for us on a page–and we want to claim those words for ourselves.

Praying God's Word gives us the hope, peace, and confidence that we're praying in alignment with His will because we remind ourselves of God's character and His promises. We then find ourselves getting on the same page with God (both literally and figuratively), praying in agreement with the Bible, aligning our hearts with His. Timothy Keller writes, "Without immersion in God's Word, our prayers may not be merely limited and shallow, but also untethered from reality. We may be responding not to the real God, but to what we wish God and life to be like ... Your prayer must be firmly connected to and grounded in your reading of the Word. The wedding of the Bible and prayer anchors your life down in the real God."[4]

Sometimes, we want God to move our mountains (see Mark 11:23) in a great demonstration and a mighty miracle. We've seen and heard of God doing mighty miracles throughout Scripture and in other peoples' lives, and we long to see it happen in our own. But God doesn't always work that way. Though Elijah experienced a great and powerful wind, an earthquake, and fire, he didn't experience God in them. Instead, Elijah felt God's power and presence in His gentle whisper (see 1 Kings 19:11-13). After recovering from God's presence in His gentle whisper, Elijah was ready to receive the new purpose God had for Him and God's provision for Elijah's journey. The mountain didn't move, but Elijah now had what he needed to go where God was sending him.

Yes, God can move the mountains we ask Him to move. Prayers are prayed and then bodies are healed, souls saved, and needs met in miraculous ways that could only be orchestrated by God. But what I've learned–and I hope you experience as well–is that sometimes the mountains God moves are the mountains in our hearts and in our minds. And having those mountains moved can be just as miraculous.

The Power of Having a Prayer Practice

Anytime the disciples found Jesus alone, it was often because He was in prayer. The disciples saw Jesus living a life of prayer and communion with God and they wanted to experience it too. Out of all the questions the disciples asked Jesus throughout the Gospels, there is only one thing they asked Jesus to teach them: "Lord, teach us to pray" (see Luke 11:1).

Like the disciples, we know prayer is a beautiful gift that helps us communicate with our Creator, but sometimes it can feel challenging and mysterious. Scripture indicates that prayer isn't always easy. Jesus sweat blood and persevered in prayer in the olive grove as He wrestled to align His will with His Father's. Paul says that we may wrestle in prayer (see Colossians 4:12). Yet despite the struggling and the wrestling we experience, we know prayer is important and powerful, and we want to learn to pray more effectively. To pray more like Jesus. Jesus is the perfect Teacher to ask for help in learning how to pray. And the Bible offers us a rich treasure trove of examples of prayer, as well as God-breathed words we can embed in our prayers.

Both Jesus' example and God's Word can help us grow in our individual prayer practices. And indeed, prayer is an individual thing, unique to each and every one of us.

Sometimes we may compare our prayer lives and long to pray more like certain prayer warriors we know and admire, and that can be paralyzing to our prayer life. Jaime Hampton offers these beautiful words of encouragement: "There are countless ways comparison or false expectations paralyze us in our prayer lives. If you want to know what a prayer warrior looks like, look in the mirror. Seriously. God has given you gifts. He's given you talents. He's given you a unique communication style and learning style and motivational style, so that there is literally no one else on this planet that can pray like you. So my challenge to you is to stop looking around at how everyone else is praying, stop trying to live up to imaginary expectations and start praying like you and nobody else."[5]

Each of us has an individual relationship with God, so that means that our methods of connecting with God and hearing from God will be different and unique. David prayed in Psalm 141:2a, "May my prayer be set before you like incense." Our prayers and the prayer practices we are drawn toward are all a unique and beautiful offering to Him. No one else can pray and worship like you do and that's to be celebrated.

No matter where you are on your prayer journey–or how you find yourself turning to God in prayer–know that He is there and He is listening. He delights in whatever you have to give Him, whether it be a tear-filled one-word prayer or a weekend-long prayer retreat. If your heart is in it, it's beautiful to Him.

While there are numerous prayer practices and formulas you could try, prayer isn't meant to be perfect or overwhelming. It isn't about how eloquently we can say our prayers, but how earnestly we can communicate with our Heavenly Father. Prayer is about sharing your heart, your mind, and your soul with God and inviting Him into your circumstances, as well as your heart, your mind, and your will. It's a sacred time of being heard, loved, and changed by the Creator of the universe and the Lover of our soul.

Praying Scripture is considered a spiritual discipline and a prayer practice, and it takes both practice and discipline to grow in and refine this transformative form of prayer.

I pray that as you practice praying Scripture, you'll freshen and deepen your prayer life and find great delight and satisfaction in Him. I pray that you would find the Bible to be a treasure trove of prayer possibilities, rejuvenating your faith and your prayer life. And I pray that you'll find mountains moving as you find yourself more and more on the same page as our loving Father.

Scripture Prayers for a Mountain-Moving Prayer Life

God, our glorious Father, and our Lord Jesus Christ, may You give me the spirit of wisdom and revelation as I read Your Word, and may I grow in my practice of praying Scripture so that I may know You and Your heart better. I pray that the eyes of my heart may be enlightened so that I may know the hope to which You have called me, the riches of Your glorious inheritance in the saints, and Your incomparably great power for all of us who believe. Thank You that the same power that raised Jesus from the dead is in me! May this resurrection power bring new life to my heart, my faith, and my prayers. (Based on Ephesians 1:17-20.)

God, increase my faith in You and in the power of prayer. May I say to the mountains (in my life, in my heart, and in my mindsets) to move, and may they be moved! I praise You for having the power to move mountains. (Based on Mark 11:23.)

How lovely is Your dwelling place, O Lord Almighty! May my soul yearn, even faint for Your presence and Your Word. May my heart and my flesh cry out for You, the living God. (Based on Psalm 84:1-2.)

Lord, give me a heart to know You. Help me to return to You with my whole heart. (Based on Jeremiah 24:7.)

Heavenly Father, help me to approach Your throne of grace with confidence and receive all that You have for me. (Based on Hebrews 4:16.)

May I call upon You and come and pray to You, knowing that You will listen to me. May I seek You and find You when I search for You with my whole heart. (Based on Jeremiah 29:12-13.)

As I seek You in prayer and in Your Word, may You put a new heart and a new spirit inside me. Remove my heart of stone and give me a heart of flesh. (Based on Ezekiel 36:26.)

Chapter 2

Benefits of Praying Scripture

Prayer does change things, all kinds of things. But the most important thing it changes is us. [6]

–R.C. Sproul

A few weeks after the women in my Bible study had introduced me to the power of praying Scripture, I was driving my two- and four-year-old boys down a country two-lane road to a therapy appointment. My car suddenly slowed, and I heard a steady bump-bump-bump-bump right outside my driver's side window.

My anxiety skyrocketed. I pulled over, and a quick check of my front tire confirmed my fear. I called the therapists' office to let them know we had a flat tire and wouldn't be able to make it to our appointment. I didn't call anyone to come help because as providence –or God–would have it, I had pulled over right in front of a family-owned auto shop.

With my confused kids and their belongings in tow, we entered the auto shop, and I told the friendly man at the service desk what had happened. He promised to have it fixed within two hours and pointed me toward the tiny, toyless waiting area that smelled of motor oil and burnt coffee. Two hours of unplanned screen time later, the car was fixed. As I was paying the bill, the kind service guy casually mentioned, "We threw in an alignment for you as well."

I smiled, thanked him, and we trudged back to the car, eager to go home. But as I was driving home, that word "alignment" resonated over and over again in my spirit. I knew my newfound practice of praying Scripture was helping me align my will with God's will–or 'getting on the same page' as God, both literally and figuratively–as I shared about in the previous chapter.

Going through life–filled with its share of potholes and obstacles –we will naturally get out of alignment. Spending time with God in prayer and in His Word helps us get our hearts and minds back into alignment with God's heart and mind.

Just as a mechanic can align our tires when we bring our cars into their shop, God can gently align our hearts with His heart as we pray His words back to Him. And just as there are many benefits for our cars when we get the wheels aligned, so there are many benefits for our prayer life when we get our prayers aligned with God's Word.

Praying Scripture Focuses and Freshens Our Prayers

Prayer is a powerful gift and an incredible privilege. It allows us to personally connect with the God of the universe and move mountains in the circumstances around us or in our hearts. But, sometimes, prayer can feel a little boring, especially when we find ourselves praying the same requests over and over. Sometimes discouragement can set in as we wonder if our prayers are lined up with God's will for us. And sometimes our minds are pulled in many directions, making it difficult to focus on our prayers.

Praying God's Word can help us overcome many of those challenges. Donald J. Whitney writes that because we can trust God's Word and the character of God, the practice of praying Scripture will help our prayers "be far more biblical than if [we] just make up [our] own prayers. We tend to say the same old things about the same old things. And without the Scripture to shape our prayers, we are far more likely to pray in unbiblical ways than if we pray the thoughts that occur to us as we read the Scripture ... The Spirit of God will use the Word of God to help the people of God pray increasingly according to the will of God."[7]

After my transformative experience with the ladies in my Bible study—when they powerfully included Scripture in their prayers for me and my family—I was eager to do the same. I had been praying for my childrens' speech for years, but now I was determined to pray God's Word over their speech. My older son has a diagnosis of apraxia—a neurological speech disorder that requires years of frequent and intensive speech therapy to learn to speak. My younger son has a speech delay that accompanies an autism diagnosis.

I looked up and recorded every verse about words, speaking, and the mouth. There were hundreds. But two verses in particular really stood out to me: "How sweet are your words to my taste, sweeter than honey to my mouth!" (Psalm 119:103), and "a word fitly spoken is like apples of gold in settings of silver" (Proverbs 25:11 NKJV).

When each of my children said his first word and then slooooowly added to his vocabulary, I viewed each of those words as both something sweet to savor and a precious treasure. I combined the words I liked from both of these verses—"sweet" from Psalm 119:103 and "apples of gold" from Proverbs 25:11—to form my new prayer for my children. I prayed for "new sweet apples of gold" in my prayer time with God and on the way to speech therapy, and praised God for "new sweet apples of gold" after my children said a new word or phrase.

Finding God's own words to pray for my childrens' words brought a refreshing joy to my prayer life. The Bible became a rich library full of prayer possibilities, and learning to pray God's Word revived my prayer life and my faith. I found delight in praying again. Honestly, part of this joy was because I was witnessing God answer my heart's desire for my kids' speech. There were new "sweet apples of gold" from my sons each month, and each was a treasure. Seeing God answer your prayers does wonders for your faith. But a large part of what brought me joy was that the practice of praying the very words of God's own heart and mouth drew me so much closer to Him.

Just as my sons needed speech therapy to learn to effectively communicate with us, learning to pray Scripture helped me effectively communicate my prayers to God in a new and powerful way. Just as my sons persevered and slowly learned to string new sounds, then words, then phrases together to better express themselves, I slowly added new words and phrases from Scripture into my prayers to better articulate my desires, hopes, prayers, and praises to the Almighty. Just as my sons grew more confident in their speech the more they practiced, I gained confidence in my prayer life, knowing that I was praying God's Words and His will and His promises, rather than praying according to my own desires.

Joni Eareckson Tada writes, "I have learned to ... season my prayers with the word of God. It's a way of talking to God in his language–speaking his dialect, using his vernacular, employing his idioms ... This is not a matter simply of divine vocabulary. It's a matter of power. When we bring God's word directly into our praying, we are bringing God's power into our praying ... God's word is living, and so it infuses our prayers with life and vitality. God's word is also active, injecting energy and power into our prayer."[8]

I believe God feels honored when He hears the very words He has shared with us in Scripture included in our prayers. It shows Him that we're taking His Word and Him seriously, but also that we have such a familiarity with His words that they become part of our prayer vocabulary. It activates His power into our prayers.

Praying Scripture is a Powerful Weapon Against Spiritual Warfare

Whether we want to admit it or not, we are in a spiritual war. Our enemy is Satan, and his goal is to steal, kill, and destroy (see John 10:10) your faith, your family, your marriage, your purpose, your identity in Christ, and everything else that is God-given. Satan's mission is to leave us doubting God's goodness and His ability. Bob Sorge writes, "The nature of the enemy's warfare in your life is to cause you to become discouraged and to cast away your confidence. Not that you would necessarily discard your salvation, but you could give up your hope of God's deliverance. The enemy wants to numb you into a coping kind of Christianity that has given up hope of seeing God's resurrection power."[9]

God does not want us to be victims of Satan when He created us to be victors with Christ. God ensured that we have both protection and weapons to fight against this spiritual warfare, and the knowledge that ultimately this war against Satan will end in victory. Near the end of the Bible, we see Satan's defeat: "And the devil, who deceived them, was thrown into the lake of burning sulfur" (Revelation 20:10a).

In Ephesians 6:10-18 we are urged to suit up in the whole armor of God to protect ourselves. Then Paul tells us to "take the sword of the Spirit, which is the word of God. And pray in the Spirit on all occasions with all kinds of prayers and requests. With this in mind, be alert and always keep on praying." Many sources will say that there are six pieces of armor, with the Word of God, our sword, being our only offensive weapon. But Priscilla Shirer informs us, "There aren't only six pieces of armor. There are seven. Prayer is the linchpin that holds our armor together. It is what activates all the other pieces and fortifies you as a soldier in battle. It is the device that empowers and 'charges up' every other piece so they can be used effectively against the enemy. Without prayer ... your armor cannot, will not, be infused with the power that only God's Spirit can give."[10]

2 Corinthians 10:3-4 tells us, "For though we live in the world, we do not wage war as the world does. The weapons we fight with are not the weapons of the world. On the contrary, they have divine power to demolish strongholds." We'll learn more about spiritual warfare and the armor of God in chapter 8, but here we're focusing on the fact that we are provided with two weapons to fight against Satan's schemes–God's Word and prayer. Beth Moore describes the power of these two weapons combined: "God has handed us two sticks of dynamite with which to demolish our strongholds: His Word and prayer. What is more powerful than two sticks of dynamite placed in separate locations? Two strapped together."[11] Praying Scripture is how we strap those two pieces of dynamite together, lit by our faith and detonated by God's power to stop Satan's work in our lives.

Praying Scripture Bears Fruit in Our Hearts and in Our Lives

In elementary school, we learn about the water cycle. The rain and snow have a purpose: to nurture the seeds and plants below for our nourishment before returning back to the heavens. Isaiah 55:9-11 says,

> As the heavens are higher than the earth,
> so are my ways higher than your ways
> and my thoughts than your thoughts.
> As the rain and the snow
> come down from heaven,
> and do not return to it without
> watering the earth
> and making it bud and flourish,
> so that it yields seed for the sower

and bread for the eater,
so is my word that goes out from my mouth:
It will not return to me empty,
but will accomplish what I desire
and achieve the purpose for which I sent it.

God's Word also has a cycle. His Word is intended to teach, instruct, and nourish us. And then, when we live His words, speak His words, and pray His words, they return to Him having done what they were intended to do in our lives. Imagine how beautiful that is for God, to know that He spoke a word thousands of years ago that brings you so much hope and encouragement today. Or that brings conviction and puts you back on the path He wants you to be on, drawing nearer to His heart.

Everything God says has power and a purpose. God's Word will accomplish what it was intended to do, for all people, if we're open to listening to and learning from His Word. We are reminded that "all Scripture is breathed out by God and profitable for teaching, for reproof, for correction, and for training in righteousness, that the man of God may be complete, equipped for every good work" (2 Timothy 3:16-17 ESV).

God often gives us the Scriptures we need to read or hear exactly when we need them. Sometimes, we may have to wait a while before the Scripture we need is revealed, but when it comes, it is powerful—sometimes life- and faith-changing. Sometimes it's a verse we discover anew in our Bible reading, or one we hear in a worship song or sermon. Sometimes it's a verse a friend shares with us or we read in a book or see in a post on social media. Such is the power of God's Word and His desire for His Word to work in our lives.

We can be encouraged and transformed by hearing and reading His Word, but in praying His Word back to Him, we demonstrate that the Word is doing its work in our hearts and our lives. The cycle will continue over and over as we read and then pray Scripture, accomplishing the purposes that God's Word has intended for us.

As we abide in His presence (see John 15:5-8) and in God's Word, His Word takes root in our hearts and our prayers to bear fruit in our lives. As we pursue growing in our relationship with God through reading His Word and prayer, He molds us more and more into the image of His Son. As we seek the heart of God, we find ourselves exhibiting more of the character of Christ in the fruit of the Spirit (see Galatians 5:22-23). Jesus exhibited each of the fruit of the Spirit perfectly, and when we are abiding with Him, rooted in Him and His Word, the evidence will show through the fruit of the Spirit we bear in our own lives. Jesus says, "By this my Father is glorified, that you bear much fruit and so prove to be my disciples" (John 15:8 ESV).

The process of remaining in Him gives us the authority to pray mountain-moving prayers for the things we know are aligned with the will of God (see John 15:7)

Psalm 1:1-3 tells us, "Blessed is the one ... whose delight is in the law of the Lord, and who meditates on his law day and night. That person is like a tree planted by streams of water, which yields its fruit in season and whose leaf does not wither–whatever they do prospers." Being still in God's presence and soaking up His Word equips us to bear fruit and leaves that do not wither.

E. M. Bounds writes that "faith, and hope, and all the strong, beautiful, vital forces of piety are withered and dead in a prayerless life. The life of the individual believer, his personal salvation, and personal Christian graces have their being, bloom, and fruitage in prayer."[12]

As we remain in Him and His Word remains in our humble and prayerful hearts, we'll find ourselves being molded more and more into the character of Christ, bearing fruit for His glory.

Scripture Prayers for Your Prayer Life

Help me to be delighted in Your presence and Your character. May You align the desires of my heart with Yours, and give me the desires of my heart. (Based on Psalm 37:4.)

Help me to not pray empty phrases as the Gentiles do, but to pray Your words according to Your will. (Based on Matthew 6:7 ESV.)

Lord, help me take up both of my weapons of spiritual warfare: the sword of the Spirit, which is Your Word, and prayer. Help me to pray in the Spirit on all occasions, with all kinds of prayers and requests. (Based on Ephesians 6:17b-18.)

Oh Lord, may I remain in You and Your words remain in me. May I pray according to Your words and will. May my prayers and Your Words bear much fruit in my life and my heart, that I would show myself to be one of Your disciples. (Based on John 15:4-5, 7-8.)

Lord, thank You that prayer is powerful and effective. (Based on James 5:16b.)

God, as the heavens are higher than the earth, so are Your ways higher than my ways and Your thoughts than my thoughts. As the rain and the snow comes down from heaven and does not return to it without watering the earth and making it bud and flourish so that it yields seed for the sower and bread for the eater, so Your Word goes out from Your mouth. May Your Word not return to You empty, but may it accomplish what You desire in my life and my heart and achieve the purpose for which You sent it. (Based on Isaiah 55:9-11.)

Lord, I thank You that all Scripture is God-breathed, and I pray that You would use it in my life to teach me, correct me, and train me for righteousness, that I could be made complete, equipped for every good work. (Based on 2 Timothy 3:16-17 ESV.)

Father, soften my heart to hear and receive Your Word. May Your Word go down deep in the soil of my heart and in my prayers. May Your Word bear a fruitful crop in my heart, my life, and my prayer life. (Based on Matthew 13:8.)

Chapter 3

Praying with the Father, Son, and Holy Spirit

You cannot pray without the Trinity. If the full work of salvation requires a Trinity, so does that very breath by which we live. You cannot draw near to the Father except through the Son, and by the Holy Spirit. [13]

–Charles Spurgeon

I've read the story of Jesus' baptism many times, but recently while reading through the book of Luke I noticed something new. After Jesus was baptized, He began to pray. "And as he was praying, heaven was opened and the Holy Spirit descended on him in bodily form like a dove. And a voice came from heaven: 'You are my Son, whom I love; with you I am well pleased'" (Luke 3:21-22).

For a little over 400 years (from the end of the Old Testament until the beginning of Jesus' ministry), God's chosen people hadn't heard a single word from God. Until Jesus prayed. Jesus spoke to His Father, and the heavens were opened, and God's voice was heard by all those who were near. And the Holy Spirit descended upon Him. Jesus' prayer initiated the Holy Trinity all uniting together: Father, Son, and Holy Spirit. The whole Trinity is reunited and activated every time we pray too.

The concept of the Holy Trinity–or three persons in one–is hard to grasp but is foundational to our Christian faith and to our prayer life as well. We pray *to* the Father, *through* the Son, *by* the power of the Holy Spirit. Knowing the role each member of the Trinity plays as we pray is helpful as we begin or continue growing in our prayer journey.

The Father

One day, when my boys were about two and four years old, we went to a playground near their speech therapy clinic after their appointment. My older son wandered the perimeter of the playground and discovered sweet gum balls–a spiky, green fruit on the sweetgum tree that dries out and turns brown before dropping to the ground. He would pick up a prickly pod, inspect it between his fingers, then fling it at a tree, and walk a few steps until he found another gum ball. Another child, probably a year or so younger than my son, decided to join in.

"Mommy, what are these things?" he shouted toward his mother.

She didn't respond, preoccupied with caring for a baby in a stroller. I watched his head and shoulders droop in defeat, so I answered his question. He grinned at me and asked a few more questions about trees and fruit and seeds. He stared at the gum ball in his hand and then the tall tree above him, his mouth wide open in wonder. Then he giggled, sat down on the bench next to me, and shared with me his favorite facts about trees and dinosaurs and his new baby sister.

"Leave the nice lady alone," the mom said to him after a while, and he scampered off to play with the other kids. I watched my children play in their individual silence. My heart ached to know what was going on in my sons' heads, to hear them say mama, to hear their stories, their requests, their thoughts about the things that excited them, and the funny expressions they would say as they began to grasp language. I wanted to know what questions they had about the world around them and what they worried and wondered about.

And I realized, that's what God our Father wants from us too. He wants us to share our thoughts even though He already knows them. He wants us to ask our questions so He can supply the answers in His own way. He wants us to share our requests and petitions with Him. Nothing is too big or too small to bring before our Heavenly Father.

Jesus wanted everyone to know God was His Father, and He wants us to have that kind of relationship with God as well. He taught His disciples and followers that God is our Heavenly Father too. He longs for us to ask Him for everything we need so that He can be involved in our lives. Jesus also shows us that God is the one we pray to. In Luke 11 and Matthew 6 Jesus begins His prayer with "our Father, who art in heaven ..." He also states in Matthew 6:6, "But when you pray, go into your room, close the door, and pray to your Father, who is unseen. Then, your Father, who sees what is done in secret, will reward you."

That doesn't mean we can't talk directly to Jesus or to the Holy Spirit. We indeed can. My older son opens each of his prayers with, "Dear God and Jesus ..." and I adore it. But most of the time throughout Scripture, prayers are recorded as being prayed to God the Father.

Our Heavenly Father didn't just create us and leave us; He wants to be involved in every detail of our lives. Psalm 145:18a tells us, "The LORD is near to all who call on him." He's available and accessible to us. And not only that, but He loves us and is mindful of us (see Psalm 8:4). His heart is all about drawing near to our hearts.

I think sometimes we picture God as a tired or overwhelmed parent preoccupied with other situations. Or maybe as a mighty King sitting on His throne, only acknowledging us and our needs when it fits in with His schedule and priorities. But it's not an accurate picture of God. Timothy Keller eloquently said, "The only person who dares wake up a king at 3:00 AM for a glass of water is a child. We have that kind of access."[14] God isn't too busy to listen to our prayers, and He doesn't find our prayers tiring or overwhelming.

King David wrote one of my all-time favorite verses about prayer: "I love the Lord because he hears my voice and my prayer for mercy. Because he bends down to listen, I will pray as long as I have breath!" (Psalm 116:1-2 NLT). God wants to hear what we have to say so much that He bends closer to us to hear us. What an incredible picture of God's love for us and the relationship He desires to have with us as His beloved children.

Paul tells us, "You can tell for sure that you are now fully adopted as his own children because God sent the Spirit of his Son into our lives crying out, 'Papa! Father!' Doesn't that privilege of intimate conversation with God make it plain that you are not a slave, but a child? And if you are a child, you're also an heir, with complete access to the inheritance" (Galatians 4:4-7 MSG). We can go to our faithful heavenly Father with whatever is on our hearts. He has an abundance of good things He wants to bless us with as our loving Father. He won't spoil His children and give us everything we ask for, but He wisely and generously can provide us with everything we need and which are for our ultimate good.

The Son

One day I was experiencing an unusually hard day. I was frustrated with my children, who had missed their nap because we had been at an appointment that lasted longer than we expected. Now they were fussy and tired. I spent over an hour on the phone with a doctor's office and insurance and still hadn't resolved the issue. I was tired and cranky myself, and I asked God, "Where are you in all of this? Why aren't you helping me?" I desperately wanted to be alone with God, but the kiddos needed dinner and attention. And then bedtime rolled around.

After my older son, about four years old at the time, was all snuggled in bed and we had read his book, we prayed together. Sometimes I did the praying, and sometimes I did it fill-in-the-blank style, as he could only say one- or two-word phrases. That night, I decided to go with the fill-in-the-blank prayer. I prompted him, "Thank You, God, for _____."

He stared at me for a few seconds, then grinned and proudly declared, "Eesus!"

I choked back tears as I told him, "Yes! Thank You, God, for Jesus."

I'd never had any indication that he understood anything relating to God, Jesus, or Bible stories, except for identifying "baby Eesus" at Christmas time. I'd never prayed before using the words, "Thank You, God, for Jesus." It was his own spontaneous thought and prayer, and it filled my heart with hope and joy.

We finished our prayers, and I kissed that precious little guy goodnight. As I left his room it hit me: God had answered my angry prayer through the mouth of a child who would need years of speech therapy to be able to talk like his peers. I had demanded God tell me where He was and why it felt like He wasn't caring for us. And He gently reminded me that He loved me and my children so much He gave us Jesus.

Jesus left the comforts of heaven to become Immanuel, or "God with us," to live and dwell with us in our messy, sin-filled world because He wants to be with us. That kind of relationship and desire to be with us hasn't changed. Jesus knows each of us intimately. He listens to our prayers. He loves us. When we pray, we can imagine He is right beside us because He is! He longs to hear every word we pray, and He longs to help us experience all the victories of the spiritual realm that are available to us because of Jesus' death on the cross.

Timothy Keller writes in his book *Prayer*, "The only time in all the Gospels that Jesus prays to God and doesn't call him Father is on the cross, when he says, 'My God, my God, why have you forsaken me?' Jesus lost his intimate relationship with his Father so that we could gain access to a relationship with our Father. That is the great cost of prayer."[15] Jesus died so that by the power of His blood and in the power of His name we can approach the throne of God with confidence (see Hebrews 4:16). The curtain in the temple that separated all people (except the high priest) from the unapproachable holiness of God, was torn from top to bottom when Jesus breathed His last breath on earth (see Matthew 27:51), removing that separation forever. Before Jesus' death, only the high priest could enter the temple once a year and pray on behalf of the people. But now, we can pray on behalf of ourselves and our loved ones and pray for whatever is on our heart, because of Jesus' death on the cross.

Now we can pray whenever and wherever we want in Jesus' name. He told his disciples, "You can ask for anything in my name, and I will do it, so that the Son can bring glory to the Father. Yes, ask me for anything in my name, and I will do it!" (John 14:13-14 NLT).

In his book *A Praying Life*, Paul Miller writes, "The name of Jesus gives my prayers royal access. They get through. Jesus isn't just the Savior of my soul. He's also the Savior of my prayers. Asking in Jesus' name isn't another thing I have to get right so my prayers are perfect. It is one more gift of God because my prayers are so imperfect."[16] When we pray in Jesus' name, we are recognizing that we are able to pray because of Jesus. We come to the Father not by the sweat of our brow but by the blood of his Son. We can knock on the door and God will answer (see Matthew 7:7-8) because of the precious blood and the powerful name of Jesus. We can have personal access and an unbreakable relationship with God because of Jesus.

The Holy Spirit

My husband and I were contemplating a move to an area that would open doors for new opportunities for our children. There would be better support for our children in their future schools and even a special needs preschool we'd heard amazing things about that we were told our older son would be able to get into immediately if we applied. But the thought of moving away from friends, family, our church, and all that was familiar was daunting. So we went to the Lord in prayer.

Heads bowed, hands clasped, my husband prayed that God would give us wisdom and direction. And as he prayed, I heard a single word whispered in my heart: "Flourish." I strongly believed that the place we moved to would offer us a place where our family would flourish. It filled me with peace and excitement about the move. I couldn't wait to share with my husband what I had heard during our time of prayer. But he beat me to it.

"Jenn, when we were praying, I heard the Holy Spirit give me the word 'flourish.' I believe that if we move we are going to have a season of flourishing."

I occasionally have a word or phrase dropped into my heart that I know has to be a whisper from heaven because I would not think of it on my own. But to have my husband receive a word? And the same one as mine? A beautiful word we could cling to and remember God's goodness toward us? Priceless. Such is the love of God and the Holy Spirit working in our hearts.

We find in Isaiah 11:2 that the Holy Spirit provides us with wisdom and understanding, counsel and might, and with knowledge and fear of the Lord. Paul reassures us that the Holy Spirit helps us to pray when we don't have the words: "And the Holy Spirit helps us in our weakness. For example, we don't know what God wants us to pray for. But the Holy Spirit prays for us with groanings that cannot be expressed in words. And the Father who knows all hearts knows what the Spirit is saying, for the Spirit pleads for us believers in harmony with God's own will. And we know that God causes everything to work together for the good of those who love God and are called according to his purpose for them" (Romans 8:26-28 NLT).

When you feel at the end of your rope, overwhelmed by circumstances, and you have no idea what words to pray, the Holy Spirit is working and praying on your behalf. When all you can pray is, "Lord, help," or all you can do is cry before the Lord, the Holy Spirit is telling God exactly what it is you need.

The Holy Spirit is so important to our faith that Jesus told His disciples, "It is for your good that I am going away. Unless I go away, the Advocate will not come to you; but if I go, I will send him to you" (John 16:7). Everything Jesus did, people found amazing, and yet while He was on earth, He couldn't minister to every person individually like the Holy Spirit can. Jesus' death provided us all with the gift of the Holy Spirit to help us.

The Holy Spirit may seem mysterious. We rely on our senses to understand our world and make decisions, and the Holy Spirit is such an abstract being that He's hard to understand, let alone understand how and when we are praying in the Spirit. We use He/Him pronouns for the Holy Spirit because the Holy Spirit is a holy person of the Holy Trinity. In fact, author Dr. Saundra Dalton-Smith simply says Holy Spirit and leaves off the article 'the' all together, since Holy Spirit is a living being and not a thing.

Have you ever been praying and then suddenly a Scripture popped into your mind? Or you are praying and suddenly find yourself overwhelmed with an emotion, such as being moved to tears or feeling joy bubbling up within you? Have you ever suddenly found yourself boldly claiming the promises of God in your prayers? Have you ever felt you were suddenly in a different place while praying, as if you were right in the presence of God? Have you ever had the strong indication you needed to pray for someone or something in particular at a certain time?

Those are all some of the many ways that the Holy Spirit can move in your prayers. He helps make your prayers come alive with energy that goes straight to your heart and the throne of God. Sometimes it will feel amazing and electrifying, an incredible experience that we don't want to end. Other times it will indeed feel like groans, an inability to even find the words to say what your heart and mind are dealing with. It will look and feel different for all of us because the Holy Spirit is a personal being, bringing us into oneness with God in a way that aligns with our heart, giftings, and personality. Luckily, we have a whole lifetime to learn how to "pray in the Spirit on all occasions with all kinds of prayers and requests" (Ephesians 6:18a).

The Word of God

While reading my Bible one day in college, I discovered a verse I loved. So much so that I claimed it as my life verse. 1 Corinthians 1:5 declares, "For in him you have been enriched in every way." To me, it was a beautiful image of what it means to be a Christian, of God providing us with every physical and spiritual blessing we need.

It wasn't until almost a decade later, when I began searching for Bible verses that mentioned speech so that I could pray for my boys' speech, that I realized to my surprise that there was more to the verse. The verse in all its fullness states, "For in Him you have been enriched in every way, in all speech and all knowledge" (1 Corinthians 1:5 BSB). I don't remember if my heart skipped a beat or two, or if it started pounding, but surely it did one of the two. How had I missed this?!

I had been feeling a heavenly nudge to share the things God was teaching me about parenting my neurodiverse children with other moms of children with special needs, and this was confirmation.

One of the many amazing features about the Word of God is that it will mean different things to us in different seasons: "For the word of God is living and active, sharper than any two-edged sword, piercing to the division of soul and of spirit, of joints and of marrow, and discerning the thoughts and intentions of the heart" (Hebrews 4:12 ESV).

When I was a college student, my life verse reminded me that God provides us with everything we truly need. As an overwhelmed mom feeling an intimidating call to write about the things God was teaching me amidst all the challenges of being a special needs parent, my life verse informed me that God's provision includes the equipping to do and say the very things He has called us to complete.

Paul E. Miller reminds us that "we need the sharp-edged absolute character of the Word and the intuitive, personal leading of the Spirit.

The Word provides the structure, the vocabulary. The Spirit personalizes it to our life."[17]

The Word has the power to convict, to crush the hardness in our hearts, and bring about repentance. "'Is not My word like a fire?' says the Lord, 'And like a hammer that breaks the rock in pieces?'" (Jeremiah 23:29 NKJV).

The Word also has the power to gently mold us more into the image of Christ. We are told that God is the potter and we are the clay (see Isaiah 64:8). I'm not a potter, but I have seen how potters add a bit of water to the clay to keep it soft and malleable. Throughout the Bible, water is sometimes used as a symbol for God's Word, having the power to revive us, to soften our hearts, to wash us clean, to shape us according to His will and His purpose for us.

God's Word can also be wielded to defeat Satan, as Jesus demonstrated while being tempted in the wilderness (see Matthew 4:1-13).

The Bible has the power to teach, correct, guide, encourage, and protect us. Every time we read our Bibles, the Holy Spirit will help us glean something new from it, something we need to read for the current season we find ourselves in. Every time you open your Bible it can seem fresh, if you're open to letting the Holy Spirit lead you into new truths. His Word will continually guide you toward being on the same page with our heavenly Father.

Scripture Prayers to the Trinity

I love You, Lord, and I thank You that You hear my voice and my prayer for mercy. Because You bend down to listen to my prayers, may I pray as long as I have breath! (Based on Psalm 116:1-2 NLT.)

Heavenly Father, may I approach Your throne of grace with confidence, receiving mercy and finding grace and help in my time of need. (Based on Hebrews 4:16.)

Thank You, Jesus, that whatever we ask our Father in Your name, it will bring glory to the Father. Thank You that You will do what we ask in Your holy, precious, and powerful name. (Based on John 14:13.)

Thank You, Jesus, that because of You we have access in one Spirit to our Heavenly Father. (Based on Ephesians 2:18.)

Thank You, Christ Jesus, that You are at the right hand of God and are interceding for us in prayer. (Based on Romans 8:34.)

Thank You, Holy Spirit, that You help us pray in our weakness. We do not know what we ought to pray for, but You intercede for us with groans that words cannot express. You intercede for us in accordance with God's will. (Based on Romans 8:26-27.)

Holy Spirit, may I grow in my ability to pray in Your Spirit at all times and on every occasion. May I pray with persistence. (Based on Ephesians 6:18 NLT.)

Thank You, God, that Your Word is living and active, sharper than any two-edged sword, piercing to the division of soul and of spirit, of joints and of marrow, and discerning the thoughts and intentions of my heart. (Based on Hebrews 4:12 ESV.)

Heavenly Father, may Your Word not return to You empty, but accomplish all You desire in me, and achieve the purposes for which You sent it. (Based on Isaiah 55:11.)

Chapter 4

The Practice of Praying Scripture

For me it is absolutely essential that my prayers be guided by, saturated by, and sustained and controlled by the word of God. [18]

–John Piper

George Mueller was a Christian evangelist and director of several orphanages in England in the 1800s. He cared for thousands of orphans in his lifetime, never asking the community to meet the needs of his orphanages or his ministry, but instead taking all of his needs to God. He would spend hours in prayer and often felt like he hadn't connected with God during that time.

But then he discovered the life-changing practice of praying Scripture. He wrote, "For my heart being nourished by the truth, being brought into experiential fellowship with God, I speak to my Father and my Friend (vile though I am, and unworthy of it) about the things that He has brought before me in His precious Word. It often now astonishes me that I did not sooner see this point."[19]

R.A. Torrey further explains, "George Mueller never prayed for a thing just because he wanted it, or even just because he felt it was greatly needed for God's work. When it was laid upon George Mueller's heart to pray for anything, he would search the Scriptures to find if there was some promise that covered the case ... And then when he found the promise, with his open Bible before him, and his finger upon that promise, he would plead that promise, and so he received what he asked. He always prayed with an open Bible before him."[20]

Mueller recorded over 50,000 prayer requests in his prayer journals and would indicate the date each prayer was answered. Over 30,000 of his prayer requests were answered within twenty-four hours of his initial prayer request.[21]

I've heard the story of George Mueller and his mighty practice of praying Scripture numerous times, and each time I found his passion for praying Scripture an incredible, and admittedly, unattainable example of what my prayer life could look like.

It sounds amazing; to include God's Word in our prayers and see over half of them answered immediately in such miraculous ways that there are books filled with them. However, there's more to the story, one that may offer encouragement to those of us who are praying for certain things and not seeing the results we want.

While George Mueller prayed Scripture often and saw God provide in miraculous ways for his ministries and orphanages, he also experienced the heartbreaking loss of two of his sons born stillborn, and another son who died shortly after his first birthday. His only daughter survived to adulthood, but died before she was able to have any children. After about forty years of marriage and ministry together, his wife Mary experienced a devastating illness and died. A few years later, Mueller remarried, and twenty years later his second wife also died.

I don't know the Scriptures and prayers that Mueller pleaded for his family, though I'm sure he did pray for his family often. Despite loss after painful loss, he still clung to his faith, to his God, and to his daily practice of praying for the needs of his ministries, and he did indeed experience many mountains moved.

While George Mueller grieved the loss of his loved ones, he also delighted in God's character, His presence, His provisions, and his own transformation. Mueller, in his youth, was guilty of lying, stealing, and gambling, yet God moved numerous mountains in Mueller's life so that Mueller's heart was now focused on God's will and on God receiving all the glory.

Mueller was able to care for and educate over 10,000 orphans in his lifetime, travel on numerous missionary trips to five different continents, and deliver many sermons. He has become an incredible example to many Christians, bearing much fruit for God's kingdom. He may have lost his whole family and his biological legacy, but God gave him an incredible spiritual family and legacy.

Life will have its hard moments and challenges that our human flesh will fight against. Mueller shows us that praying Scripture will help us not only to align our hearts with God's most glory-filled plan, but also to grow in satisfaction and delight with God and all that He has done for us.

Mueller's example is meant to be an encouraging one, not one that leads to guilt or condemnation. Most of us don't have hours to spend in Scripture and in prayer like Mueller did, and that's OK. When the disciples asked Jesus how to pray, Jesus didn't teach them to pray for hours. He didn't pray the loud, fancy, formal prayers of the religious leaders. Instead, He prayed a simple prayer from His heart that God's will be done.

Finding Scriptures to Pray

The Bible is a treasure trove of verses we can pray, filled with truths and encouragement that can help us get on the same page with God's heart and His desires for us. Sometimes, certain Bible verses will come to mind when we need them or while we're praying. Other times, we'll need to search for them.

Perhaps you want to pray for a particular topic, such as your marriage, your children, your business, or your health. You can record verses that come to mind about that topic or search online for Scriptures for the specific topics you want to pray for. Keep a list of your favorite Scriptures to pray in your Bible or near where you often pray. The Scriptures I have included at the end of each chapter are some of my favorite verses to pray for that chapter's topic. They can help you in building up an arsenal of your own Scriptures to pray with.

You may want to invest in a Bible concordance, a book where you can look up a word related to the topic in the Bible you want to pray for. Underneath, it will list the main verses that include that variation of the word. For you fellow word nerds out there, I highly recommend *Strong's Concordance*, as it will also help you understand the Greek or Hebrew origin of the term you're researching. Some study Bibles include a concordance at the back of the book. You can also find online Bible concordances.

Sometimes, to find a Scripture, or several, to pray for yourself or for loved ones will require you to consider the character trait or heart state or fruit you'd like to see become more evident in that person's life. For example, my older son struggles a lot with writing and spelling; there are no Bible verses about becoming a better speller in any of the sixty-six books of the Bible. But there are plenty of Scriptures about growing in wisdom and knowledge, and about growing in diligence and self-discipline, and in persevering and working hard. So I can pray these Scriptures as he continues working on his writing and spelling.

Sometimes the easiest Scriptures to pray are from the book of Psalms. Many of the psalms were written as prayers that remind us it's OK to share our emotions with God.

We can also use the words and prayers of our Bible heroes throughout Scripture, as we ourselves can identify with their highs and lows, and their praises and petitions. We're praying to the same God.

And of course, we can't forget about Jesus' prayers. If you want to align your heart with the Savior, then join Him in praying for the things that mattered to Him, such as the Lord's Prayer (see Matthew 6:9-13), Jesus' prayer for Himself, for His disciples, and for all believers (see John 17), and that God's will be done (see Luke 22:42).

The prayers of Paul are great to pray for yourself and your loved ones. Paul was an incredible intercessor who often wrote the specific prayers he prayed for individuals and whole churches in his letters, making them especially easy to pray. Colossians 1:9-12, Ephesians 1:16-19, Ephesians 3:16-21, and Philippians 1:9-11 are wonderful prayers we can pray for our loved ones.

Praying Scripture While Reading the Bible

I was going through a season where I no longer found joy in reading my Bible. It felt like a daily obligation, something I had to check off my to-do list and keep up with in my Bible reading plan. Some days, I neglected the practice completely. I prayed that my passion for reading God's Word would return. A day or two after I made this prayer request, I realized that while I was learning to incorporate Bible verses into my prayers to refresh and power up my prayers, maybe I could also be incorporating prayers into my Bible reading. It felt like a novel thought, a huge light bulb moment, but it isn't new.

In approximately 605 B.C. Daniel read the Scriptures and it led him to turn immediately to the Lord in prayer. Daniel was reading in the words of the prophet Jeremiah that their people would be in exile for seventy years due to their sin but that God would restore them to their land (see Daniel 9:2 and Jeremiah 29:10). We often focus on and claim the words of Jeremiah 29:11, but Daniel stopped at Jeremiah 29:10, moved by the promise of restoration for his people. Those words caused him to turn immediately toward prayer and petition, lamenting over the sin of his people and asking that God would restore them as promised to their land (see Daniel 9:3-19). Daniel was moved by God's Word and claimed God's Word, asking that God would receive all the glory.

In the sixth century A.D. a group of monks began a spiritual practice called *lectio divina*, a Latin phrase which means 'divine reading.' *Lectio divina* is a spiritual practice in which you read a passage of Scripture, reflect on it, and then pray it. You don't merely read the

Bible for intellectual and spiritual gain, but for spiritual connection with God.

Donald J. Whitney writes, "Reading Scripture and praying are often disjointed when they should be united. We read the Bible, close it, and try to shift gears into prayer. But many times it seems as if the gears between the two won't mesh. In fact, after some forward progress in our time in the Word, shifting to prayer sometimes is like suddenly moving back into neutral or even reverse. Instead, there should be a smooth, almost unnoticeable transition between Scripture input and prayer output so that we move even closer to God in those moments."[22]

We can enjoy this spiritual practice as well. To practice *lectio divina*, choose a small section of Scripture to focus on. A chapter or less. While this first step isn't usually mentioned as part of *lectio divina*, it's a good idea to pray before you even start reading the Bible. A beautiful verse to pray before reading is Ephesians 1:17-19, but make it personal to you and your time in the Bible. For example: "God, I ask that You would give me the Spirit of wisdom and revelation as I read Your Word so that I may know You better. I ask that the eyes of my heart would be enlightened by Your Word so that I would know the hope to which You have called me, the riches of Your glorious inheritance in the saints, and Your great power available for me and all who believe. Amen."

Then, read slowly through a passage of Scripture. Read until a verse challenges or encourages you, and stop to meditate on it. Or, read through the entire passage you've selected to read. You may need to read through that passage a few times. Listen or look for a word or phrase in the passage that speaks to you, that feels significant to you, though you may not initially know why. God's Word is alive and active, and that means that different phrases and words will resonate with our hearts and our minds according to the season we are in.

Once you have a word or phrase that you have connected with, think about why you connected with it. Does it encourage or convict you? Does it give you a fresh new understanding about something? Is it a new concept you haven't thought about before? Is it relevant to something you've been thinking about or worrying about lately? As you contemplate and meditate on why your heart has resonated with this particular word, phrase, or line of Scripture, you will find, before long, your spirit is talking to God about it.

Read slowly through the chapter you've selected to read, and know that it's OK to read only a small portion of Scripture before you stop to reflect and pray. *Lectio divina* is an invitation to slow down your Bible reading and connect with the heart of God, rather than checking off several passages on your Bible reading plan. Reading less can often help you reflect more and make His Word more meaningful to your own life and situations. You can always pick up where you left off next time you sit down to read the Word, but don't rush through what the Spirit wants you to learn from this portion of the Bible.

The psalms and prayers of our Bible heroes make praying the Scriptures easier. But most of the Bible is filled with narrative stories, and these can feel harder to pray. While reading narrative stories in the Bible, I find it best to reflect on what that story is teaching me, letting that guide my prayers. Does it convict me of a particular sin that I need to confess? Does it make me feel thankful for a particular attribute of God or Jesus' character? However my heart is feeling stirred after reading that Bible story will guide me into a time of prayer.

I've recently started using *The Prayer Bible*[23] in my Bible reading and prayer time. This Bible provides in the margin a prayer prompt based on the content in each and every chapter. That's approximately 1,200 prayer prompts, which I find especially helpful for reading, meditating on, and praying the narrative stories in the Bible. It has been a great tool for me, encouraging the dual focus on God's Word and on prayer that is presented in the discipline of *lectio divina*.

Paul E. Miller wrote about a time when he felt overwhelmed by challenges in his life, making it difficult for him to focus on prayer. He writes:

I stopped trying to have a coherent prayer time, and for weeks on end during my morning prayer time, I did nothing but pray through Psalm 23. I was fighting for my life. I didn't realize it at the time, but I was following the habit of *lectio divina*, which was developed by the early church. By praying slowly through a passage of Scripture, I was allowing Scripture to shape my prayers.

As I prayed through Psalm 23, I began to reflect on the previous day and to look for the Shepherd's presence, for his touches of love. Even on hard days, I began to notice him everywhere, setting a table before me in the presence of my enemies, pursuing me with his love.[24]

If you haven't tried practicing *lectio divina* yet, reading and praying through the familiar and comforting Psalm 23 is a great place to start. If you read through it several days in a row, you may find yourself being drawn to a different line each day, or you may find yourself drawn to the same one.

Mark Batterson writes in his book *The Circle Maker,* "The Bible wasn't meant to be read through; the Bible was meant to be prayed through. And if you pray through it, you'll never run out of things to talk about."[25]

Like all spiritual practices, *lectio divina* will take some practice to get used to. Some days you may have a beautiful divine reading experience, connecting with God and the words in your Bible, and other days you may not. I encourage you to keep diving into this transformational spiritual practice and continually find new things to talk to God about.

Listening to and Praying God's Word

During the early days of the pandemic, I injured my eye. It watered and stung, especially when exposed to bright lights. I knew I needed to get it checked, so I found myself stumbling into an urgent care wearing both a mask and sunglasses, tears streaming down the side of my face.

An eye exam indicated I had a corneal abrasion. I was prescribed anti-bacterial eye drops and told it would take about a week to heal. Reading and exposure to light–including light from any TV, computer, or phone screens–made my eye sting and water, so I spent the next week or so in near darkness, accompanied by audiobooks and podcasts.

Unable to read my Bible, I began listening to the Bible on audio and to Christian podcasts, especially ones about praying Scripture. David Platt's podcast *Pray the Word* became a wonderful tool in helping me grow in my practice of praying Scripture. Each podcast episode is only a few minutes long and begins with David Platt reading a few verses from the Bible, giving a short commentary on it, and then praying that Scripture for all his listeners. Mary DeMuth also has a podcast called *Pray Every Day*, where she reads a chapter from the Bible and then prays for each of her listeners.

At first, I missed being able to open the pages of my Bible and read the Word, but before long I began to enjoy this fresh new practice of listening to His Word. I would listen to the Bible passages being read aloud and–just like with *lectio divina*–usually a line or two would stand out, something that uplifted or convicted my heart. I would pause the audio to meditate on those words and turn them into a prayer.

Numerous verses throughout Scripture indicate the importance of listening to God's voice, His Law, His instructions, and to the words of Jesus. In fact, the Israelites and early Christians didn't read God's Word for themselves; they had it read to them or recited to them from memory. This practice began in Exodus 24:7 with Moses reading what they called The Book of the Law or The Book of the Covenant (believed to be either the first five books of the Bible or perhaps just the book of Deuteronomy) to the Israelites. In Deuteronomy 31:10-12, Moses commanded the Levite priests to assemble all the people to hear The Book of the Covenant read to them during the Festival of Tabernacles (an event celebrated every seven years). Several kings and religious leaders would repeat this practice of reading The

Book of the Covenant to the nation (see 2 Chronicles 34:29-33 and Nehemiah 8:3-9). This may have been the only time some of the Israelites heard the Word of God in their lifetime. Hearing God's Word would often lead to both personal and national conviction and revival.

Paul urged Timothy to "devote yourself to the public reading of Scripture" (see 1 Timothy 4:13), a practice we see sprinkled throughout the Old Testament and the New, and that we may practice in our own churches.

Just as we learn to listen to God's voice or the Holy Spirit's prompting in our lives, we can listen to God's Word and see how it stirs our hearts toward prayer. As you listen to the Word of God being read to you, "think of Him as present and speaking to you, disclosing His emotions and mind and will. God is articulate: He speaks to us through His Word. Meditate on His Words until His thoughts take shape in your mind ... Then, listen carefully to the words that touch your emotions and cause you to meditate on His goodness. 'Feed on His faithfulness' (Psalm 37:3 NKJV). ... Savor His words. 'Taste and see that the Lord is good' (Psalm 34:8)."[26]

In our world, we are often surrounded by noise, whether it be that of those around us, music, podcasts, TV, or audiobooks. What better sound to fill our world with than the very Word of God.

Scripture Prayers for Your Prayer Practice

Father, may You give me the Spirit of wisdom and revelation as I read Your Word and seek You, so I may know You better. May the eyes of my heart be enlightened so that I would know You, Your calling, and the riches of Your glory more. (Based on Ephesians 1:17-18 NKJV.)

Thank You that Your Word is living water to my soul. May it refresh my soul, my faith, and my prayer life. (Based on John 4:14.)

Lord, give me a heart to know You and Your Word. Help me to return to You with my whole heart. (Based on Jeremiah 24:7.)

May I be devoted to prayer and to reading Your Word. May I be watchful as to how You are working in my life and my faith, and may I be thankful for Your work in my life. (Based on Colossians 4:2.)

May I hide Your word in my heart that I might not sin against You. Lord, teach me Your decrees. (Based on Psalm 119:11-12.)

Open my eyes as I read Your Word, that I may see wonderful things in Your Word. May my soul be consumed with longing for Your Word at all times. (Based on Psalm 119:18, 20.)

Help me to hear Your Word and put it into my prayers and into practice, like the wise man who built his house on the rock. (Based on Matthew 7:24.)

Part 2

Types of Prayer

Chapter 5

Prayers of Praise and Thanksgiving

Enter his gates with thanksgiving and his courts with praise; give thanks to him and praise his name. For the LORD is good and his love endures forever; his faithfulness continues through all generations.

–Psalm 100:4-5

I'm involved in a local Moms in Prayer[27] group that begins with a time of Scripture-based praise, then shifts into a moment of silent confession, a time of joint thanksgiving, and finally, a time of intercession in which we pray for our children/grandchildren and their schools and teachers. Each week we are handed a worksheet that lists a different attribute of God that we praise Him for, as well as a few Scriptures to pray related to that character trait. The first week I went, the attribute of God we focused on was God our Shepherd. We read a passage about God being our shepherd (see Psalm 23), and we spent time praising God and thanking Him for being our shepherd. Then we moved on to a few more Scripture passages that mention Him being our Shepherd: Psalm 79:13, Psalm 28:9, and Matthew 18:12-14.

This time of praise and then thanksgiving has become my favorite part of our prayer time. I get to listen to how the others in the group pray these Scriptures and praise God for who He is, before we then thank God for what He is doing in our lives. It's a time where I don't seek anything of God, but simply savor the wonder of who He is and who He wants to be in my life. It's a time where I let go of my worries and prayer requests and just revel in the awesomeness and love of God.

When we start with praise and thanksgiving and then move on to the intercession part of our prayer time–where we pray for our children–my concerns and worries don't seem like such a big deal anymore. My mind and my heart have settled while I praise God and thank Him for what He has done, and I am reminded that He is in control and on His throne. My prayer requests and worries for my children do not seem as huge, heavy, or burdensome.

This formula of prayer helped me realize how often I go to God in prayer when I need something, rather than go to Him because I'm thankful for who He is and what He has already done in my life.

Thankfully, Richard J. Foster indicates I'm not alone in this feeling, writing that "prayer of adoration must be learned. It does not come automatically. Notice our own children! They do not need to be trained to ask for things ... What endless effort it takes to help our children cultivate a habit of gratitude ... The same is true for us."[28]

It takes practice to learn to praise God and cultivate a thankful heart. But as we learn more about the heart and character of our Heavenly Father, Foster says it should "draw us into praise and thanksgiving more often ... Our God is not made of stone. His heart is the most sensitive and tender of all ... Like the proud mother who is thrilled to receive a wilted bouquet of dandelions from her child, so God celebrates our feeble expressions of gratitude ... It brings joy to the heart of God when we grip that pierced hand and say simply and profoundly, 'Thank you, bless you, praise you!'"[29]

Praising God Through Worship Songs

Growing up, my favorite part of church was when we'd open our song books and sing a song to the Lord. I had my favorite songs, the ones I'd quickly memorize and which would be stuck in my head for the next week.

Throughout Scripture we see that songs were sung to the Lord often. Most of the psalms were songs. When God parted the Red Sea for the Israelites to cross safely, Moses and Miriam led the Israelites in a song of praise (see Exodus 15). When the prophetess Deborah experienced victory, she burst into song (see Judges 5). When David experienced trials and victories, he wrote songs. When King Jehoshaphat and his army marched toward battle, they were singing hymns of praise (see 2 Chronicles 20:21). When Paul and Silas were imprisoned, they "were praying and singing hymns to God, and the other prisoners were listening to them" (Acts 16:25b). And in the book of Revelation, we see angels and people of all nations, tribes, and tongues praising God in song (see Revelation 7:9-12).

When I'm feeling discouraged, I find turning on some worship music helps my mood and mindset greatly. Just like our Bible heroes realized, music helps to lift the spirit, reminding us of God's character and that He is in control.

I've sung worship songs and hymns that have brought me to tears, others that have brought me to my knees, and yet others that have made me want to dance or lift my hands up in praise or jump up and down in awe and wonder of our God. These songs have the power to move our bodies, as well as our hearts. Music is powerful, and we can use it to help us connect with God. The words of worship songs and hymns can help us verbalize what we may be unable to say or help us remember what is true of our God.

Music can speak to us in a way that many other mediums of communication cannot. It has the ability to elicit emotion and carry memories. It has been shown to create new pathways in the brain for communication for those unable to or struggling to speak.[30] There are many testimonies of men and women who have dementia and can barely remember their loved ones, yet when they hear their favorite hymns and worship songs they can remember and sing every word.

Many of the psalms indicate that we should be singing people. In Psalm 40:1-3, David writes that when God "lifted me out of the slimy pit ... He put a new song in my mouth, a hymn of praise to our God." God rescuing us should lead us to praise Him in song. In Psalm 100:2, the psalm of thanksgiving and praise, we are invited to "worship the LORD with gladness; come before him with joyful songs." And in Psalm 126:2, in celebration of God bringing back the captives to Zion, the psalmist wrote that "our mouths were filled with laughter, our tongues with songs of joy."

God's work in our lives can lead us to burst into songs of praise. And sometimes, when we least feel like singing songs of praise, songs of praise and thanksgiving can be just the thing we need to help us remember the faithfulness and goodness of God. They can bring us comfort, encouragement, inspiration, and lead our hearts toward praise.

No matter how you feel about your singing voice, our songs of praise and worship are a beautiful gift to the Lord. Martin Luther wrote, "Music is a fair and glorious gift of God ... I am strongly persuaded that after theology there is no art that can be placed on a level with music; for besides theology, music is the only art capable of affording peace and joy of the heart ... The devil flees before the sound of music almost as much as before the Word of God."[31]

Often the lyrics in our favorite worship songs and hymns come straight from Scripture, so when we sing them, we're singing the very Word of God. These heartfelt words can work their way into our hearts and can become our prayers to the Lord.

Also, just as we can pray Scripture, we can also pray the words of our favorite worship songs or hymns. Instead of singing the words, we can read or recite them in our prayers. The familiarity of the words of these songs can take on new meaning when we forget about singing them and just focus on the words and what they mean. Meditate on the words of "Amazing Grace" or "How Great Thou Art" or another favorite hymn and turn those words into a prayer of praise.

Prayers of Praise

Prayers of praise and adoration celebrate the grandeur of who God is, what He has done, and what He is doing. It's recognizing God's greatness, holiness, and His power. When we praise God, we focus solely on His character and our love for Him, rather than focusing on ourselves. We let go of any expectations we have of what God could do for us, and instead focus on our Almighty God. It cleanses our mind of our own cares and puts us in the presence of God. Praise beats back the power of darkness and thwarts the work of Satan.

The founder of Moms in Prayer, Fern Nichols, further identifies why praise is both important and powerful:

> Within each of us is the desire to be valued, admired, and honored for our virtues. But how much more our heavenly Father deserves recognition and admiration ...
>
> Nothing is as powerful as praise. Praise gives glory due His name; draws us more intimately to the Father's heart; causes us to look up–setting our minds on things above; changes our attitude; brings an awareness of God's presence; defeats Satan; releases God's power; brings a victorious perspective; provides peace; wards off the spirits of self-pity, depression, and discouragement; and produces strength in an anxious heart. Through praise we find hope in what seems like impossible situations.[32]

Throughout Scripture, we see numerous examples of our Bible heroes praising God for His miraculous works and His Almighty character, and praising Him for His mighty provision. Sometimes, they praised God when good things happened, and other times they praised God through the pain and the unknown.

For eighteen verses in Exodus 15 Moses praised God after the miraculous parting of the Red Sea.

When Nehemiah learned of the wall in Jerusalem being destroyed and found himself grieving the state of Jerusalem, he turned to prayer, praising God before making a request.

David wrote entire psalms of praise, and even when he poured out his true feelings of grief and anger and repentance to God, he often ended these psalms of lament with praise, remembering who God is despite his pain. David's Psalm 139 includes eighteen beautiful verses of praise and adoration before ending his last six verses with petition.

King Jehoshaphat, when praying about an upcoming battle about to take place in which they were vastly outnumbered (see 2 Chronicles 20), praised God's character and His provision, rather than asking God to be with them and give them victory in battle. They went into battle singing and praising God, and God gave them an incredible victory.

Hannah praised God for ten verses (see 1 Samuel 2) when she left her son Samuel with the priest Eli, focusing not on the gift of her son whom she'd prayed for for years, but on the character of the Giver of such gifts.

Daniel praised God for giving him wisdom and insight into the king's dream in Daniel 2:19-23.

Mary praised God with Elizabeth (see Luke 1:46-55), recognizing His work in their miracle pregnancies and praising the faithful works God has done for His people and would do through their children.

When the disciples asked Jesus how they should pray, Jesus taught the Lord's prayer, in which the first three statements praise God as our heavenly Father, holy, and our King.

In Luke 19:37, the disciples and others following Jesus praised Him for the miracles He had done.

When Paul and Silas were in prison, they sang songs of praise (see Acts 16:16-40). In fact, their songs of praise broke their prison chains and caused their prison door to swing open, before they were set free. Praising God, even in our painful circumstances, has the power to either change us or to change our circumstances. Just like Paul and Silas experienced, praising God in the midst of your painful circumstances can unlock chains that have been keeping you captive.

If you were to take an inventory of your prayers, or search through your prayer journal, how much would be filled with praising God? Have you ever prayed an entire prayer of praise without asking God for anything?

We have a limited view of who God is, and finding and praying verses that remind us of God's character, faithfulness, and attributes help us remember how much bigger and better He is than our minds can grasp this side of heaven.

A fun way I've found to praise God is to think of a characteristic or a name for God for each letter of the alphabet. For example: Almighty. Beautiful. Compassionate. Defender. Eternal. Father. Good. Holy. Etc. You can do the same thing for Jesus too, or any member of the Holy Trinity. God, Jesus, and the Holy Spirit all have such wonderful names and attributes that your alphabet praise will end up being different each time. (Hint: If you get stuck at the letter X like I did, you can use a word that has X in it. I also discovered after a little research that Xristos means Christ in Greek.) This is also a great activity to do with your whole family around the dinner table or on a road trip. Oh, and if you find yourself having a hard time falling asleep, I've found the alphabet praise a great practice. Your whirlwind of thoughts will settle and there's nothing quite like falling asleep praising God.

David–known as the man after God's own heart–wrote in Psalm 27:4, "One thing I ask from the Lord, this only do I seek: that I may dwell in the house of the Lord all the days of my life, to gaze on the beauty of the Lord and to seek him in his temple." David simply wanted to experience more of God.

Dillon Burroughs wrote, "Even if God never did another good thing in our lives, we could spend the rest of this life praising Him for what He has already done."[33] There are times when I agree wholeheartedly with Burroughs' words, and other times where I feel like God is holding out on me. Sometimes it's easier to want more–to long for the answer to the prayer you've been praying for a long time–than it is to be in awe of the One who has given us everything we do have and who is worthy of our praise and adoration. As we seek to delight in God's presence and praise God for who He is, it elicits further awe of God's character and His involvement in our lives.

Prayers of Thanksgiving

In Luke 17, Jesus heals ten lepers. I can't imagine the joy they must have felt to have their body and their place in society instantly restored. And yet, only one of those former lepers returned to tell Jesus thank you. Interestingly enough, we're told in verse 16 that he was a Samaritan. Yet he found Jesus and fell at His feet thanking Him and praising God. "Jesus asked, 'Were not all ten cleansed? Where are the other nine?'" (Luke 17:17). Those other nine were off enjoying their healing and restoration and didn't take the time to thank Jesus for answering their deepest prayer. Unfortunately, there are times we can be like those other nine. Whether huge answered prayers or daily blessings, we can sometimes take for granted God's provision and gifts in our lives.

Thanksgiving is one of my favorite holidays. I love the fun times with family gathered around the table. I love the food. And I adore the beauty of the autumn season–the crisp weather and the kaleidoscopic display of leaves contrasting the beautiful blue sky. But what I love most is the spirit of Thanksgiving. Of cherishing all the blessings in your life; of utter and complete contentment and peace with the awareness of how blessed we are. Honestly, I wish every day was Thanksgiving. Not the whole smorgasbord of food each day (though, I honestly wouldn't complain. I love Thanksgiving dinner!), but I wish each day we simply took time to acknowledge the things we are thankful for.

As much as I love Thanksgiving, praying prayers of thanksgiving don't often come naturally to me. I find it much easier to bring my requests to God than acknowledge the giver of all my gifts. We're invited to bring our requests to God, but to do so with a heart of thanksgiving. Philippians 4:6 tells us, "Do not be anxious about anything, but in every situation, by prayer and petition, with thanksgiving, present your requests to God." Philippians 4:7 continues on to say that if we present our requests to God with thanksgiving, "the peace of God, which transcends all understanding, will guard your hearts and your minds in Christ Jesus."

I don't know about you, but whenever I'm feeling anxious about something but choose instead to focus on the things I'm thankful for and how God has provided for us in the past, it helps me to let go of a lot of those worries and trust that He's in control.

One way I've found helpful in cultivating a heart of thankfulness is to keep a gratitude journal. Once or twice a week I record the things I'm thankful for. They could be something specific that happened to me or a loved one. Or something more general, like I'm thankful for my family. Taking time to reflect on our blessings elicits thankfulness and contentment.

The God who created our minds and our bodies has long known what our bodies need, and now, scientists are learning about the benefits of practicing thankfulness. In 2003, two psychologists wrote about an experiment they had conducted where they divided hundreds of people into three groups. The first group was told to write about things they were grateful for each day. The second group was told to write about the things that bothered them each day. And the third group could write about anything they wanted from their day. After ten weeks the psychologists noted that those in the first group experienced less anxiety, stress, and depression, proving that practicing gratitude was beneficial for mental health. What surprised the researchers was how beneficial gratitude was to their physical health as well. The members in the first group had reduced their cortisol (stress) hormones by an average of twenty-three percent. A little over half of the participants in the first group had lowered their blood pressure. All of the members in the first group reported better sleep and digestion as well as less stress and anxiety in their lives.[34]

Praise and thanksgiving not only remind us of God's goodness but also that God created us to praise and thank Him for our own physical and spiritual health and well-being. A heart of gratitude and thanksgiving helps us turn our minds away from our worries and needs, and onto the Giver of our many gifts and blessings. It helps us experience contentment and peace in our lives, letting go, if only temporarily, of our continual striving for more. It helps our bodies, our minds, and our faith as we remember all the wonderful things He has done for us. Practicing and praying with thanksgiving and gratitude gives us peace, reminding us that God has been there and met our needs before, and He will do it again in whatever situation we find ourselves in.

Scripture Prayers of Praise and Thanksgiving

Oh Lord, there is no one like You among the gods. Who is like You, majestic in holiness, awesome in glorious deeds, and able to work wonders. (Based on Exodus 15:11 ESV.)

Lord, You are my God; I will exalt You and praise Your name, for in perfect faithfulness You have done wonderful things, things You planned long ago. (Based on Isaiah 25:1.)

One thing I ask, this alone I seek: that I may dwell in Your house all the days of my life, to gaze upon Your beauty and to seek You in Your temple. (Based on Psalm 27:4.)

Praise and glory and wisdom and thanks and honor and power and strength be to You, our God for ever and ever. Amen! (Based on Revelation 7:12.)

Because Your love is better than life, my lips will glorify You. I will praise You as long as I live, and in Your name I will lift up my hands. (Based on Psalm 63:3-4.)

I praise You, Lord, with all my soul; all my inmost being, praise Your holy name. I praise You, Lord. May I forget not all Your benefits–You who forgives all our sin and heals all our diseases, who has redeemed my life from the pit and crowned me with love and compassion. (Based on Psalm 103:1-4.)

I thank You, Lord, for You are good; Your steadfast love endures forever! (Based on 1 Chronicles 16:34 ESV.)

Father of heavenly lights, thank You for every good and perfect gift from above. Thank You for _____. (Based on James 1:17.)

God, thank You that You take care of me. You will supply all my needs from Your glorious riches. Thank You for _____. (Based on Philippians 4:19 NLT.)

Lord, thank You for the surpassing grace You have given us. Thank You for this indescribable gift! (Based on 2 Corinthians 9:14b-15.)

Chapter 6

Prayers of Confession and Salvation

We come to prayer with a tangled mass of motives ... God is big enough to receive us with all our mixture. We do not have to be bright or pure or filled with faith or anything. That is what grace means, and not only are we saved by grace, we live by it as well. We pray by it.[35]

–Richard J. Foster

I'm not much of a baker or a cook but one day I decided to make red velvet cupcakes for an upcoming party. As if that wasn't lofty enough, I somehow got it in my mind to make the cupcakes by following a recipe with raving five star reviews, rather than from a box like I usually do.

I followed the recipe carefully and everything was going splendidly until it was time to add the red food coloring. And then spoon the red batter into the cupcake holders. Somehow, in the process of those two steps, I got red stains all over my fingers and a few splotches on my white countertops. A later glimpse in the bathroom mirror would inform me that I had a bright red highlight in my hair and a constellation of three red freckles on my cheek as well.

I scrubbed at my fingers and my face and those counter tops while the cupcakes baked and felt like an utter failure. Those stains quickly led to a spiral of all the other areas where I was failing, where I felt I wasn't good enough.

Once the cupcakes had cooled, I opened up the container of white cream cheese frosting, grabbed a knife, and swirled it over each and every cupcake. I watched the white frosting cover up the red cupcakes, and I wanted it to miraculously remove the red dye from my fingertips and countertops, too.

And that random thought led to a sudden spiritual epiphany. The red dye in those cupcakes reminded me of our sin, leaving behind a stain that invades our souls and leaves us trapped in guilt. But the white cream cheese frosting reminded me of God's grace, which makes us clean.

That thought wasn't new. They are God's words to Isaiah: "Though your sins are like scarlet, they shall be as white as snow; though they are red like crimson, they shall be as wool" (Isaiah 1:18b NKJV). Coming to God in confession–sharing with God our sins that stain not fingers and countertops but our soul and our mind, leaving us full of shame and feeling like failures–opens the door to Him being able to make us clean. It covers us with His grace and His righteousness, making us as white and clean as fresh snow.

As I covered those red cupcakes with that white frosting, I thought about how both elements–the red cake and the cream cheese frosting–were important and meant to be balanced to make the proper decadent dessert. God's gift of grace, and making us righteous and clean before Him, is to be balanced with our responsibility to repent of our sin in striving to be more like Christ.

We unfortunately can fall into two traps when it comes to God's forgiveness. One, we can think our sin is so bad that God can't forgive it, that our guilt and our shame are deserved. In this way, we forget the gift of God's extravagant grace and become like a red velvet muffin with a smidge of frosting on top.

Or two, we can think our sin isn't that bad and because of God's great love and the gift of grace, we can freely sin knowing we'll be forgiven. In this way, we forget the power of God's holiness and become like a tiny red velvet cupcake smothered in rich cream cheese frosting.

By focusing on only one element–either our guilt and shame or His unending mercy–we miss out on an important aspect of God, either His holiness or His amazing gift of grace. Both are meant to be savored together.

And in case you were curious, the cupcakes were delicious and I was able to remove all the red stains.

Prayers of Confession and Repentance

A few months after my second son was born, and only a few weeks after my older son had received his diagnosis of apraxia, I found myself overwhelmed with both situational and postpartum anxiety. My life revolved around my boys' plethora of appointments, our home felt messy and unorganized, meal planning and cooking was a daily struggle, and I was barely holding on. My faith and my marriage were both struggling under the stress.

I learned from a friend at church about a discipleship class called God of Order®.[36] It was a year-long discipleship class focused on getting your home organized and your family under God's order (God first, husband second, children third), with practical assignments to help you get your home into order. I jumped at the chance to join.

Our teacher was an incredible woman of God named Jo Hancock, who at our very first class reminded us that God is indeed a God of order. From the largest galaxy to the smallest cell, to the family structure and all things in between, everything has a design, a place, and a purpose that aligns with His will.

And then she shared that the most important thing God wants to bring into order is our heart. At the end of our first lesson, Jo gave us our very first assignment. We were to read through a two-sided worksheet called "Put Off ... Put On,"[37] which listed different sins and attitudes we were to put off, and the types of qualities, character, and mindset we were to put on (such as put off pride and put on humility), with a Bible verse to read about each. This assignment was based on Ephesians 4:22-24: "You were taught, with regard to your former way of life, to put off your old self, which is being corrupted by its deceitful desires; to be made new in the attitude of your minds; and to put on the new self, created to be like God in true righteousness and holiness."

Jo told us that we needed to get our hearts in order before we could get our homes in order, and this list would help. I'll admit I went home disappointed. I was drowning at home and in desperate need of practical help, and instead I had an assignment to do a deep dive into Scripture and into my heart. But every day that week while the boys napped, I dutifully gathered my Bible and my "Put Off ... Put On" sheet and dug in.

Arranged in alphabetical order by sins and attitudes we were to put off, it took me weeks to get past the B's. Not because I stopped doing the assignment. No, it was because anger and bitterness were among the first sinful attitudes I had to confront, wrestle with, and put off. I spent months parked in Scriptures about anger and bitterness, journaling, praying, weeping, confessing, and repenting of the bitterness and anger I had toward the circumstances in my life, my husband, and with God Himself.

My greatest takeaway from the discipleship class wasn't anything practical like I had anticipated. Confessing my sins of anger and bitterness to both God and my husband changed my heart, my marriage, and my home more than any amount of meal planning or home organization ever could.

I learned that a clean heart is foundational to our spiritual well-being and in helping us to love others the way we were created to. God's Word is great at both convicting and cleansing our hearts. Jodie Berndt writes:

> The more we employ different parts of God's Word, letting them 'soak' into our hearts and minds, the more they can work together to refresh and renew us. To teach us right from wrong ...
>
> And here's the really remarkable thing about the cleansing power of Scripture. When we open our Bibles, we are not the only ones doing the reading. God's Word is actually ... examining us. Powerful, penetrating, and sharper than any double-edged sword, the

Bible exposes our innermost thoughts and desires ... God won't force us to come clean. He doesn't make us confess. But He can make us clean.[38]

It's important to recognize and confess our mistakes in prayer, acknowledging our hearts were not in alignment with our Father. God's love for us is so strong that He runs toward us with a lavish love and open arms at the first glimpse of our hearts returning to His. We do nothing to earn that love. We simply are in right standing with Him because of His unfailing love and Jesus' shed blood for us.

Acts 3:19 says, "Repent, then, and turn to God, so that your sins may be wiped out, that times of refreshing may come from the Lord." The prodigal son in Luke 15 repented from his time of sin by returning home to his father. The son was fully embraced and celebrated not for the confession he had prepared, but for simply turning back to his father. He felt broken and ashamed and not worthy to be a son, but that's not how his father saw him.

When we turn toward God ready to confess all our sins, we find He hasn't turned away from us and our sin. He doesn't scold or shame. He's a faithful Father, waiting for us to return to Him, to make us clean, and to reassure us of our identity as His beloved children.

Repentance isn't just about confessing your sins to God and doing your best to not sin in that area anymore. It's also about embracing the gift of God's grace, which offers us a fresh start every time we need it: "The steadfast love of the LORD never ceases, his mercies never come to an end; they are new every morning; great is your faithfulness" (Lamentations 3:22-23 ESV). Each time we admit and turn away from sins, we receive a new start full of God's love and grace. This fills our hearts with joy and keeps us bending our knees toward confession and repentance.

King David saw the importance of having his heart cleansed and the value of confession and repentance. Praying as David did–"create in me a pure heart, O God, and renew a steadfast spirit within me.

Do not cast me from your presence or take your Holy Spirit from me. Restore to me the joy of your salvation and grant me a willing spirit, to sustain me" (Psalm 51:10-12)–will have the power to transform our hearts and our lives.

Embracing the Gift of Salvation

As we confess our sin to God, it leads to another type of confession: "If you confess with your mouth that Jesus is Lord and believe in your heart that God raised him from the dead, you will be saved" (Romans 10:9b ESV).

It was at a Christian teen retreat up in the snowy mountains with some of my friends that I heard the gospel presented in a way that seemed too simple to be true. Sure, I had grown up in church, I knew and believed that Jesus died for my sins, but I also believed I had to work for my salvation–that I had to go to church and read my Bible and be a 'good girl' to go to heaven.

One evening during the retreat, my friends and I were seated around the table after dinner, laughing and chatting until it was time for our final session of the night, when the air was pierced with the shrill sound of a fire alarm. We looked at each other and the leaders in confusion, hesitant to go outside into the snowy mountains on a freezing December evening.

Then the alarming scent of smoke wafted into the cafeteria and we rushed outside, away from the blaring fire alarm and into the biting cold, to see to our horror that the retreat center's steepled chapel was spouting billows of smoke.

We watched in mixed horror and fascination as the orange flames devoured the chapel's walls. One of the retreat leaders told us to get into a circle and pray while we waited for the fire department to arrive. We shivered and prayed and huddled together for warmth.

While the firefighters fought to put out the fire before it affected any other buildings, we were sent to our cabins to pack up our belongings, get back on the bus, and solemnly drive back to our own church a day early.

The bus was eerily quiet. The scent of smoke still clung to our clothes and hair, and memories of the events replayed in our minds. And then one of the retreat leaders rocketed out of her seat.

"Oh my goodness," she cried out. "You guys, my watch stopped!"

Why that mattered in light of everything that had happened, we didn't know, but before we had a chance to ask, she explained, "I checked my watch during dinner because I knew we needed to head to the chapel for our final meeting of the night. I didn't realize my watch had stopped. If it hadn't, we could have been in that chapel when that fire started."

My arms were covered with goosebumps, but this time not from the cold. I realized then that the God who saved me from a physical fire had also saved me from my sins and an eternal fire, and I prayed the prayer of salvation right there on that school bus.

If you have not accepted the gift of salvation, perhaps now is the time. You don't have to do anything to work for it or earn it. All you have to do is confess that you are a sinner and you know that Jesus died for your sins, though you don't deserve it. As the Bible says in John 3:16, "For God so loved the world that he gave his one and only Son, that whoever believes in him shall not perish but have eternal life."

If you were in a church, they might ask you to boldly step forward to the altar where you could declare you were ready to receive the gift of salvation. Every time that happens, I get teary eyed as I watch new brothers and sisters join the family of Christ. But you don't have to do that. You can pray the prayer of salvation right where you are, whether it's at home or work or even on a school bus.

Here is a sinner's prayer filled with God's Word that you can pray. I added the Scripture references if you want to look them up. Feel free to personalize this prayer and humbly make it your own:

"Father, it is written in Your Word that if I confess with my mouth that Jesus is Lord and believe in my heart that You have raised Him from the dead, I shall be saved (see Romans 10:9). Therefore, Father, I confess that Jesus is my Lord. I make Him Lord of my life right now. I believe in my heart that You raised Jesus from the dead (see Romans 8:11). Thank you for forgiving me of all my sin (see 1 John 1:9). Jesus is my Lord, and I am a new creation. Old things have passed away; now all things become new in Jesus' name (see 2 Corinthians 5:17). Amen."[39]

Embracing How Salvation Transforms Our Identity

Several years ago, I joined a group for Christian moms of young children. At the beginning of the first meeting we were to introduce ourselves to the other moms at our round table by saying our name, how many children we have, and three facts about ourselves.

When it was my turn I said, "My name is Jenn and I have two boys and I'm a special needs mom and ... um ..." I froze. My life revolved around both of my young sons' endless needs and appointments, and I couldn't think of a single other thing to say myself.

The table leader gently added, "And you're a beloved child of God," before calling on the next mom to introduce herself.

I smiled gratefully at her, but the whole situation and her words left my mind whirling. How easy it is to become consumed by our hard circumstances. To get lost in our labels and end up losing track of our true identity. Or how easy it is to claim our insecurities as part of our identity and forget how God feels about us.

When I got home from that meeting I was determined to reclaim my spiritual identity, beginning with that beautiful name, Beloved. I looked up the definition; it means "to be deeply and dearly loved. To have great worth, value, and esteem to the beholder."

God loves and values us so much He sent His son to die for us. When He looks at us, He doesn't see those lies and labels we carry with us. He feels a love for us that is so vast we cannot even comprehend it this side of heaven. He looks at us, His beloved children, with such love and delight it makes Him break out into song over us (see Zephaniah 3:17).

Salvation transforms our identity. The same words that God proudly declared from heaven at Jesus' baptism and again at Jesus' transfiguration, God declares over us too: "This is my Beloved ... with whom I am well-pleased and delighted" (see Matthew 3:17 NKJV, Matthew 17:5 AMP). And that terrifies Satan. The devil will do whatever he can to make us doubt that identity, or to make us focus on our work and our roles for our identity. Psalm 139:17-18a tells us, "How precious to me are your thoughts, God! How vast is the sum of them! Were I to count them, they would outnumber the grains of sand."

God thinks wonderful thoughts about us, and we need to get on the same page as Him, reading and reminding ourselves of what our Heavenly Father thinks about us. That's our true identity. Reading, praying, and declaring the Scriptures that tell us who we are in Christ can help guide us toward walking in confidence and victory as God's children.

Here are some of my favorite Scriptures about our spiritual identity that we can be praying and declaring:

Beloved: "Beloved, we are God's children now" (1 John 3:2a ESV).

Child of God: "See what kind of love the Father has given to us, that we should be called children of God; and so we are" (1 John 3:1a ESV).

Chosen: "He chose us in him before the foundation of the world, that we should be holy and blameless before him" (Ephesians 1:4b ESV).

Friend: "I no longer call you servants ... I have called you friends" (John 15:15).

Heir: "Now if we are children, then we are heirs–heirs of God and co-heirs with Christ" (Romans 8:17a).

Holy: "To all ... who are loved by God and called to be his holy people: Grace and peace to you from God our Father and from the Lord Jesus Christ" (Romans 1:7).

Workmanship: "For we are God's workmanship, created in Christ Jesus to do good works, which God prepared in advance for us to do" (Ephesians 2:10).

Wonderfully Made: "I praise you because I am fearfully and wonderfully made; your works are wonderful, I know that full well" (Psalm 139:14).

And so many more!

Ephesians is one of my favorite books of the Bible because it reminds us of our spiritual identity and the spiritual blessings we receive when we accept Him as our Lord and Savior. I highly recommend you read and pray through the book of Ephesians (or at least the first chapter) so you can more fully embrace your spiritual identity and know that you are worthy of all the spiritual blessings God generously pours out on us.

Scripture Prayers of Confession and Salvation

Thank You, God, that though my sins were like scarlet, You have made them white as snow. (Based on Isaiah 1:18.)

God, thank You for calling me to forget the former things and to not dwell on the past, because You are doing a new thing! May I perceive the work You are springing up in and around me. (Based on Isaiah 43:18-19.)

May I exalt You, Lord, and praise Your holy name. Thank You that Your anger lasts only a moment, but Your favor lasts a lifetime. Thank

You that my weeping may last for a night, but rejoicing comes in the morning. (Based on Psalm 30:4-5.)

Oh God, create in me a pure heart and renew a steadfast spirit within me. (Based on Psalm 51:10.)

God, I ask that You would help me put off my old self, which is being corrupted by its deceitful desires. I ask that I would be made new in the attitude of my mind, putting on the new self, which has been created to be like You in true righteousness and holiness. (Based on Ephesians 4:22b-24.)

Lord, I thank You that because of Your Son's obedient sacrifice on the cross, I can now approach Your throne of grace with confidence, so that I can receive mercy and find grace to help me in my time of need. (Based on Hebrews 4:16.)

Lord, thank You that because You gave up Your life for us, I am now a beloved child of God. Help me to fully embrace my identity in You. (Based on 1 John 3:1.)

Thank You, God, that because of Your great love for us, You who are rich in mercy, made us alive with Christ even when we were dead in transgressions—it is by Your gift of grace we have been saved. (Based on Ephesians 2:4-5.)

I pray that I would not take advantage of Your grace and keep on sinning so that grace may increase. I have died to sin; help me to not live in it any longer. (Based on Romans 6:1-3.)

Chapter 7

Prayers of Petition and Intercession

I believe God has heard my prayers. He will make it manifest in His own good time that He has heard me. I have recorded my petitions that when God has answered them, His name will be glorified. [40]

–George Mueller

When my children first started talking, it was thrilling. Each word was a treasure, a connection into their world, and I was eager to show them I heard and understood and loved them.

When my older son was about to turn five we asked him what he wanted to do for his birthday. We took him to Party City for inspiration, and after happily walking the birthday party aisles, he grinned and declared, "Chee Chee! Min cay! Boons!!"

It was the first time he could tell us what he wanted for his birthday, and though he may not have articulated the words perfectly, my husband, Tim, and I knew exactly what he wanted for his special day. As his parents, we had a few ideas of what we could offer our son for his birthday, but we wanted to give him the birthday desires of his heart. So we listened to those desires and planned a birthday party at Chuck E. Cheese (Chee Chee), my mom made him a Minion cake (min cay), and we bought a bouquet of balloons (boons), including a Minion balloon. We all had a grand ol' time at Chuck E. Cheese. Tim and I were excited to give our son the desires of his heart and see him experience such delight at receiving them.

I think that's merely a glimpse of how God feels when we ask Him for something. He already knows our hearts and our thoughts perfectly, and He is already attentive to our needs and our desires, but He delights in having us share them with Him. He wants to show us how much He loves us. And He delights in seeing our hearts' desires met. He joins in our joy as we delight in the good gifts He has given us.

In 1 Kings 18, Elijah has a prayer stand-off with the prophets of Baal. Whichever God or god can light a sacrificial bull on fire on the altar will win. The prophets of Baal prayed and danced and shouted, trying to get their god to answer. Elijah taunted them: "Shout louder! ... Perhaps he is deep in thought, or busy, or traveling. Maybe he is sleeping and must be awakened" (1 Kings 18:27).

So the frantic prayers kept up, increasing in intensity with the prophets cutting themselves to get their gods' attention. "But there was no response, no one answered, no one paid attention" (1 Kings 18:29b). When they gave up, Elijah stepped up to pray.

God paid attention to Elijah's prayer. He not only lit the sacrifice on the altar on fire, but the wood, the stones, the soil, and the water in the trench around it. Such is the attention, the affection, the action of God in response to our prayers.

When we ask God for something for ourselves, that is petition, and when we ask God for something on behalf of someone else, that is intercession. We can ask God for anything or anyone that matters to us, because it matters to God as well. He wants us to ask, and He wants to hear what is on our hearts.

Ron Hutchcraft writes regarding the goodness and generosity of our heavenly Father: "God has thrown open His storehouse to His children. He's unlocked His infinite resources and promised that our prayer of faith would unleash those resources and aim them at the need we have, the situation we face, or the person we love. When you are praying, don't ever forget—you really are touching heaven, changing earth."[41] Our Heavenly Father is generous and willing to give us that which is for our ultimate good.

Petitioning the Lord Through the Lord's Prayer

The Lord's Prayer is an incredible model of petitionary prayer. When one of Jesus' disciples eagerly asked Him to teach them to pray, Jesus taught them the words to what we call the Lord's Prayer, found in Matthew 6:9-13 and Luke 11:1-4.

I grew up in a denomination where we would pray the Lord's Prayer every Sunday. We would all reach along the wooden pews and across the aisles, clasping hands with family members and fellow church members, until we were all connected in one united body. Then, we would all recite the familiar words. In fact, the words were so familiar that I'll admit, they often lost their meaning, or maybe as a child I never understood what they meant to begin with.

Even though I may not have understood what all the words of this all-too-familiar prayer meant, the act of the entire church holding hands and praying this prayer together made it clear this was a prayer intended for us to pray as a collective unit. The plural pronoun words 'our' and 'us' are further confirmation this is a prayer for the body of Christ to pray together. This doesn't mean we can't pray the Lord's Prayer by ourselves. The Lord's Prayer is full of petitions that show us what was on Jesus' heart when He prayed, things that we can join Him in praying for, too.

The first three lines of this prayer have to do with God's glory, His kingdom, and His will. Kelly Minter explains, "Each of these petitions is a slight variation of the same request. Like three tributaries running into the same river, our desire for God's renown, reign, and rule all flow toward His throne."[42] It seems obvious that we should focus on God's character and will first, but how often our hearts are inclined to jump right into our requests for ourselves and the people we care about and the things we want to see happen. Once we've given God His proper place, then all other things will fall into their proper places. Once we've focused on the Person, then we can focus on our petitions.

While reading a chapter in *Prayer* by Timothy Keller recently, I uncovered many gems about what the Lord's Prayer is about. Keller has done a lot of research and gleaned incredible insight from some of the spiritual greats (namely, Martin Luther, Augustine, and John Calvin) regarding the Lord's Prayer. I'd like to share some of those nuggets with you, as well as a few more modern Bible study teachers' insights into the Lord's Prayer. Understanding what each of these familiar phrases and petitions truly means will provide you with a plethora of prayers, using God's Word and Jesus' Prayer as our foundation and guide.

Our Father

Jews typically addressed God as Almighty God or Yahweh, or viewed Him as too holy to even say His name, so referring to God as 'our Father' would have been revolutionary, ushering in a whole new relationship paradigm.

Just as many prayer patterns begin with praise or adoration, so too does The Lord's Prayer. By remembering that He is our loving Father, and addressing Him as such, we remind ourselves that He is trustworthy and He will provide us with what we need. He may not always give us the things we want, but He will care for us and provide us with what is for our good and His glory. As Martin Luther said, this prayer opening "is a call to not plunge right into talking to God but to first recollect our situation and realize our standing in Christ before we proceed in prayer."[43]

Who Art in Heaven

We continue the prayer addressing where God both resides and reigns. Remembering that He is an Almighty God who reigns in heaven encourages both praise and humility. It reminds us that He is in control and we are not. It reminds us to approach Him with not only the intimacy of our Father, but with awe-struck wonder.

The combination of these first six words remind us that He is both our loving Father and Almighty God. Honoring both aspects of God's character and His care for us are important.

Hallowed Be Thy Name

In this part of the prayer we recognize that God and His name are holy (hallowed), which means to be set apart, or sacred. A.W. Tozer reminds us that "holy is the way of God. To be holy, He does not conform to a standard. He is that standard. He is holy with an infinite, incomprehensible fullness of purity that is incapable of being other than it is. Because He is holy, all His attributes are; that is, whatever we think of as belonging to God must be thought of as holy."[44]

Luther, Calvin, and Augustine agree that not only is this part of the prayer about praising and declaring that God and His name are holy, but it is also meant to be a petition that God's name would be holy and glorified to all others as well in all nations.

Thy Kingdom Come

Jesus spoke often of His Father's kingdom. He lived out what he said in Matthew 6:33 ESV: "Seek first the kingdom of God and his righteousness." Since God is everywhere and is in control of everything, that means His kingdom is wherever God reigns. God's kingdom is in heaven and on earth and in you and me, if we've invited Him to rule there. To pray "thy kingdom come" means to invite His rule and Lordship into your life and into the whole world.

The kingdom of God is so complex and so important that Jesus used numerous parables to explain it to His various audiences, describing it as a mustard seed, a hidden treasure, a priceless pearl, a vineyard, a wedding feast, a fisherman's net, and more. What we get from all these illustrations is that God's kingdom is good and we should eagerly desire to be a part of it.

According to Revelation 19:16, Jesus will return as King of kings and Lord of lords, establishing a new kingdom and rule forever. Luther believed "the reign of God is only partial now, but the fullness of the future kingdom is unimaginable. All suffering, injustice, poverty and death will be ended. To pray thy kingdom come is to yearn for the future eternal kingdom of God."[45] We can often get distracted by the things we want to see happen on earth, building our own mini-kingdoms. This part of the prayer reminds us that it is all temporary, and we must be focused on God's kingdom, as Jesus did.

Thy Will Be Done

This is a prayer that Jesus Himself would pray in the Garden of Gethsemane hours before His excruciating death. Jesus taught it, prayed it, and lived it, and it was for our benefit–our salvation.

It is an acknowledgement that God knows best. We have a limited vantage point, but God sees the whole picture and how it fits in with His kingdom. Our flesh may want circumstances to turn out differently, but this prayer acknowledges that God knows best. It allows you to surrender your own desires and will to embrace that of God's for your life. Calvin said, "Praying 'thy will be done' is to submit not only our wills to God, but even our feelings, so that we do not become despondent, bitter, and hardened by the things that befall us."[46] God's goal is always for us to be sanctified and shaped more into the likeness of Christ.

On Earth as it is in Heaven

This phrase combines both the Kingdom of God and the will of God, making it relevant to our role in it. How wonderful would it be if things happened here on earth in the same way they do in heaven. We are told in Revelation 21:4 that there is no death, struggle, pain, or tears in heaven. God's dwelling place is more amazing than we can ever try to grasp or imagine with our limited minds. That is, until we one day are called home to live with Him forever.

Heaven is a perfect place, the ultimate reward and destination for each Christian. Knowing that God's will is perfect and complete in heaven offers us hope, comfort, and confidence in His will for us here on earth. Kelly Minter writes, "As God's perfect will is being worked in heaven, we are to pray for its inbreaking right here in our everyday lives. Because the kingdom of heaven is at hand or has come near through Christ, we have access to pray that all that is true in heaven will be made so on earth."[47]

Give Us This Day Our Daily Bread

The pronouns shift from addressing God to now addressing our own needs. Jesus pivots from focusing on God's greatness to our weakness, but in this line He teaches us how important our physical needs are to our heavenly Father. He reinforces this idea in the Sermon on the Mount (shortly after teaching them the Lord's Prayer), telling the listeners not to worry about what they will eat or drink or wear, for their Heavenly Father will take care of them (Matthew 6:25-34).

This line would have reminded His audience of when God told the hungry, grumbling Israelites, "I will rain down bread from heaven for you" (Exodus 16:4a). Every morning the daily provision would rain from heaven–precisely enough bread to satisfy their family's needs, with a double portion on the sixth day so they could rest on the Sabbath. In fact, God met all the Israelites' greatest needs, providing guidance, healing, bread, meat, and even sandals that never wore out.

In this line of the prayer, we acknowledge we are utterly dependent on God for life, sustenance, provision, and protection. God faithfully provides for us the physical and spiritual nourishment we need.

Luther adds that there's a social component to this prayer as well. We are praying not only for our own needs or that of our family but for the needs of all people. "To pray 'give us our daily bread' is to pray for the needs of all the people of the world ... it is to pray for a prosperous and just social order."[48]

Forgive Us Our Sins as We Forgive Those Who Sin Against Us

Right after Jesus reminds us of the physical needs that God can meet, He reminds us to focus on our spiritual and relational needs as well. As John Stott says, "Forgiveness is as indispensable to the life and health of the soul as food is for the body."[49]

This line of the prayer reminds us of the gospel foundation of forgiveness and grace. God is faithful to forgive us when we sin. And we are called to forgive others when they sin against us. It's hard to do. We want to hold onto the anger and bitterness or forget it ever happened. It often requires prayer to be able to let go of any unforgiveness we are carrying in our hearts. Forgiveness is possible for us because we know we have received it when we didn't deserve it.

Jesus saved us from our sin so we could be reconciled to Him and to one another. It may be a struggle in our flesh sometimes, but pursuing reconciliation, love, and forgiving others comes through prayer and a grateful heart that we ourselves have been forgiven. Kelly Minter writes:

> The body of Christ can't exist without forgiveness flowing in and out of us. Without seeking regular forgiveness from God, our relationship with Him is hindered. And without giving it and receiving it amongst ourselves, we can lose our most precious gift–each other ...
>
> Whenever it's possible, we want to be people who seek reconciliation and healing in our relationships (2 Corinthians 2:5-11). God's forgiveness for His people and our forgiveness toward one another are what hold our relationships together.[50]

Lead Us Not into Temptation

Jesus then teaches us that we should pray for protection and provision in the fight against our temptations. Temptation is relentless. Even Jesus experienced it. These temptations come from the schemes of Satan and from circumstances in our lives, neither of which we have the strength to resist on our own, as Jesus did. Our flesh is strong, and we need God's strength to resist the temptations that will lead us into sin.

Jesus used the Word of God to fight against temptations and Satan's lies (see Matthew 4:1-11). He also demonstrated through His words and actions how to live out this line of the prayer. We must pray against temptation and fight it using the Word of God, which reminds us of God's best for us.

Deliver Us from Evil

Augustine indicates that "while praying to 'lead us not into temptation' helps protect us from the evil in us, this petition asks for protection from evil outside of us, such as spiritual warfare, enemies who wish us harm, poverty, dishonor, and death."[51]

We may not want to think about it, or maybe we think too much about it, but Satan and sin and evil are all around us. Thankfully, when Jesus died on the cross and rose again, He defeated sin and Satan and evil. We have access to that same victory power because we are covered by the blood of Jesus. We aren't merely victims of Satan's schemes, but rather we can stand victorious in Christ, fully equipped with the armor of God. You'll read more about the armor of God and spiritual protection in the next chapter.

The Lord's Prayer is only sixty-six words, and yet each phrase of the Lord's Prayer offers a plethora of prayer possibilities.

John Calvin made it a practice to pray the Lord's Prayer daily, while Luther preferred to go line by line, paraphrasing and personalizing as he prayed. Calvin says that "the Lord's Prayer must stamp itself on our prayers, shaping them all the way down."[52]

Whether you pray the Lord's prayer word for word or you personalize the Lord's prayer, may Christ's prayer become your own, leading you to praise and petition God more like Christ.

Interceding in Prayer for Others

Recorded in all four Gospels we read the story of several men who carried their paralyzed friend to Jesus for healing. Jesus was teaching in a house surrounded by people listening to His teachings. Desperate for their friend to get to Jesus, these faithful friends carried him up onto the roof, and then lowered him through the roof on his mat. These friends were willing to do some heavy lifting and some house reconstruction to get their friend before Jesus.

In the same way, when we pray for others, or intercede for them, we are lifting them and their needs up to the throne of God and laying them before the feet of Jesus. When we intercede for others, we are taking our focus off our own needs and focusing on those of others.

Paul encourages Timothy (and us today) "that supplications, prayers, intercessions, and thanksgivings be made for all people, for kings and all who are in high positions, that we may lead a peaceful and quiet life, godly and dignified in every way. This is good, and it is pleasing in the sight of God our Savior, who desires all people to be saved and to come to the knowledge of the truth" (1 Timothy 2:1-4 ESV).

Paul himself was an incredible intercessor. His letters begin and end with prayers of blessing, and sprinkled throughout his letters are the prayers he is praying in intercession for those he loves. Paul would "kneel before the Father in prayer," (see Ephesians 3:14) interceding for those he loved. D. A. Carson writes, "If we follow Paul's example, we will never overlook the monumental importance of praying for others ... We will see it is part of our job to approach God with thanksgiving for others and with intercessions for others. In short, our praying will be shaped by our profound desire to seek what is best for the people of God."[53]

Paul interceded for the spiritual well-being of those he prayed for, recognizing that it was ultimately what mattered. He prayed that Christ would dwell in their hearts (see Ephesians 4:17); that they would comprehend the depths of God's love for them (see Ephesians 4:17b-19); for spiritual wisdom and enlightenment (see Ephesians 1:17-18), and much more.

Jesus was also an incredible intercessor. He prayed for His disciples "for their protection, for the full measure of Christ's joy within them, and for their sanctification by God's Word. Those words in John 17:6-19 are what a parent would pray for their child."[54] He also prayed for us in John 17:20-26, for our unity, for our witness to the world, and for our relationship with Him and our Heavenly Father. It's incredible and humbling to think of our Lord and Savior praying two thousand years ago for you and for me hours before He would go to the cross for us. He was headed toward His death, and yet He took the time to focus on and pray for you and for me and all other believers.

Jesus was praying and interceding for us then, and even more incredibly, He still intercedes for us today. Romans 8:34 says that Jesus "is at the right hand of God and is also interceding for us." In 1 John 2:1 we read that Jesus is our "advocate with the Father," and from Hebrews 7:25 we learn that Jesus "always lives to intercede" for us.

Richard J. Foster explains Jesus' ministry of intercession this way:

> Jesus makes it unmistakably clear to his disciples that His going to the Father would catapult them into a new dimension of prayer ... Jesus is entering his eternal work as Intercessor before the throne of God, and as a result, we are enabled to pray for others with an entirely new authority.

> Our ministry of intercession is made possible only because of Christ's continuing ministry of intercession.[55]

Lifting others up in prayer to the throne of God is a selfless and beautiful way of caring for individuals, whether they are loved ones or strangers we may never meet. Richard J. Foster says that intercession is not only an act of love but a "priestly ministry ... As priests, appointed and anointed by God, we have the honor of going before the Most High on behalf of others ... It is a sacred obligation—and a precious privilege."[56]

Jesus—our Lord, Savior, and great High Priest (see Hebrews 4:14-16)—engages in priestly prayer and ministry for us today from heaven. I don't know about you, but that makes me want to spend more time in prayer, thanking Jesus for the gift of salvation and prayer, and also to spend more time interceding for others as Jesus does.

Using Prayer Cards to Intercede for Others

I've tried many different systems when it comes to recording and keeping track of prayer requests and areas I want to pray. Prayer lists, notebooks, prayer journals, even prayer calendars have been helpful. Trying to keep them all in my head can work sometimes but can also feel overwhelming. So when I read Paul E. Miller's book *A Praying Life* and learned about using prayer cards, I was excited to try it.

Miller shares that one day, when he was struggling to focus his prayers:

> A thought suddenly came to me. *Put the Word to work.* I got some three-by-five index cards and on each one wrote the name of a family member, along with a Scripture that I could use to shape my prayers for that person ...
>
> A list is often a series of scattered prayer requests, while a prayer card focuses on one person or area in your life. It allows you to look at the person or situation from multiple perspectives. Over time, it

helps you reflect on what God does in response to your prayers. You begin to see patterns, and slowly a story unfolds that you find yourself drawn into ... When I pray, I have only one card in front of me at a time, which helps me concentrate on that person or need.[57]

I first started using a prayer card to pray for my husband. I have a long list of Scriptures that come to mind when praying for my children, but sadly Scriptures to pray for my husband don't come as easily to my mind. Creating a prayer card with several areas I wanted to pray for Tim—with a Scripture to pray for each of those areas—has helped me stay focused and reminds me of the specific Scriptures I want to pray for my husband.

I found that prayer card so helpful, I began making them for other areas and people I wanted to pray for. Each family member has a card, as well as friends and individuals in my prayer group and Bible study at church.

I also started making cards to pray for specific topics. For example, I have a card with names of people I would like to see saved and a few Scriptures about salvation. I have a card with names of people I'd like to see experience physical healing and Scriptures to pray about healing. When I learn about natural disasters, wars, and examples of injustice around the world, I look up verses to pray for that particular topic and write down specific prayer requests and Bible verses to help me intercede for those people with God's Word. I have a card for missionaries and mission-based organizations I want to pray for with verses to pray.

Prayer cards have been a wonderful tool to help me stay focused while praying and to ensure I'm interceding for others on the same page as our heavenly Father. And when a prayer request has been answered, I jot a quick note about the answer to prayer with the date in a different color ink next to the prayer request. Sometimes we need those visual reminders that God answers prayers. This then encourages us to continue interceding in prayer.

Scripture Prayers of Petition and Intercession

Thank You, Heavenly Father, for listening to my prayers when I call out to You. (Based on Jeremiah 29:12.)

Thank You, God, for supplying all my needs, according to the riches of Your glory in Jesus Christ. (Based on Philippians 4:19.)

Help me to cast all my anxieties and cares on You because You care for me. (Based on 1 Peter 5:7.)

Help me to not worry about _____. May I always seek Your kingdom, knowing You will provide all I need, just as You feed the birds and clothe the grass of the field. (Based on Matthew 6:25-34.)

Help me to pray in the Spirit on all occasions with all kinds of prayers and requests. Help me to be alert and keep on praying. (Based on Ephesians 6:18.)

Lord, help me to lift up others with all types of petitions, prayers, intercession, and thanksgiving, that we may live peaceful and quiet lives in all godliness and holiness. (Based on 1 Timothy 2:1-2.)

Lord, help me to be thankful for those in my life, and help me to continually lift them up in my prayers. (Based on 1 Thessalonians 1:2.)

Help me to not worry about anything but instead pray about everything. (Based on Philippians 4:6 NLT.)

Our Father in heaven,
    Hallowed be Your name.
Your kingdom come.
Your will be done
    On earth as it is in heaven.
Give us this day our daily bread.
And forgive us our debts,
    As we forgive our debtors.
And do not lead us into temptation,
    But deliver us from the evil one.
For Yours is the kingdom and the
    power and the glory forever.
Amen. (Matthew 6:9-13 NKJV)

Part 3

Praying Scripture by Topic

Chapter 8

Praying for Spiritual Protection

Put on the full armor of God, so that you can take your stand against the devil's schemes ... Take ... the sword of the Spirit, which is the word of God. And pray in the Spirit on all occasions with all kinds of prayers and requests. With this in mind, be alert and always keep on praying ...

–Ephesians 6:6-11, 17-18

Whether we want to admit it or not, we are in a spiritual battle. Satan is our enemy, keeping us from living the life of freedom and victory that Jesus offers us. Recognizing that we are at war, knowing who our enemy is, and knowing the strategies and the spiritual weapons we have been provided to fight this battle are critical for spiritual protection and victory.

Ms. Clara says in the opening scene of the movie *War Room*:

War. It's been part of humanity in every age ... There always seems to be something to fight for. But one thing that has been true of every war–behind the field of battle, someone has developed a strategy ...

I find myself amazed that of the many battles we engage in to-day ... very few of us know how to fight the right way, or understand who we're really fighting against. To win any battle, you've got to have the right strategy and resources because victories don't come by accident.[58]

Ms. Clara isn't wrong. Paul wrote about the war we are in and the strategies and weapons we need for this battle: "For we are not fighting against flesh-and-blood enemies, but against evil rulers and authorities of the unseen world, against mighty powers in this dark world, and against evil spirits in the heavenly places. Therefore, put on every piece of God's armor so you will be able to resist the enemy in the time of evil" (Ephesians 6:12-13 NLT).

A Battle Fought Through Prayer

In a time of spiritual battle we can feel exhausted, alone, powerless, and absolutely desperate for God to show up powerfully. Let's spend some time paying attention to how some of our Bible heroes prayed when they encountered a physical or spiritual battle, and consider how that can help us as we fight our own spiritual battles.

Pray for Opened Spiritual Eyes

In 2 Kings 6, Elisha the prophet has been summoned to see the king but discovers that he is completely surrounded by horses, troops, and chariots. Elisha's servant is terrified, and Elisha tells him, "'Don't be afraid! ... For there are more on our side than on theirs!' Then Elisha prayed, 'O LORD, open his eyes and let him see!' The LORD opened the young man's eyes, and when he looked up, he saw that the hillside around Elisha was filled with horses and chariots of fire" (2 Kings 6:16-17 NLT). A few chapters later, Elisha prays that the Arameans would be blinded, and God answers that prayer, too.

Elisha's prayers show us it's important to see what is really going on around us, not in the physical realm but the spiritual realm. I honestly think it would be terrifying to see what was really happening in the spiritual realm around us. But like Elisha's servant experienced, we would be comforted knowing we have angel armies also at work around us.

Thank God that He is working, even when you can't see it. Pray that God would open your eyes to see what Satan and his armies are doing around you. Pray that your eyes would be opened to the spiritual resources you have available around you to help you defeat Satan's lies and power in your life and to find victory in this battle. Seek what God is doing and what He's trying to teach you in your battle.

Persevere in Prayer and Spiritual Understanding

In Daniel 10 we learn that Daniel received a vision and a revelation that a great war was coming. Daniel didn't have the details about the war or any idea how to stop this great war from coming, but he knew the new king would expect him to have the answers. Only, Daniel didn't. He could have tried to form his own plans or strategies to fight a war he knew little about. He could have found experts to help him formulate a plan. But Daniel knew He needed understanding that came from God and the spiritual realm, not the worldly one which didn't hold the answers he needed.

At least three times a day for three weeks Daniel prayed, as was his custom. He fasted. He waited. Until finally, Daniel got an answer through an angel who appeared before him. The angel tells him, "Do not be afraid, Daniel. Since the first day that you set your mind to gain understanding and to humble yourself before your God, your words were heard, and I have come in response to them. But the prince of the Persian kingdom resisted me twenty-one days" (Daniel 10:12b-13).

God heard Daniel's prayer from the very first day Daniel started praying for wisdom. Things were happening in the spiritual realm that Daniel was not aware of, but God was listening, and He was in control.

Daniel couldn't see that angels were engaged in a spiritual war while he was striving to help the king prepare for a physical one, which reminds us that during our storms and battles God is working in ways we may not see until further down the road, when we can look back and see how God was at work.

Sometimes God answers our prayers immediately. Many times, He does not. It's not because He doesn't care; He just sees a bigger picture than we can. He sees all the spiritual warfare and everything happening in the spiritual realms. He knows how everybody's lives fit together, including the impact your life has on others. He sees all the details. He knows how many hairs are on your head, how many tears you've cried, and how many days you've been praying for something. And one day, we will be able to see how God was at work in that situation and our lives.

Pray with Other People

King Jehoshaphat was hard at work reforming the nation of Judah according to God's holy standards and bringing peace to the land when he discovered three enemy armies coming up to surround and attack them. "Alarmed, Jehoshaphat resolved to inquire of the Lord" (2 Chronicles 20:3a).

After some time in prayer, he tells all the people of Judah to fast and to gather together at the temple in Jerusalem. They didn't gather to create battle plans and to prepare for battle, but instead "the people of Judah came together to seek help from the LORD" (2 Chronicles 20:4a).

I love that his first response is to turn to prayer, and I also love that he calls people to pray with him. There is power in praying together and power in other people battling with you in prayer. There is also power in admitting your need for prayer. Sometimes, just admitting to someone you are in a spiritual battle and need prayer brings enough light into your situation that Satan loses his grip on you. Then, when you couple that with prayer, he's in trouble!

Pray with Praise and Trust in God's Character

Continuing where we left off, King Jehoshaphat prays a powerful prayer with his people, praising God for His character and His faithfulness. He ends his passionate prayer by humbly acknowledging their trust in God. He concludes his prayer with the statement, "For we have no power to face this vast army that is attacking us. We do not know what to do, but our eyes are on you" (2 Chronicles 20:12b).

He didn't pray for any specific outcome. Prayer and praise were their battle plan. Worship was their weapon. They put their complete trust in God, remembering the things He did for the Israelites in the past and praising Him for the victory they believed they would receive.

God answered their prayer. He tells them, "Do not be afraid or discouraged because of this vast army. For the battle is not yours, but God's" (2 Chronicles 20:15b). God was with them and gave them victory in a way that could only have been God orchestrating it (see 2 Chronicles 20:14-30).

Remember and praise God's faithfulness and His character as you fight your battles. Praising God will remind you of who He is and what He has done, and give Him room to work in your current situation, too.

Pray Big, Specific Prayers

Joshua and the Israelites had several battles to fight in order to claim the Promised Land. This time, Joshua and the Israelites were battling five armies that were ready to attack their allies, the Gibeonites. Joshua boldly prayed to the Creator of the moon and the sun that He would make the sun and the moon stop their orbit until they had won the battle (see Joshua 10:12). And the Creator of the earth, sun, and moon honored Joshua's prayer!

Joshua could have simply prayed that they'd have success in battle or for protection. But it would have been a little harder to see if God was answering their prayers or if it was their own effort that led to their success. Instead, Joshua chose a very specific prayer request, one where if God answered, they'd be sure to know it was God at work. He also could have kept that bold prayer to himself, but instead he courageously prayed it aloud for everyone to hear, so that if and when God answered, they'd all be in awe of God at work. In fact, Israel's enemies worshiped the gods of the sun and the moon, so seeing the sun and moon stop moving would have proven the power of the one true God.

In contrast to Jehoshaphat, who did not pray for a specific outcome and put his full trust in the Lord, Joshua prayed for a very specific result. Both types of prayer are good, for different reasons. In one, we give God full control to do His work in the way and the timing that brings Him the most glory. Sometimes, God is able to do far more than we could ever ask or imagine (see Ephesians 3:20).

On the other hand, when we pray specific prayers, we know exactly if and when it has been answered. Joshua knew that God helped them fight and find victory because God answered his specific prayer by making the sun stand still so the Israelites could continue fighting and find victory.

In the book *Streams in the Desert*, Lettie Cowman writes "aimlessness in prayer accounts for so many seemingly unanswered prayers ... Fill out your check for something definite, and it will be cashed at the bank of Heaven when presented in Jesus' name. Dare to be definite with God."[59]

Praying on the Armor of God

In Ephesians 6, Paul reminded us of the spiritual battle we are in, and then concludes with the truth that we are to "put on every piece of God's armor so you will be able to resist the enemy in the time of evil" (Ephesians 6:13 NLT).

Each piece of the armor of God can be found by having a relationship with Jesus. When you give your life to Jesus, you are clothed in the whole armor of God, but we need to keep intentionally putting on our armor to protect us from Satan's schemes. In her Bible study *Armor of God*, Priscilla Shirer writes, "Prayer is the linchpin that holds our armor together. It is what activates all the other pieces and fortifies you as a soldier in battle. It is the device that empowers and 'charges up' every other piece so they can be used effectively against the enemy. Without prayer ... your armor cannot, will not, be infused with the power that only God's Spirit can give."[60]

Here's a little about each piece of the armor of God and a Scripture-based prayer to help you put on and activate each piece of the armor through prayer.

Belt of Truth

"Stand firm then, with the belt of truth buckled about your waist" (Ephesians 6:14a).

The belt holds many of the pieces of the armor in place. It is crucial to have this piece in place, and it comes by knowing God's Word and having its truths remind you of God's will, your salvation, and what He says about you.

Heavenly Father, I buckle myself up with the belt of truth. May I have spiritual eyes that are open and aware of Satan's schemes and lies in my life (2 Kings 6:15-17). Show me Your ways, oh Lord, and teach me Your paths. Guide me in Your truth and teach me (Psalm 25:5). I thank You that You are the light of the world who helps me to not walk in darkness, but to walk according to the light of truth (John 8:12). Help me to hold fast to Your truths, for the truth is able to set me free and helps me walk in victory (John 8:31-32). Amen.

Breastplate of Righteousness

"Stand firm then ... with the breastplate of righteousness in place" (Ephesians 6:14).

The breastplate covers our most vulnerable areas–the heart, lungs, and gut. Because of Jesus' sacrifice on the cross, we can walk boldly, covered in righteousness, which covers our guilt and shame. Righteousness is upright living that aligns with God's expectations—we can't be righteous on our own, but because of Jesus' death on the cross, we are made righteous and holy.

God, I thank You that I am covered by the breastplate of righteousness. I thank You that You have provided a way for me to be righteous and holy before You, thanks to the precious blood of Your son, Jesus. Help me to guard my heart (Proverbs 4:23) and to be made new in the attitude of my mind, to put on my new self, created to be like God in righteousness and holiness (Ephesians 4:22-23). Protect me from the temptations I battle, for in Your faithfulness You will not let me be tempted beyond what I can bear (1 Corinthians 10:13). Amen.

Footwear of the Gospel of Peace

"Stand firm ... with your feet fitted with the readiness that comes from the gospel of peace" (Ephesians 6:14-15).

The sandals soldiers wore protected their feet as they traveled, giving them security. In the same way, the good news of the gospel gives us peace and security, helps us move forward in faith, and compels us to share our source of peace, the good news of the gospel, with others.

Father, I pray that I would put on the gospel of peace and carry it with me wherever I go and to whomever I interact with today. Help me to let go of all fearful and anxious thoughts and let the good news of the gospel flood my heart and mind with a peace that transcends all understanding (Philippians 4:6-7). I pray that words may be given me so that I would fearlessly make known the mystery of the Gospel (Ephesians 6:19). I pray that I would courageously bring good news that proclaims peace to others (Nahum 1:15). Amen.

Shield of Faith

"In addition to all this, take up the shield of faith, with which you can extinguish all the flaming arrows of the evil one" (Ephesians 6:16).

The shield allows you to protect yourself from an enemy's weapon. When Satan lies to us or makes us feel weary, fearful, or discouraged, it is our faith and God's truths that have the power to stop Satan's lies in their tracks. Our faith is what allows us to stand firm on what we believe in. It encourages us forward, confident that God is with us and that His Word is true and trustworthy.

Heavenly Father, I pray that I would take up Your shield of faith that will extinguish all the darts and threats hurled my way by the enemy. Help me to stand firm against the enemy's lies and threats, to resist him and stand firm in my faith (1 Peter 5:8-9). I thank You that Your word is flawless and is a shield for all those who take refuge in You (Proverbs 30:5). I admit that I do believe, but help my unbelief (Mark 9:23-24). Help my faith to grow (Luke 17:5-6). Amen.

Helmet of Salvation

"Take the helmet of salvation" (Ephesians 6:17a).

A helmet is something you wear to protect your head and your brain from injury, just as remembering the truth of your salvation and your standing with God can protect your mind and your thoughts. Salvation is rescue from a state of danger. By remembering our salvation, thanks to Jesus' death on the cross, we are able to live according to our standing with God–as His beloved child, an heir, and fully equipped to fight against our enemy.

My Redeeming God, I put on the helmet of salvation, confessing that Jesus died to set me free from sin (Romans 10:9-10). Help me to stand firm and not get burdened again by a yoke of slavery (Galatians 5:1). Thank You for Your great love for me, for Your mercy, for Your grace, that makes me alive in Christ (Ephesians 2:4, 8). Thank You that my salvation is a gift and not something I can earn (Ephesians 2:8). I pray that I would continually be transformed by the renewing of my mind so that I would know God's good, pleasing, and perfect will for me (Romans 12:2). Amen.

Sword of the Spirit

"Take ... the sword of the Spirit, which is the word of God" (Ephesians 6:17).

The sword of the Spirit is an offensive weapon in the armor of God. All the others we've mentioned are defensive and protective. We can't always be in a defensive posture, though. We have the power to be victorious in Christ simply by using the powerful word of God to stop Satan in his tracks, like Jesus used Scripture to fight Satan's temptations in the wilderness in Matthew 4.

Heavenly Father, I take up Your sword of the Spirit, Your very Word, which has the power to demolish strongholds, arguments, and every pretension that sets itself up against the knowledge of God (2 Corinthians 10:3-5). I thank You that man does not live on bread alone, but on every word that comes from Your mouth (Matthew 4:3-4). Help me to use Your Word to refute the devil's lies as Jesus did (Matthew 4). Thank You that Your Word has the power to teach, rebuke, correct, and train me in righteousness so that I can be equipped to do Your good works (2 Timothy 3:16-17). Thank You that Your Word is alive, active, and sharper than any double-edged sword (Hebrews 4:12). Amen.

Prayer

"And pray in the Spirit on all occasions with all kinds of prayers and requests. With this in mind, be alert and always keep on praying" (Ephesians 6:18a).

As mentioned in chapter 2, many sources will say that there are six pieces of armor, with the Word of God being our only offensive weapon. But prayer is also a powerful weapon we have in spiritual warfare. Prayer helps us put on our spiritual armor, and it allows us to tap into God's power and His ability to fight on our behalf. Charles

Spurgeon writes, "Prayer brings inner strength to God's warriors and sends them forth to spiritual battle with their muscles firm and their armor in place."[61]

> Heavenly Father, I thank You that You gave us the gift of prayer, a form of communication and connection with You. I pray that I would devote myself to prayer (Colossians 4:2), that I would not be anxious about anything, but in every situation, by prayer and petition, with thanksgiving, present my requests to You (Philippians 4:6). I thank You that I do not pray alone, but that the Spirit intercedes for me with groans that words cannot express (Romans 8:26). I thank you that Jesus intercedes for me in prayer (Romans 8:34), and I thank You, Heavenly Father, for bending down to listen to my prayers (Psalm 116:2). Help me to grow in prayer and may my heart grow in alignment with Your heart as I pray. Amen.

Fighting from Victory

All this talk about a spiritual enemy we can't see and spiritual battles we can't completely understand can be overwhelming and even frightening. But we have hope.

The good news is that while a battle rages around us, we are not alone. God does not want us to be victims of Satan, but rather victors with Christ. We are not fighting for victory; we are fighting from a place of victory. Jesus says in Revelation 3:21 NLT, "Those who are victorious will sit with me on my throne, just as I was victorious and sat with my Father on his throne." Jesus shares His victory with us. He wants us to be victorious, too. And He gave us authority, weapons, and armor to aid us in claiming that victory.

James urges us to "humble yourselves before God. Resist the devil, and he will flee from you" (James 4:7 NLT). How do we resist the devil? By reminding him of what Jesus did for us. By saying Jesus' name aloud when we know Satan is attacking. By praying on our spiritual armor. By reminding him that Jesus has already won, and one day, Satan and all his evil angel friends will be vanquished, thrown into the lake of fire that was prepared for them.

We are victors not victims as we resist Satan and his evil schemes with Jesus' name, our prayers, and the Word of God at our disposal.

Scripture Prayers for Spiritual Protection

Help me to not be afraid or discouraged because of the spiritual battle I am facing. For the battle is not mine, but Yours, and You will handle it. (Based on 2 Chronicles 20:15b.)

God, help me to not wage war as the world does. Thank You for providing us with two weapons to fight with–spiritual weapons that are stronger than any worldly weapon. The weapons You provide have divine power to demolish strongholds. With Your Word and prayer, help me to demolish arguments and every pretension that sets itself up against You, and help me take captive every thought to make it obedient to Christ. (Based on 2 Corinthians 10:3-5.)

Help me be sober-minded and watchful, for my adversary the devil prowls around like a roaring lion, seeking to devour me. Help me to resist him and stand strong in my faith. (Based on 1 Peter 5:8-9 ESV.)

Lord, open my eyes and let me see the spiritual warfare going on around me so I can battle it properly with Your Word and prayer. (Based on 2 Kings 6:17.)

Thank You that since the first day that I set my mind to gain understanding and to humble myself before You, my words were heard by You, and You come in response to them. (Based on Daniel 10:12.)

Help me to put on Your full armor so that when the day of evil comes, I may be able to stand my ground. Help me to stand firm then, with the belt of truth buckled around my waist, with the breastplate of righteousness in place, and with my feet fitted with the readiness that comes from the gospel of peace. Help me to take up the shield of faith, with which I can extinguish all the flaming arrows of the evil one. Help me take the helmet of salvation and the sword of the Spirit, which is Your Word. And help me to pray in Your Spirit on all occasions with all kinds of prayers and requests. With You is the victory! (Based on Ephesians 6:14-18.)

Thank You that in Jesus we have peace. Even though in this world we will have tribulation, I thank You that we can take heart because You have overcome the world. (Based on John 16:33.)

Thank You, Lord, that the demons submit to us in Your precious and powerful name. Thank You that we have power over the enemy. (Based on Luke 10:17-19.)

Chapter 9

Praying for Your Family

Prayer is the mortar which keeps our house together. [62]
—Saint Teresa of Avila

When God created us, He designed us to live and grow within a family unit. Our families are important to our own well-being, as well as foundational to society's well-being. Our families have the ability to reflect the character and the glory of God. The relationship between husband and wife can show us the depths of God's love, care, and faithfulness toward us. The relationship between parent and child can show us a beautiful picture of God's endless love and patience toward us.

We know it's important to care for our family's physical needs. The never-ending bills, meals, dishes, and laundry are evidence of the care our family needs and of our role in meeting these needs. Each of these repeated acts, not always fun or glamorous, are a way for us to humbly serve our family and God.

It's also important to care for our family's spiritual needs. We can set aside intentional time to grow in our faith together, whether it be through attending church, prayer, serving others, or reading and discussing the Bible together.

Right now our families are in a spiritual battle and need our prayers. Satan doesn't like a family who prays and who loves God, and He will try to steal, kill, and destroy the sacred family unit. But he loses his power when our families and our homes are prayed over, covered by the powerful name of Jesus.

Nehemiah told his warriors when they were preparing to protect the broken wall around Jerusalem from an enemy army, "Don't be afraid of them. Remember the Lord, who is great and awesome, and fight for your families, your sons and your daughters, your wives and your homes" (Nehemiah 4:14b). He then provided each soldier with weapons they could use to protect both the wall around Jerusalem and his own family.

The weapons we've been provided are prayer and God's Word, and we can use them separately or together to protect and fight for our families against Satan's schemes.

Praying Through Your Home

We take measures to protect our home and our loved ones. We lock windows and doors, install security systems, and we buy insurance in case something should happen. We can also take spiritual measures to protect our home and our family.

Years ago, our family felt like it was struggling in many ways. My anxiety was keeping me up at night. My husband and I were stressed and arguing more than normal. Something just didn't feel right, and I wasn't sure what it was. But then, at a Bible study session I attended, I learned about the practice of praying through your home and anointing it with oil. When I got home, I decided to try it. The results were immediate. As I went through the house praying, I felt my anxiety lift and I felt joy in my heart. I felt God's presence in a way I hadn't in a while. I found joy in praying over my home, each family member, my marriage, and our sleep. Afterward, I felt closer to my husband than I had in a long time. That night, we all slept well.

The practice of using anointing oil to pray over your home began at Passover, when the Israelites anointed their doorposts with lamb's blood, marking their home as holy and belonging to God, while also protecting their family members inside. After that first time of anointing, God established the use of anointing oil to indicate a place or an object as holy and sacred. God commanded Moses to "take the anointing oil and anoint the tabernacle and everything in it; consecrate it and all its furnishings, and it will be holy" (Exodus 40:9).

You can buy anointing oil (oil that has been blessed) or you can use essential oils or even olive oil or another cooking oil. You don't need anything special, unless that's your preference. You have the power and the authority to pray over the oil and it will become consecrated anointing oil. Pray over the oil that it will be holy and anointed. After you have purchased and/or prayed over the oil, then you can begin to rub a dab of oil over door frames and other places you want to anoint or set apart as holy, praying aloud as you go.

I'll share a few of my favorite Scriptures that you can use as you pray over your home and various places and rooms within your home, but feel free to use whatever verses the Lord brings to mind and pray as you feel led.

As you begin, John Eldridge recommends praying a prayer of consecration and authority for your home like this one:

Father, thank you for the blessing and provision of this home. We bring it under our authority now, and the authority of Jesus Christ. The keys to this home have been given to us–authority has been given to us. We renounce all ungodliness and sinful activity that has ever taken place in this home ... We cancel every claim the enemy can make here, by the blood of Jesus Christ. We cleanse this home with the blood of Christ–everything spiritual, everything physical. We consecrate and dedicate this home to the rule of Jesus Christ and to the Holy Spirit ... Come Holy Spirit, come and fill every part of this home with the glory of your kingdom, with love, with peace, with holy rest. Jesus, we ask your angels to establish your kingdom here, to build a shield of protection around our home. In the mighty name of Jesus Christ the Lord, we now proclaim this home and everything in it the property of the kingdom of God.[63]

After praying a prayer similar to the one John Eldridge shared, dedicate your home to the Lord, inviting Him into it, that He would make it holy, that it would be a sacred place where He abides with your family. God says, "I have set this Temple apart to be holy–this place you have built where my name will be honored forever. I will always watch over it, for it is dear to my heart," (1 Kings 9:3b NLT). God also says, "Now My eyes will be open and My ears attentive to the prayer offered in this place. For now I have chosen and consecrated this house so that My name may be there forever, and My eyes and My heart will be there perpetually" (2 Chronicles 7:15-16 NASB).

Anoint your door frames leading into and outside the house with oil as you pray for protection over your home. Pray for Jesus' blood and protection over your home just as the blood of the lamb protected the Israelites at Passover. After anointing both front and back doors, I grab my Bible and recite Psalm 91 aloud over my home. Also, pray that all who enter your home will "go out in joy and be led forth in peace" (Isaiah 55:12a).

Pray that God would post angels to watch over your home: "The angel of the LORD encamps around those who fear him, and he delivers them" (Psalm 34:7) and "he will command his angels concerning you to guard you in all your ways; they will lift you up in their hands, so that you will not strike your foot against a stone" (Psalm 91:11b-12).

Pray for your home itself, that it would be a safe and peaceful place for your family to thrive, for "the fruit of that righteousness will be peace; its effect will be quietness and confidence forever. My people will live in peaceful dwelling places, in secure homes, in undisturbed places of rest" (Isaiah 32:17-18).

Pray that each member of the home would love the Lord and that the Lord would show you how to use your home to serve you and those around you. Boldly declare "as for me and my household, we will serve the LORD" (Joshua 24:15b).

Pray in your kitchen, thanking Him for the food He has provided, and then asking Him to continue to "give us this day our daily bread" (Matthew 6:11 NKJV). Pray that each member of your family would be able to "taste and see that the Lord is good" (Psalm 34:8a) and that your family wouldn't "live on bread alone, but on every word that comes from the mouth of God" (Matthew 4:4b). Pray that when your family gathers to "eat or drink or whatever you do, do it all for the glory of God" (1 Corinthians 10:31).

Anoint your dining room table, praying it would be a sacred space where you can grow closer together and to God as you eat and study God's Word around it. Anoint your dining room and the living room (or wherever your family has the majority of their conversations), praying that "your conversation be always full of grace, seasoned with salt, so that you may know how to answer everyone" (Colossians 4:6b).

Pray in each bedroom for any specific requests for that family member. Anoint the tops of window sills and door frames, praying for protection and specific needs for the occupant of that room. Anoint bedposts or pillowcases with oil and pray for the sleep of each person, for "in peace [_____] will lie down and sleep, for you alone, oh Lord, make [_____] dwell in safety" (based on Psalm 4:8).

In your bedroom, anoint your bed posts or pillowcases, lifting up specific areas you want God to move in your marriage. Pray that you and your spouse will grow in unity, and that God would give you both "singleness of heart and action, so that [we] will always fear [God] and that all will then go well for [us] and for [our] children" (based on Jeremiah 32:39).

As you move around the house, anointing various areas and praying, ask God to reveal any darkness or evil in your home, and be sensitive to what you feel Him leading you toward. Remove any items you come across and feel convicted to remove from your home, such as books or movies or objects that you think are inappropriate or that have a connection to evil spirits, believing that "the yoke will be destroyed because of the anointing oil" (Isaiah 10:27b NKJV). I have heard several testimonies of people whose rebellious or troubled children found peace, or of marriages that were restored, when certain objects were removed from their bedrooms and homes.

Anoint desks, workspaces, homeschooling/homework spaces, etc, praying God blesses the work done there. Pray for those using those spaces that the work they do will bring God glory, that each person would "work at it with all your heart, as working for the Lord, not for human masters" (see Colossians 3:23).

You can also walk your yard, or the perimeter of your yard, thanking God for every square inch of land He has provided, and ask that He would protect it based on the Scripture in Joshua 1:3 and 1:5. "I will give you every place where you set your foot ... No one will be able to stand against you all the days of your life. As I was with Moses, so I will be with you; I will never leave you nor forsake you."

Pray boldly for anything else the Spirit brings to mind as you go through your home. This is a sacred and spiritual time, so stay sensitive to whatever the Spirit is guiding you to pray for or do or remove.

Sometimes I'll play worship music while I pray throughout our home; other times I'll start in silence and feel led to start singing a particular worship song or hymn. Both are invitations and personal reminders that the Spirit of God is welcome in my home.

I personally anoint my house in this way about once a year, or whenever I feel like there is something off around the home, such as when we're feeling anxious or sad or sick. I have a friend who anoints her house every New Year's Eve, praying not only for her home and her family, but for the new year.

I know people who anoint their new homes in this way before they even move a single box in. I know others who while having their homes built wrote verses into wood beams or on the concrete floor of their home. In this way, God's Word becomes a part of the foundation and framing of your home.

I know of someone who felt an evil presence in their basement, so they avoided going into it. But then they anointed their home and the basement, and now she has her office and a gym in the basement, and she finds it a place of joy and purpose.

Anoint your home whenever and however the Spirit leads you to. Prepare to feel His peace and guidance and joy in your heart and home as you do so.

Establishing Rhythms of Family Prayer

I highly encourage you to institute or continue a time of family prayer. Mother Teresa encouraged Christians, "Let us love one another as God loves each one of us. And where does this love begin? In our own home. How does it begin? By praying together."[64]

Whether you meet as a family weekly or daily, whether it's around your dinner table or in the living room or before bed, the details don't matter. What matters is that you are praying together and praying for each other in a way that works for your family. It's a special time that you set aside to focus on your family's relationship with God and with each other, so that you can learn more about each other's cares, needs, and spiritual well-being. It may not seem like much is happening during these prayer times, but you are creating a safe and sacred place for the spiritual well-being and growth of each member of your family. Each family member is having their hearts opened to each other and to God as they pray together and for each other. Each family prayer is inviting God's presence and protection into our hearts and our home. Each family prayer has the ability to bind hearts and families together.

Dr. James Dobson reminds families that "there is nothing more important than parents passing on a generational legacy of faith and values to their children."[65] Holding times of family prayer and Bible study are wonderful opportunities where we can live out the words of Proverbs 22:6 KJV: "Train up a child in the way he should go." We can teach and model for our children how to study the Bible, how to live for God's kingdom, and how to pray when we set aside intentional times of family prayer and Bible study.

In our family, we gather every weekend to read a Bible story or watch an episode of *The Chosen*.[66] We discuss it together and then share our prayer requests and pray for each other. My boys nicknamed this our "home church time," and it is a special time for our family that strengthens our faith and our relationship with each other.

In addition to praying as a family, we can also pray for our families on our own, such as during our normal Bible reading and prayer time. I've found one of the best ways to grow in the habit of praying for your loved ones is to pray as you go about your normal routines. I try to pray for my family while doing the dishes, thanking God for the food and blessings He has provided and also lifting up our family's current needs. When I'm hanging my husband's freshly laundered clothes on their hangers in our closet, it reminds me to pray for my husband and his work. When I'm folding my boys' clothes, it reminds me to say a quick prayer for them. When the kids are heading to school, I try to say a quick prayer about their school day and pray for their teachers.

I also love praying the prayers of Paul over my family, but personalizing them. Inspired by the words in Ephesians 3:16-21, they might look something like this:

Heavenly Father, I pray that out of Your glorious riches, You would strengthen our family with power that comes from Your Holy Spirit, so that Christ may dwell in our hearts through faith. (Take some time to thank God for Jesus and for the salvation of your family members, or pray for any family members that haven't found salvation yet). I pray that each of us would be rooted and established in Your love and have power along with all the saints to grasp how wide and long and high and deep is Your love. I pray we would know this love that surpasses knowledge, so that we would be filled to the measure of all the fullness of You, Father God.

Thank You, God, that You can do immeasurably more than we ask or imagine, according to Your power at work within us, for Your glory. (Take some time thanking God for the mighty things He is doing in your family members or ways He has provided and blessed your family. Lift up any specific prayer requests you have for your family).

May You be glorified forever and ever. Amen.

You'll find several of my favorite Scriptures to pray for your family below. You can also check out my website *www.embracing.life* and sign up to receive a printable calendar with thirty-one Scripture-based prayers to help you pray for your family. Let's protect our families with both of the weapons we've been provided–God's Word and prayer.

Scripture Prayers for Your Family

Lord, I pray that each member of our family would believe in the Lord Jesus, and that our whole household would be saved. I pray that our whole family would rejoice because we all believe in You. (Based on Acts 16:31, 34.)

I pray that our whole family, as Your chosen people, holy and dearly loved, would be clothed with compassion, kindness, humility, gentleness, and patience. Help us bear with each other in love and forgive whatever grievances we may have against one another. Help us forgive each other as You have forgiven us. And I ask that over all these virtues, we would put on love, which binds us all together in perfect unity. (Based on Colossians 3:12-14.)

May our whole household fear You and choose to serve You wholeheartedly. (Based on Joshua 24:14-15 NLT.)

Write the commandments You have given us upon our hearts. Help us to impress them upon our children/grandchildren. May we have many family conversations about You as we sit at home and walk along the road, when we lie down and when we get up. (Based on Deuteronomy 6:6-7.)

Oh, Most High Lord, I pray that You would be our dwelling and our refuge. I pray that no harm would overtake our family and no disaster come near our home. Command Your angels to guard and protect us. (Based on Psalm 91:9-11.)

I pray that our family would enjoy good health and that all may go well with us physically as well as spiritually. (Based on 3 John 1:2.)

Help us to grow in each of the fruit of the Spirit: love, joy, peace, patience, kindness, goodness, faithfulness, gentleness, and self-control toward one another. (Based on Galatians 5:22-23.)

May our family be devout and God-fearing; may we give generously to those in need and pray regularly. (Based on Acts 10:2.)

May You bless our family and keep us, may Your face shine on us and be gracious to us, may You turn Your face toward us and give us peace. (Based on Numbers 6:24-26.)

Oh, Lord, may You help our family to flourish. May we be blessed by You, the Maker of heaven and earth. (Based on Psalm 115:14-15.)

Chapter 10

Praying for Your Marriage

Father, not my will, but your will be done in my marriage. Amen. [67]
                                                    –Laura Gethers

I attended a bridal shower a few years ago where each attendee was to write on a little card a piece of advice for the bride-to-be. Toward the end of the shower, the maid of honor read the advice to the bride-to-be. Some were silly or made the bride-to-be blush. Others were words of wisdom that I agreed with or knew I needed to take to heart myself. And then the maid of honor read one card that simply said, "Pray Scripture for your marriage."

I didn't write those words on that card, but I wished I had. It's fantastic advice. I believe if I had practiced praying Scripture earlier in my marriage, it would have saved me and Tim a lot of heartache and struggles. If I'm ever asked again to give a bride-to-be advice, I will echo those five words written by a wise woman because I have seen and experienced how powerful and transformative it can be to pray Scripture for your marriage.

I knew it was important to pray for our marriage and to pray for my husband, Tim, but a lot of the time I didn't know what I should be praying for. We had different personalities, expectations, communication styles, love languages, and different ideas about how to load the dishwasher. I found our differences the easiest to focus on and to pray about, but then I got bitter with both God and with Tim when nothing seemed to change.

It wasn't until I learned to pray Scripture for my marriage and for Tim that I began to see God working, but not in the way I expected.

Praying Scripture for Your Marriage

Jodie Berndt writes in her book *Praying the Scriptures for Your Marriage*: "From the union between Adam and Eve to the language in Song of Solomon to the fact Jesus' first miracle took place at a wedding to the Revelation promise of Christ's triumphant return to marry his people, the Bible is one big wedding story. God loves marriage–and he loves your marriage."[68]

Our marriages–a covenant that is so beautiful and special and made for God's glory–will send Satan scrambling to divide husband and wife. Our marriages can quickly turn into a battleground in which it's easy to view our spouse as the one we're fighting against, when in reality, we are fighting against Satan's schemes and our own sin natures within our marriage.

It's important to note that if you are experiencing any form of intentional abuse from your spouse, they are in sin and you should get outside help. God does not want any of His children to be hurt, and that includes you and your children. God loves you and cares about your heart and your safety and protection. The biblical role of submission is meant to be a source of love and protection, but if it is one of abuse or of keeping you a victim, that is not God's way.

If your marriage is struggling in any way, know that God has resurrection power and He can resurrect anything, including your relationship. While praying for our marriage is powerful, sometimes we may need help from trained counselors or others we trust to help us restore our relationships to a place of health and victory. There's no shame in seeking marriage counseling, if needed, and in fact, it shows how much you desire to invest in the health and well-being of your marriage and your spouse.

After I had been praying Scripture for a while for my children and their speech and seen God moving in those prayers, I decided I needed to find a Scripture or two to claim and pray for my marriage.

When we were dating, Tim and I had claimed Romans 1:12 as our verse: "that you and I may be mutually encouraged by each other's faith." We would write it on the bottom of greeting cards we would give to each other, but now I began to pray it for us. Yet, I felt I needed to find a verse that defined our mission for our marriage.

I prayed for a verse and came across a plethora that I could pray, so I decided to keep a running list on a sheet of notebook paper tucked into my Bible. But one day, while doing my Bible reading in the book of Jeremiah, a particular verse stood out that I knew was exactly what I was looking for: "I will give them singleness of heart and action, so that they will always fear me and that all will then go well for them and for their children after them" (Jeremiah 32:39).

I prayed that verse and sought to live it out in my interactions with Tim as we cared for our children and our home together, and over time, we were able to communicate with each other better. We even found ourselves on the same page more often regarding what our family needed to be doing. We found restoration and victory and joy in knowing we were working as partners and teammates, both fighting for our family instead of fighting each other, our hearts united in our desire to have a healthy marriage and a healthy family.

The more I found myself praying God's Word for my husband and our marriage, the more I found my heart changing toward Tim. As I prayed, I found my heart being knit together with him. Our communication improved, and I found that I had a greater desire to show him the love and encouragement he needed. The more I prayed Scripture, the more I found myself being molded into the Christlike teammate and wife God wanted me to be. The more I prayed Scripture and tried to live it out, the more I found myself on the same page with my husband and with God regarding His will for our marriage.

Tim and I found healing and restoration in our marriage, but it didn't come easily. It took years of persevering in prayer, continuing in conversation, and attending several marriage counseling sessions. It took years of learning to love each other more like Christ, as well as in understanding what would speak to our spouse's heart and their love language. Tim and I still have our share of struggles. We still have wounds we have given each other, especially in those earlier years of our marriage. But as we continue to invest in our marriage, to listen to each other, to love and serve each other, to pray together and for each other, we see God's faithfulness in knitting our hearts closer together and bringing healing to our marriage.

Praying for Your Spouse

Tim and I met during college through an organization called Campus Crusade for Christ (Cru). Our final year of college, after we'd been dating about a year, I started experiencing an intense spiritual battle. I didn't tell many people about it, but I entrusted it to Tim, and he prayed for me and supported me beautifully during that time.

I don't remember if we were at his dorm or mine, but one night we were watching the *Lord of the Rings: The Return of the King*. There's a scene near the end where Frodo is supposed to carry the One Ring up Mount Doom and throw it into the fire to destroy it forever. But Frodo is exhausted. He's been traveling for a long time, and the evil power of the One Ring has taken its toll on him. He's so close to finally ending this challenging chapter of his life and returning home to the safety of the Shire, and yet he has no strength left.

His friend and companion, Samwise (Sam) Gamgee tries to encourage him. But his words are not enough to get Frodo back on his feet. Frodo tells Sam it's too much for him. So Sam tells him, "Then let us be rid of it, once and for all. I can't carry it for you. But I can carry you!"[69]

And so Sam lifts Frodo onto his shoulder and struggles up the rocky mountain, fire falling all around them, instrumental music swelling. As I watched this scene unfold, I found tears in my eyes. I turned to Tim and told him, "You're my Sam. Thank you for carrying me when I can't climb anymore on my own."

When we marry, we become both life and prayer partners, helping each other along the journey of life. Sometimes one may be struggling and the other can be a Sam. Sometimes we both may need help up the mountains of life and in overcoming spiritual battles.

One way I can be my husband's Sam is to carry him in prayer to the throne of God. To let Tim know I'm praying for him and with him, that he's not alone against the spiritual forces and the struggles of life. It is a privilege to be a champion of your spouse in both life and in prayer; to not just hold their hand through the ups and downs of life, but to hold them close in our prayers. As it says in Ecclesiastes 4:12, "Though one may be overpowered, two can defend themselves. A cord of three strands is not quickly broken."

My friend Laura Gethers is an author and marriage coach who often prays, "Lord, help me to pray your will, not mine, for my spouse."[70] That prayer would have saved me a lot of heartache in the early, challenging years of our wedded life, as I prayed for my husband and our marriage to be changed according to my will, rather than God's.

Sharon Jaynes shares that prayer isn't about gaining control over our spouse; instead praying for our spouse is "relinquishing control to God ... the Master Potter. He certainly doesn't need you or me to tell Him how to shape and mold that marvelous piece of pottery called [your spouse]. Oh, we'd like to. That's for sure. But God's ultimate goal is for that lump of clay to be fashioned according to His design and His purposes, not ours ... God shapes and molds. You pray and intercede."[71]

As I began to pray Scripture for Tim, I found that it wasn't my husband who was doing most of the changing, it was me. The very areas where I had wanted Tim to change were the same areas that God had uniquely created him to provide for and protect our family. And the areas that I believed to be sin in Tim's life were discovered not through my accusations or our arguments or my selfish prayers but through the Holy Spirit's conviction and the Lord's gentle molding in Tim.

I found myself growing to understand and appreciate my husband more. I found myself convicted of ways I wasn't supporting and encouraging Tim the way I should be, or being given fresh ideas of how I could let him know I loved and appreciated him. We both have grown a lot since the day we said "I do," and most of that growth has come through prayer, communication, and offering each other a ton of grace. Nancy Guthrie explains that "as we pray instead of worry, pray instead of complain, pray instead of strategize, we find that God is not only doing a work in our spouse; he's doing a work in us too."[72]

In the movie *War Room*, Elizabeth and her husband Tony are having marital and financial struggles. They argue a lot and let each other know what they could be doing differently to make the other happy. No amount of arguing and nagging changes either of them. It only drives them farther apart.

Then, Elizabeth receives a text from her friend saying she saw Tony at a restaurant with another woman. Elizabeth, understanding the implications of that text, grabs her Bible and sits on the floor in her prayer closet/war room and begins to pray. She can't change the path her husband is on, but she knows Someone who can.

She prays about her own heart and how much she needs God. She confesses how angry she's been with Tony lately and asks for forgiveness. Then, with open hands and tears rolling down her cheeks, she prays, "Please, God, please, don't let him do this ... Help him to love me again. Help me love him. If he's doing something wrong, don't let him get away with it. Stand in his way."[73] And then she begins claiming Scripture aloud throughout her home in one of the most powerful prayer scenes I have ever experienced on the screen.

I'm not going to spoil the movie for you and tell you what happens, but by praying such a specific prayer, Elizabeth will either see God moving in her husband's life and his heart, or she will continue to see God moving in her own heart. However God answers her fervent prayer will be miraculous evidence of God at work in their marriage.

For the remainder of this chapter you'll find extra Scripture prayers to help you pray for your marriage, for your wife or your husband, and for an unbelieving spouse. May you experience health, growth, transformation, restoration, and victory in your own heart and in your marriage as you pray.

Scripture Prayers for Your Marriage

May You give us singleness of heart and of action so that we will always fear You for our own good and the good of our children and grandchildren. (Based on Jeremiah 32:39.)

Thank you, Lord, for creating marriage. Help us to cleave to one another and to become one flesh. Make us one and bind us together so that nothing can separate us. (Based on Mark 10:7-9.)

Lord, show us how to abide in You as a couple so that we can bear much fruit and glorify Your name through our marriage. (Based on John 15:5, 8.)

Holy Father, I pray that You would cause all things in our marriage to work together for good, according to Your purpose. (Based on Romans 8:28.)

May we be like-minded, having the same love, being one in spirit and of one mind. Help us to do nothing out of selfish ambition or vain conceit, but in humility consider each other better than ourselves. May we look not only to our own interests, but to the interests of each other. (Based on Philippians 2:2-4.)

Help us to speak words of life to one another, words that will build each other up that it may benefit those who listen. (Based on Ephesians 4:29.)

May we be humble and gentle with each other, patient and bearing with one another in love. May we make every effort to keep the unity of the Spirit through the bond of peace. (Based on Ephesians 4:2-3.)*

Protect us from the love of money. Help us to always keep it in proper perspective. (Based on 1 Timothy 6:10.)

May we love and submit to one another out of reverence for Christ. (Based on Ephesians 5:21-22, 25.)

May we rejoice in one another and satisfy each other's physical needs. May we be captivated by each other's love. (Based on Proverbs 5:18-19 NLT.)

May we be kind and compassionate to one another, quick to forgive each other just as You forgave us. (Based on Ephesians 4:32.)

May our love overflow and increase for each other and for others. (Based on 1 Thessalonians 3:12.)

May we be mutually encouraged by each other's faith. (Based on Romans 1:12.)

Scripture Prayers for Your Unbelieving Spouse

May I love _____ so well so that s/he may be won over without words, but by my heart and actions when s/he sees the purity and reverence in my life. (Based on 1 Peter 3:1.)

God, I ask that You would give _____ a new heart and put a new spirit in him/her. Remove their heart of stone and give him/her a heart of flesh. (Based on Ezekiel 36:26.)

Lord, please remove the blinders from _____'s mind. Help him/her to see the true light of Your gospel. (Based on 2 Corinthians 4:4.)

Come, O wind of God, and blow Your life into _____'s soul so that he/she may truly live. (Based on Ezekiel 37:9.)

May my faith bring holiness into our marriage that leads _____ toward Your holiness and sanctification. (Based on 1 Corinthians 7:14.)

Open _____'s eyes and help turn them from darkness to light, and from the power of Satan to You, so that _____ will receive forgiveness of sins and a place among those who are sanctified by faith in You. (Based on Acts 26:18.)

Scripture Prayers for Your Wife

Lord, please make _____ holy. Cleanse her through Your Word and present her to Yourself as a radiant bride without stain or wrinkle or blemish, but as holy and blameless. (Based on Ephesians 5:26-27.)

God, help _____ to delight in You and give her the desires of her heart. (Based on Psalm 37:4.)

Lord, let _____'s beauty come not from outward adornment but from her inner self, the unfading beauty of a gentle spirit which is of great worth in Your sight. (Based on 1 Peter 3:3-4.)

God, help _____ to know that she is fearfully and wonderfully made. (Based on Psalm 139:14.)

Help _____ to be a woman of character, which is worth far more than rubies. (Based on Proverbs 31:10.)

Father, please help _____ to seek first your kingdom and your righteousness. As she does, please give her all she needs. (Based on Matthew 6:33.)

Scripture Prayers for Your Husband

May You work in _____'s heart, enabling him to obey Your purpose. (Based on Philippians 3:12 GNB.)

May _____ be devoted to prayer, watchful and thankful. (Based on Colossians 4:2.)

God, help _____ to delight in You and give him the desires of his heart. (Based on Psalm 37:4.)

God, help _____ to not have a spirit of timidity, but give him a spirit of power, love, and self-discipline. (Based on 2 Timothy 1:7.)

Surround _____ with godly, trustworthy men who will speak truth into his life and be a good friend. (Based on Proverbs 28:23.)

Help _____ to lead our family and love like Jesus. (Based on Ephesians 5:25.)

Lord, help my husband to faithfully provide for the needs of our family. Bless our family and bless the work of _____'s hands. (Based on 1 Timothy 5:8, Deuteronomy 28:12.)

Chapter 11

Praying for Your Children

She (my mother) became a warrior far superior to any epic hero. She became a giant on her knees. With a sword in one hand she battled the enemies of death and disease, and with her other hand stretched toward heaven she kept beseeching God's help and His mercy. [74]

–Bishop T.D. Jakes

Note: Throughout this chapter I will be using the term "your children," but this encompasses any children in your life: children, step -children, adult children and their spouses, grandchildren, godchildren, nieces, nephews, foster children, students, etc.

When my son was five he needed to have his adenoids removed and ear tubes put in place, as he was getting frequent colds and ear infections due to his enlarged adenoids. While a necessary procedure, the thought of my little boy being wheeled away for surgery and put under anesthesia made my mama heart a little anxious.

The morning of his surgery, I sat down to read the next passage in my Bible reading plan: Isaiah 40. I quickly scanned through the passage, my mind distracted by all the tasks I needed to do before we headed off to the hospital. But Isaiah 40:11 stopped me in my tracks and brought tears to my eyes: "He tends his flock like a shepherd: He gathers the lambs in his arms and carries them close to his heart; he gently leads those that have young."

The image of God as a Shepherd holding my little lamb close to His heart when I couldn't was so special and comforting to me. It was a deeply needed image. My son was safe near His heart, a heart that beats with more love for our children than I have, and well, I love my children a lot.

But with that comforting thought also came a challenging one. The shepherd is only able to hold a lamb close if the mother will let the shepherd do so. If the mother trusts the shepherd, she knows the safest place for her child to be is in their shepherd's arms. I had to relinquish all control and surrender my precious child into the arms of the surgeon and the Great Shepherd.

As if this verse wasn't awesome and comforting enough, it continues, telling us that He will guide those who have young. It was comforting to know He would guide me and my husband so that we can do our jobs as parents well, providing us with the wisdom, guidance, strength, comfort, and provision we need if we ask, seek, and follow Him.

God doesn't love and lead us in a demanding way, but with a gentle invitation to seek Him and trust Him more completely. And so, on the way to the hospital and while watching my tiny son get checked in, prepped, and wheeled off on a gurney for his twenty-minute procedure, I clung to and prayed this verse. Throughout my son's procedure and his recovery, and still to this day, I pray Isaiah 40:11. It is one of my favorite Scriptures to pray as a parent, reminding me that we have a great Father and Shepherd who cares for our children and cares for us in ways we cannot even fully grasp this side of heaven.

The Power of Praying Scripture for Your Children

As a parent, we are wired to love, protect, and advocate for our children. But the best way we can do so is praying for our children before the throne of God, armed with the powerful, living Word of God. Mark Batterson writes, "Prayer is our highest privilege as a parent. There is nothing we can do that will have a higher return on investment. In fact, the dividends are more than generational. They are eternal. Prayer turns ordinary parents into prophets who shape the destinies of their children, grandchildren and every generation that follows. And those collective prayers are the greatest legacy you can leave."[75]

As parents, we are often our childrens' greatest intercessors, intervening for our children through prayer for their well-being and their spiritual protection and growth. Like the friends who carried the paralyzed man to the roof so they could get him before the feet of Jesus (see Mark 2:3-11), we carry our children to the throne of God with our prayers. Having the Word of God in our prayers helps us lift up our children to Him with power and confidence that we're praying according to the will and the heart of God.

As parents we can teach and love and encourage and discipline our children every waking moment of the day but, ultimately, we are powerless to change our children's hearts. That's a job that only God can do. We can share the gospel with them and teach them Bible stories and godly character but we can't save them. That's something that only Jesus can do. We can help and counsel and advise our children but we can't change them. That's a job that only the Holy Spirit can do.

And as much as we may try to protect our children, we can't protect them from everything. Hard things happen in life, and Satan is trying to claim control of our children. We must fight in prayer for our childrens' physical and spiritual protection and well-being. Stormie Omartian shares, "The battle for our children's lives begins on our knees. When we don't pray, it's like sitting on the sidelines, watching our children in a war zone get shot at from every angle. When we do pray, we're in the battle alongside them, appropriating God's power on their behalf. If we also declare the Word of God in our prayers, then we wield a powerful weapon against which no enemy can prevail."[76]

Not only does praying Scripture help us pray for and protect our children, it helps us in our parenting as well. While we pray the living and active Word (see Hebrews 4:12) for our children, the living and active Word moves in our own hearts, molding us into better parents who reflect the heart of our own great Father.

Nancy Guthrie explains, "My prayers tend to be more self-directed than Scripture-saturated ... shaped more by my stunted and sometimes selfish desires for my child, than by God's grand purposes for all His children. So I need the Scriptures to inform and direct my prayers and to encourage me to persevere in prayer. I need the Word of God to provide me with fresh words and renewed passion to pray for my child day by day ... I need the Scriptures to go to work in me to reshape my deepest longings for my child ... I need the Word to convict me of my own sin because I easily become overly focused on my child's shortcomings. I need the Word to challenge me to change because I can be tempted to think it is my child who needs to change. I need the Word to remind me of the gospel because sometimes I think my child is more in need of the gospel than I am."[77]

When I prayed for my children to be healed, to start speaking miraculously like that of the deaf/mute man in Mark 7, I was praying according to my own will and desires. But once I started praying Scripture for their speech, it was my heart that was miraculously changed, not their speech. New words and phrases emerged slowly over time, a beautiful answer to prayer, but it was my heart changing and aligning with the heart of our Father that molded me into a better parent to my children.

Praying God's Word is an incredible way to pray for your child's protection and for mountains to move in their situations and hearts and minds. And you may find mountains moving in your own, molding you more into the parent God has created you to be.

Praying for Your Child's Salvation and Faith

I find it easiest to pray fervently for my children when I'm worried about them. It might be about their safety, their health, their first day of school, or their eternal salvation, but my concern for them and their well-being draws me to the only One who can save them and protect them in a way that I cannot. Lamentations 2:19 describes it well when it says, "... Pour out your heart like water in the presence of the Lord. Lift up your hands to him for the lives of your children ..."

I shared before how the first Scriptures I really prayed for my children were verses for their speech. I also prayed for their protection and their health, for their healing, and for them to get to the next milestone I longed for them to experience. One day, God reminded me of 1 Samuel 16:7b, which says, "People look at the outward appearance, but the LORD looks at the heart." I was so convicted that I'd been focusing on and praying for the things related to my kids' health, behaviors, and milestones that I'd lost track of the most important things—their hearts, their character, their souls, and their salvation. These are the things that matter most and will have eternal impact.

One of the most important prayers we can pray for our children is that they would receive salvation, if they haven't already, and that they would grow in their faith. Salvation is a choice they alone can make, and while we can teach them the gospel, ultimately the decision to believe the gospel and receive salvation is up to them. We can teach them about having godly character, but ultimately the character building and heart work is up to God. We faithfully disciple our children in their faith, and pray they take hold of it on their own, so that they don't depart from that faith (see Proverbs 22:6). We teach, train, guide, and pray with and for our children, but the rest is out of our hands and in the hands of God and our children.

Some of my favorite Scriptures to pray regarding my childrens' salvation are:

- May You open _____'s eyes and turn him/her from darkness to light and from the power of Satan to You, so that _____ may receive forgiveness of sins and a place among those who are sanctified by faith in Jesus. (Based on Acts 26:18 ESV.)
- May _____ confess with his/her mouth "Jesus is Lord," and believe in his/her heart that You raised Jesus from the dead, so that he/she will be saved. (Based on Romans 10:9.)
- May _____ be saved by grace through faith, not of his/her own doing, but as a gift from You. (Based on Ephesians 2:8 ESV.)
- May _____ grow in the grace and knowledge of our Lord and Savior Jesus Christ. (Based on 2 Peter 3:18.)
- May _____ hear Your voice and open the door (of his/her heart to You), so that You may go in and eat with him/her, and him/her with You. (Based on Revelation 3:20.)

Once our children have been saved, we need to continue praying. Satan will try to snatch away our children's faith; we are the ones who can cover them from Satan's attacks with our prayers.

Encouragement Regarding Salvation for Children with Disabilities/Special Needs

For those whose children may be nonverbal or cognitively delayed and you are worried they may not be able to accept Christ and experience salvation, I want to reassure you of two things. First of all, God is very loving and merciful. Psalm 145:9 tells us, "The Lord is good to all; he has compassion on all he has made."

God knows what is in the hearts and minds of our children, which is a lot more than we may ever realize. We often think that our children must have an adult-like understanding of grace and salvation to be able to be saved, but Matthew 18:2-5 tells us otherwise: "He called a little child to him, and placed the child among them. And he said: 'Truly I tell you, unless you change and become like little children, you will never enter the kingdom of heaven. Therefore, whoever takes the lowly position of this child is the greatest in the kingdom of heaven. And whoever welcomes one such child in my name welcomes me.'"

Jesus also said, "... Let the little children come to me and do not hinder them ..." (Matthew 19:14 ESV). God our Father will not forsake the child He lovingly and uniquely created. He wants to have a relationship with them. While there is a Bible verse about confessing our faith with our mouths, I believe God in His great mercy meets our children at their level of ability. He knows fully what is in their hearts, and He welcomes them into His family and eternity. I don't believe a good Father would require our children to do something they are physically unable to do to gain access to salvation.

God knows our childrens' hearts. He is a good Father and He loves our children more than we will ever know or understand this side of heaven. His love and mercy are available to our children.

Encouragement for the Parent of an Unsaved or Prodigal Child

The most important decision your child can make is to accept Jesus into their heart and decide to follow Him. When the decision has been made, it brings so much joy and celebration and pride. To watch your child turn their back on that decision and their faith, or to reject that decision, is heartbreaking.

God is waiting for your child to come back to Him, just like the Father in the parable of the prodigal son. I'm sure you are waiting too, praying fervently, pouring out your heart and your prayers and your tears for the eternal security and faith of your child.

Pray for godly friends, coworkers, and mentors to share God's love and truth with them. If you helped plant the words of God in their heart when they were little, pray those words would take root in their hearts now. God's love is what will draw them back to Him, so keep sharing God's love with them and keep praying.

Here are a few biblical promises you can cling to as you wait for your child(ren) to claim or reclaim the gift of salvation:

- God, I ask that You will open _____'s eyes so _____ will turn from darkness to light and from the power of Satan to Your power. In doing so, they may receive forgiveness of sins and a place among those who have been sanctified by faith in You. (Based on Acts 26:18 ESV.)
- Thank You, Lord, that my faithful work and tears and prayers will be rewarded, that You will bring _____ back from the land of the enemy. (Based on Jeremiah 31:16-17.)
- Lord, draw _____ to Yourself, and help _____ to love You with all of their heart, soul, mind, and strength. (Based on John 12:32, Deuteronomy 6:5.)
- Bless _____ with godly friends and mentors who will encourage them, and may _____ not keep company with those who will lead them astray. (Based on Proverbs 12:26 NKJV.)
- Lord, I pray You would bring _____ out into a broad place, that You would rescue _____ because You delight in them. (Based on Psalm 18:19 ESV.)
- Satan wants to sift _____ like wheat, but I pray that _____'s faith may not fail and that _____ may turn back to You. (Based on Luke 22:31-32.)
- Lord, I thank You that You keep Your promises and that You are patient with _____, not wanting _____ to perish, but

wanting everyone to come to repentance. (Based on 2 Peter 3:9.)

- God, I ask that You will put a new spirit in _____. Soften their heart toward You, so _____ will follow You. (Based on Ezekiel 11:19-20.)

The Lord wants all to be saved, including your children. He experiences the same heartache you do over your lost or wandering child. He longs to work in their hearts and their lives to draw your children toward Him.

Praying for Your Child's Gifts and Calling

One day, after a playdate where I was reminded yet again of how far behind my children were from their peers and even children significantly younger than them, I went for a walk through a neighborhood. As I was walking, I saw a lone flower growing between a crack in the sidewalk and a brick rock wall. At first, I felt sorry for this flower. There was a beautiful garden about five feet away boasting a kaleidoscopic display of color. Surely that was where this poor flower belonged.

But then my perspective changed and I was proud of this flower. It did exactly what it was created to do: spread its roots, grow, bloom, and share its color and beauty with the world, despite its unusual circumstances. It could have withered up and died but it was flourishing.

And it got me thinking about my own children. They are not in the garden I expected them to grow in. There's a part of me that so desperately wants to scoop them up and put them in the garden with the other flowers. A part of me that fears that strangers will pluck that flower because it doesn't seem to belong there.

That perspective-changing moment with the flower helped me stop focusing so much on the skills I wanted my children to learn to help them fit in with the world a little more, and to instead become a steward of my children and the unique way they were created. It helped me focus on nurturing and encouraging the gifts and passions God crafted into them. It brought such joy and purpose to my parenting and to my relationship with my children.

Part of being a parent isn't pushing our children to be who we want them to be, but embracing exactly who God created them to be, nurturing and stewarding them toward His plan and purpose for them. As we pray for our children–for their gifts and their purpose –we find ourselves aligning with His plan for them. Jodie Berndt writes:

> Our heavenly Father longs to shower [our children] with blessings and equip them with everything they need to love him deeply and serve him effectively ... Ask God to empower them through the Holy Spirit–and then watch as he blesses them with gifts, talents, and abilities that are far better than anything you could imagine ...
>
> Be alert to the gifts and talents you see God weaving into their lives and then join him, through your prayers, as you watch these things flourish and grow.[78]

Jesus' mother treasured the miracle of Jesus and the events of His birth. She had a front-row seat to watch Him grow in favor with God and man, and she was aware of His gifts and calling. So when Mary saw that their friends were out of wine at a wedding, she knew her son could make it right. She encouraged Him to do what only He could do. Her love, her support, and her encouragement helped create a space for our Savior to begin His work and ministry because she knew her son well and knew His purpose.

What a privilege it is that, as parents, we can create an environment that allows both our children's faith and giftings to grow. What a privilege that we can pray for our children's giftings and calling, and that we can watch them bloom in their own unique way, bringing such God-glorifying color to this world.

Claiming Specific Scriptures for Your Children

I encourage you to prayerfully choose at least one Bible verse to pray for each of your children. You may want to make a list, or a prayer card, of Scriptures to pray for each child–for their character, for their faith, for the fruit you'd like to see in their lives, and anything else that is on your heart to pray for them. Keep those collected verses tucked in your Bible or in your prayer space for easy access. If you're unsure where to start, I recommend reading and praying through the book of Proverbs, recording any verses in particular you want to claim for your child.

I personally love praying Luke 2:52b over my sons, that they would grow as Jesus did "in wisdom and in stature, and in favor with God and man." With this one verse as an anchor in my prayers, I can lift up any specific ways I'd love to see each of my sons grow and mature in wisdom (biblical wisdom and knowledge, academic skills, life skills) and in stature (their physical health and well-being).

I can then pray for ways I want them to grow in favor with God (salvation, faith, and spiritual growth) and in favor with man (their social skills and manners, for godly friends and mentors, for their teachers, and their current or future spouse and children). This verse is also wonderful as a prayer of blessing to boldly proclaim over my sons: "May you grow in wisdom and stature, and in favor with God and with man."

While I love praying Luke 2:52 for both of my sons, I also have a verse that I feel God led me to during my Bible reading that I could pray for each of my sons' individually, and I work those verses into my prayers. Those verses sometimes change as we go through new seasons, but to have a verse to cling to and pray over each child is such a beautiful way to advocate for them. There's nothing like being on the same page with our Heavenly Father regarding the things we want for our beloved children.

Keep praying for your children, and do not give up. Keep lifting your children up to the throne of God, knowing that He loves your children more than you do. And keep praying God's Word for your children, knowing that it will not return void, but will accomplish exactly what God intends for it to do in their lives (see Isaiah 55:11 NKJV).

Scripture Prayers for Your Children

Thank You, God, that You tend to our children like a shepherd: You gather _____ in Your arms and carry them close to Your heart. Thank You for gently leading us as we parent our children. Help us surrender them into Your trustworthy arms. (Based on Isaiah 40:11.)

May _____ acknowledge You as God their Father and serve You with wholehearted devotion and with a willing mind. May _____ seek You and find You. (Based on 1 Chronicles 28:9.)

May _____ love You with all their heart, with all their soul, with all their mind, and with all their strength. And may they love their neighbors as themselves. (Based on Mark 12:30.)

Heavenly Father, give _____ an undivided heart and put a new spirit in them, remove from them their heart of stone and give them a heart of flesh so that they will follow You and Your decrees. May _____ be Yours, and may You be their God. (Based on Ezekiel 11:19-20.)

I pray for _____, that his/her faith may not fail. (Based on Luke 22:32.)

Help _____ grow in each of the fruit of the Spirit: love, joy, peace, patience, kindness, goodness, faithfulness, gentleness, and self-control. (Based on Galatians 5:22-23.)

Help _____ grow in wisdom and stature, and in favor with You and with man. (Based on Luke 2:52.)

May _____ enjoy good health, that all may go well with him/her, both physically and spiritually. (Based on 3 John 1:2.)

I pray that You would provide _____ friendships that are with good, godly friends who stick closer than a brother, friends who help strengthen each other in their faith. (Based on Proverbs 18:24, Proverbs 27:17.)

May _____ receive my words and the words of the Lord. Help _____ to incline their ear to wisdom and apply it to their hearts. May they cry out for discernment and listen for Your voice instead of following the ways of the world. May they seek Your treasure as silver, that they may fear You, Lord, and find Your knowledge and wisdom. (Based on Proverbs 2:1-5.)

Lord, I ask that you would give us as parents the wisdom and courage to correct and instruct our children when needed. May _____ have their hearts open to instruction. May they love wisdom and chase after understanding. (Based on Proverbs 1:8.)

May _____ grow in knowledge and skill in both books and in life. (Based on Daniel 1:17 MSG.)

May _____ live a life worthy of You, Lord, and may they please You in every way. May they bear fruit in every good work and grow in their knowledge of You. (Based on Colossians 1:10.)

Chapter 12

Praying Through the Storm

None can believe how powerful prayer is, and what it is able to effect, but those who have learned it by experience. It is a great matter when in extreme need to take hold of prayer.[79]

–Martin Luther

When I was seventeen weeks pregnant with my younger son, I felt a sharp pain in my right side that would not let go no matter what position I settled into. Within an hour, I was sweating and vomiting. I called my doctor, who urged me to go to the ER immediately. My sister-in-law graciously came over to watch my older son, and Tim raced home from work to take me to the hospital.

I lay on the gurney, curled up in agony. Doctors, nurses, and ultrasound techs kept urging me to lay down flat on my back so they could run some tests and probe the painful spot, which only made the pain intensify. Pain makes us want to curl into a ball, wrapped around our hurts, ignoring the world around us, and ready to lash out at anybody who interrupts our pain. Healing comes when we open ourselves to be examined, to get to the root of the pain.

An ultrasound revealed my appendix was close to rupturing. The surgeon told us that if my appendix ruptured, it would be dangerous to me but fatal to our baby. I needed immediate surgery. I nodded in relief, grateful to have a plan to relieve the unrelenting pain.

Tim and I prayed that God would protect me and our unborn baby through the surgery, and then I was whisked off to surgery. I hoped that once the inflamed and angry organ was removed, the pain would miraculously go away.

It didn't. Because I was pregnant, I could not take strong pain meds, so standing up straight was agony for a few weeks following surgery. So was coughing, laughing, rolling over in bed, and walking. I was told to be on limited bed rest for six weeks, so no bending over or picking up anything–including my almost two-year-old son.

On top of that, the baby inside continued to grow, stretching my skin and creating a starburst of stretch marks around my healing incisions. And he was an active fellow, who stretched, rolled around, and kicked. What had once been a joy to feel the baby moving around inside had now become agony while my muscles and skin slowly healed.

The process of healing from emotional pain and trauma can be similar. Prayer and counselors can help, but it's still a long process. Longer than we want it to take. The path toward healing isn't linear, but includes ups and downs, steps forward and backward, and layers of hurt that need to be uncovered and dealt with before healing can take place.

We live in a world where there is pain and trauma–both physical and emotional. We are not promised an easy life. In fact the Bible makes it clear that there will be pain and sorrow in our lives. Every single one of our favorite Bible heroes experienced grief.

It doesn't sound fun, but grief and lament are an important part of our journey here on earth. Life hurts sometimes and our heart longs to connect with God, especially when we're hurting. Sometimes we don't have the words to pray when we find ourselves amidst the storms of life and the pain and heartbreak they cause.

In Mark 4:35-41, when the disciples found themselves amidst a storm, they cried out to Jesus for help. He was able to calm the wind and the waves by commanding them to be still (see Mark 4:39). Sometimes, Jesus says, "Peace be still" to our circumstances. Other times, He says it to our hearts. He never rushes us toward joy, but climbs into the boat with us, sitting with us in our grief and our storms, ushering us closer to His heart. As Dr. Tony Evans says, "It often takes the darkness of a storm to show us the light of God's presence."[80]

When the waves keep coming, God is near. When we're tired and overwhelmed, God is near. When the tears won't stop and we don't even know what to pray anymore, God is near.

Embracing the Psalms as Prayer

While experiencing grief over both of my sons' multiple diagnoses, I decided to study the life of David. David had a lot of grief and painful experiences in his life. He had been appointed to be the next king as a child, had triumphantly defeated Goliath the giant (see 1 Samuel 17), and yet he wouldn't take the throne until a few decades later. He spent many years running away from King Saul (his own father-in-law), hiding in a desert. Later in life, he would lose several children. For a man after God's own heart, he sure didn't have an easy life.

We find David amid another painful experience during his time in the desert in 1 Samuel 30. David and his small, loyal army would travel from time to time to fight in various battles. This time, they had been making an alliance with the Philistine leader before returning back to their own land and family in Ziklag. When David and his men returned home, they found their town burned to the ground, the women and children taken away.

When David and his men realized what had happened to their homes and their families, they wept until they could weep no more. And then in the very next verse we read, "But David found strength in the LORD his God" (1 Samuel 30:6b). After David wept, he strengthened himself in the Lord. I like to think he wrote a psalm as one of his ways of strengthening himself.

Psalm after psalm is filled with David's emotions, pouring out his pain and his questions, but always remembering God's promises and His character and His nearness, and ending with confessing his trust in God. He always ends with praise. I find the psalms a wonderful pattern for us to practice in prayer, but whether we're able to end or begin our prayers with praise or not, it's ok. With approximately one third of the psalms considered a psalm of lament, they can give us words to pray when we're too heartbroken to think of any on our own. Poring over the psalms gives us an invitation–and the words–to pour out our hearts before God.

Tish Harrison Warren writes in her beautiful book *Prayer in the Night*:

> By praying the Psalms year after year for millennia ... the church learns to remain alive to every uncomfortable and complex human emotion. We learn to celebrate and we learn to lament. John Calvin called the Psalms 'the anatomy of all the parts of the soul.' He says there is no human emotion that 'anyone finds in himself whose image is not reflected in this mirror. All the griefs, sorrows, fears, misgivings, hopes, cares, anxieties, in short all the disquieting emotions with which the minds of men are wont to be agitated, the Holy Spirit hath here pictured exactly.'
>
> The Psalms are dramatic. And life–even ordinary life–is dramatic, drenched in meaning, full of glorious beauty and deep pain.[81]

The psalms remind us it is ok to ask God questions and to express our feelings. They remind us it is ok to lament–to express our grief and sorrow. Jennifer Rothchild reassures us:

> God isn't waiting for you to get your emotional act together so you can come to Him with a tidy presentation of trust and rejoicing. No. He has provided the path of lament for you to travel so you can arrive at those choices.
>
> Jesus laments for you, and with you by His Spirit, as we read about in Romans 8. He is wading through the ocean of tears you cry to get to you, attend to you, look after you, and give you a million reasons to trust Him and rejoice.[82]

We can pour out our hearts to God, and in the process we can be reminded that God is in control, as David often did in his psalms.

Donald S. Whitney says of the psalms that "God has inspired a psalm for every sigh of the soul. Within the breadth of 150 psalms, you can find the entire range of human emotion. You will never go through anything in life in which you cannot find the root emotions reflected in the psalms ..."

"But the main reason why the psalms work so well in prayer is that the very purpose God put them in his Word to us is for us to put them in our words to him."[83]

When Jesus hung on the cross–innocent, in agony, and separated from the love and presence of His Father–He asked in Matthew 27:46b, "My God, my God, why have you forsaken me?" This is one of the only instances where all four Gospels share the same story and words. They are the exact words of King David in Psalm 22:1.

All the words of Psalm 22 were prophesying exactly what Jesus was experiencing on that cross. While Jesus hung there, I like to think He prayed the words of Psalm 22, claiming those prophetic words for Himself in His hour of need and knowing that the ending of both the psalm, and of his death, would be victory.

And then in Luke 23:46, Jesus prayed, "... 'Father, into your hands I commit my spirit' ..." These are also the words of David, this time in Psalm 31:5. Jesus went from crying out to "my God" and feeling forsaken, to crying out to "His Father," aware that He was in alignment with His Father's will and would see His Father soon.

This is the pattern of many of David's psalms–acknowledging God, sharing his complaints or concerns with God, expressing trust in God's character, making a request, and then praising God. Jennifer Rothschild writes, "Every psalm of lament has a point where it transitions into an expression of trust in God ... Confessing trust in God is the hinge that turns our grieving into grace, tears into trust, and worries into worship."[84]

David's heartfelt words in the psalms were able to fully express what was in Jesus' heart and mind in His most desperate time. Despite His suffering and separation from God on the cross, He trusted that He would be reunited with God and in His presence.

Praying the psalms wasn't just for Jesus; they are a great gift and practice for us, too. Donald S. Whitney recommends praying through a psalm a day and demonstrates how to do that in his small but powerful book *Praying the Bible*. You may instead choose to focus on a psalm that reflects your current situation or emotions, or on one that provides you comfort for your present moment.

Embracing Tears as Prayer

Sometimes, when we're overwhelmed with thoughts or emotions, we have no words. Sometimes, all we have is tears, and tears can be a beautiful and holy prayer to God. When you bring your tears and your broken heart to the throne of God, seeking His help, His answers, and His comfort in your pain, He draws near to you.

Jennifer Rothschild writes, "Our prayers are often disordered, messy, and vulnerable. That's why God so graciously gave us a path and pattern [through the psalms] for our messy emotions to travel in prayer. Letting your tears travel the path of lament will draw you closer to God."[85]

King David wrote, "You keep track of all my sorrows. You have collected all my tears in your bottle. You have recorded each one in your book" (Psalm 56:8 NLT). God knows how many hairs are on our heads, every prayer we've ever uttered, and how many tears we've ever cried. Whether they were tears of grief and sorrow or of joy and awe at God's majesty, they all matter to God.

The Holy Spirit is fluent in the language of tears and is able to translate them on your behalf. "Likewise the Spirit also helps in our weaknesses. For we do not know what we should pray for as we ought, but the Spirit Himself makes intercession for us with groanings which cannot be uttered" (Romans 8:26 NKJV). God knows our hearts; He knows the groanings of our Spirit, the ache in our hearts, and the prayers we cannot verbalize contained in each and every tear.

Psalm 34:18 reassures that "the LORD is close to the broken-hearted and saves those who are crushed in spirit." It may feel He is not involved in whatever has caused us such grief, but He is so faithful and compassionate and near when we are in such grief all we can do is cry.

Hannah experienced grief over her infertility and went to the temple to pray. "In bitterness of soul, Hannah wept much and prayed to the LORD," (1 Samuel 1:10). Being able to share her feelings, her heart, and her tears with God helped her regain her trust in Him. As a result, she found peace, regained her appetite, and was filled with hope (see 1 Samuel 1:15-18).

Jesus worked, worshiped, and wept, and we tend to overlook the last bit. Tears are viewed as a sign of weakness rather than as a spiritual language that connects us to the heart of God. At the death of Lazarus, when Jesus saw his friends weeping, it led Him to weep as well (see John 11:33-35). He also wept when He saw people struggling under their sin (see Luke 13:34 and Luke 19:41-42). He wept in the garden before His crucifixion, sharing His heart, His grief, and His fear with God. Jesus "offered up prayers and petitions with fervent cries and tears to the one who could save him from death" (see Hebrews 5:7). Despite knowing that these stories would ultimately end in resurrection and victory, Jesus experienced the brokenness of grief and death and expressed lament through tears.

Jesus loved people so much their tears brought Him to tears. And He loved people so much He went obediently to the cross, even though He wanted God to find another, less painful way for their sins to be removed. Jesus was sent to "... bind up the brokenhearted ... to comfort all who mourn, and provide for those who grieve ... to bestow on them a crown of beauty instead of ashes, the oil of joy instead of mourning, and a garment of praise instead of a spirit of despair. They will be called oaks of righteousness, a planting of the LORD for the display of his splendor" (Isaiah 61:1-3).

We see throughout Scripture many of our Bible heroes–both men and women–experienced grief and wept before God. Let's embrace our tears as a way to connect with our Father God, who is faithful and compassionate and near in our brokenness, our sorrow, and our grief. God is there in our grief, drawing near to us in our pain, listening to our heart cries, considering every tear as precious, comforting us with His presence, with friends, with a song, or some other form of encouragement we need during our time of grief.

If you find it hard to cry, give yourself grace. Tears are not a requirement of a life devoted to God and to prayer; they are merely a manifestation of what's in your heart. But they are not the only way. Richard J. Foster shares that if shedding tears doesn't come naturally to you, to "shed tears before God in your intention. Have a weeping heart. Keep your soul in tears. Even if the eyes are dry, the mind and the spirit can be broken before God ... You are building new habits of prayer and patient, kind, firm persistence is what you need with yourself."[86]

Tears are indicators of what really matters to our hearts, and no one knows our hearts more than the Holy Spirit, our Father God, and our Advocate, Jesus Christ. The whole Trinity is near us, working on our behalf when we pour out our tears (both our physical tears and those in our hearts) before His throne.

Embracing Prayer Journaling

When life takes an unexpected turn, or we are stressed and busy, it's easy to focus on all the responsibilities we have before us and end up burying our emotions. We keep pressing on, going to work, caring for our families, and putting one foot in front of the other.

Because we're in survival mode during that time, it's easy to not spend intentional time seeking God. But it is vital that we process those emotions rather than holding them in until we explode or hit a breaking point. Whether shared with other people or alone on the pages of a notebook, our emotions and thoughts need to be processed. Felt. Dealt with. And released.

Writing is an incredible way to help us focus and process our thoughts and our honest prayers while reconnecting us with the heart of God. David was considered a man after God's own heart. He wrote many of the psalms, which are full of his struggles, questions, confessions, and worries, but he always came back to declaring his trust in God and praising God. We see from his life that writing is a creative form of worship.

It only takes a few minutes to sit down in front of a computer or a notebook with a blank page in front of you and start writing whatever comes to mind. Be honest and vulnerable, the page is a safe place for you to spill your thoughts, your heart, your tears. He can handle it all.

After I've written my honest thoughts and processed for a while in my journal, I find my emotions spent and my thoughts turning back toward Scripture and God. I ask Him for help, guidance, wisdom, peace–whatever it is I need in that situation. And most of the time, I end with declarations of trust and praise for the evidence of His character in my life. Like David and the other psalmists, we have to get our doubts, questions, and angry thoughts out of the way so we can be reminded that He is indeed good and trustworthy. Ending your journaling with words of praise and worship, if possible, will do you and your faith a lot of good.

Don't worry about making each word eloquent or editing while writing. Don't worry about your handwriting or about your spelling; just share your heart with God and keep going. Get the words out and onto the paper. God already knows what you're thinking, and He wants you to share your heart with Him so He can help you move forward with Him.

While journaling can be a wonderful healing practice while we're in seasons of grief, it is also a great prayer practice for any time we sit down to pray. For many of us, our minds may have a tendency to wander while we're praying, but writing your thoughts and prayers are a great way to help you stay focused during your time with God. Some people like to record a daily prayer in their journal or record a few memories or things they're thankful for each day. Some like to use their journal to keep track of the Scripture passage they read each day, including their takeaway thoughts and prayers they had from that Scripture reading. I like to write out letters to God in my prayer journal. Make your journaling practice your own.

Prayer journals are also a great tool to help you see how you have been growing, how God has been working in your heart, and how He has answered your prayers. We may not see how God is working in the present moment, but when we go back and read old journals, we see how God was working in our hearts and our circumstances.

Embracing the Life We Have

My family and I were having a wonderful and much-needed beach vacation when, on the last day of our trip, the thought of packing up our belongings and returning to our house, the mountain of laundry, and endless appointments for our young sons gave me a panic attack. A literal panic attack.

My chest felt tight and my heart pounded. Tears streamed down my face, and I couldn't catch my breath. My husband suggested I go out to the beach and spend some time by myself. I went gladly, eager to process this overwhelming anxiety with God.

I listened to the waves crash on the shore and tasted my warm salty tears. I didn't even know what to pray about. I had no words, only tears, and I poured them all out to God, my heart begging Him to speak to me and my anxiety.

I expected to hear more silence from God when I needed Him the most. Never have I been more thankful to be proven wrong. He whispered one word that banished the anxiety and grief that had gripped my heart for so long. *Embrace.*

Surely that word was from God. But what was there to embrace in my life with all that I was currently experiencing? So I asked Him. And for the next hour or so, God revealed area after area of my life that I needed to embrace. I wish I had written it all down at the time, but I don't think my pen would have flown across the pages fast enough. I was convicted. Encouraged. Loved by the God of the universe.

As I listened to the waves crash onto the shore, God gently reminded me of various areas I needed to embrace fully in my life. My children and their hearts, their gifts, their personalities. This special needs journey. Myself. My husband and the fact we were teammates together. And most importantly, God. My perspective was transformed to the biblical, rather than the worldly way of doing everything that I'd been trying to do unsuccessfully for years.

I don't know how long I spent with God, tears rolling down my cheeks, while my anxious thoughts stilled and surrender and transformation unfolded in my heart. That precious time on the beach transformed my life, my faith, and my purpose. It gave me the strength to continue forward on the path God set for me and my children, trusting that God was faithful and had given all of us a life worth embracing.

It wasn't until a few years after that encounter with God when I found a quote by John Piper that elegantly encapsulated what I had learned and experienced on that beach and in the years that followed: "Occasionally, weep deeply over the life you hoped for. Grieve the losses. Feel the pain. Then wash your face, trust God, and embrace the life that he's given you."[87]

Solomon in his wisdom tells us there's "a time to weep and a time to laugh, a time to mourn and a time to dance" (Ecclesiastes 3:4). So whether you're in a season of weeping and mourning, or a time of embracing the life you have and experiencing laughter and joy again, know that God is there with you.

Scripture Prayers for Seasons of Grief

My soul is weary with sorrow; strengthen me according to Your Word. (Based on Psalm 119:28.)

Lord, I thank You that You are close to the brokenhearted and save those who are crushed in spirit. (Based on Psalm 34:18.)

God, I thank You for keeping track of all my sorrows. You have collected all my tears in a bottle. You have recorded each one in Your book. (Based on Psalm 56:8 NLT.)

Thank You for being the Father of compassion and the God of all comfort. You comfort us in all our troubles so that we can comfort those in trouble with the comfort we ourselves have received from You. I thank You that just as the sufferings of Christ flow over into our lives, so also through Christ our comfort overflows. (Based on 2 Corinthians 1:3-5.)

Lord, may You give me a crown of beauty instead of ashes, the oil of joy instead of mourning, and a garment of praise instead of a spirit of despair. May You make me an oak of righteousness, a strong plant for the display of Your splendor. (Based on Isaiah 61:3.)

God, thank You for being with me in whichever season I currently find myself in. Thank You that I can experience both a time to weep and a time to laugh, a time to mourn and a time to dance. (Based on Ecclesiastes 3:4.)

In my distress, may I find my strength in You. (Based on 1 Samuel 30:6.)

Lord, I know that on earth we will have many trials and sorrows. But I thank You that we can take heart because You have overcome the world. (Based on John 16:33.)

May You fill me with all joy and peace as I trust in You so that I may overflow with hope by the power of the Holy Spirit. (Based on Romans 15:13.)

Chapter 13

Praying "Thy Will Be Done"

God always has and always will look for men and women who say to Him, 'I trust you so much, I'm all in. I want your way not mine. I am willing to live by faith!' [88]

–Chip Ingram

One day while preparing dinner I was listening to my local Christian radio station when Hillary Scott's song "Thy Will" came on. I had never heard the song before, and I stopped what I was doing to listen. Hillary Scott admits through her lyrics how hard and confusing it is to be in God's plan, which is so different from her own plan. She pours out her heart in each beautiful stanza, and then always comes back to the chorus in which "Thy will be done" is repeated four times.

As I listened to those words that echoed my own hurt and confusion regarding the challenges in my parenting journey, I started sobbing. I felt seen. But I also felt convicted. I hadn't been praying those four words of the chorus at all, let alone surrendered my will, or my children, to God.

When the song ended, salty tears still spilling down my face, I abandoned dinner prep on the counter and went to my computer to find and play the song again. I listened to it a second time, tears still falling. I then played it a third time, this time finding I could sing along to the chorus, truly believing the words I was singing. A peace filled my heart as I released how I wanted my life to go and learned to embrace God's will for my life and for my children.

Learning to Trust God's Will

We struggle with trusting God's will because hard circumstances and situations happen and it makes us wonder if God and His plan for us are trustworthy. God's will is always for our ultimate good and His glory. We see throughout Scripture how–despite the challenges so many of our Bible heroes go through–God has a plan for each of them, and each of them fit into a much larger story than they can see. Andre Yee says, "We find the meaning of our own story in the context of his epic. If you are in Christ, you have a blessed story–not because of your unique experiences, but because your story is a microcosm of God's great story. And just as God is the hero of every biblical narrative, you can be confident that he will be the hero in your personal story as well."[89]

There are hundreds of examples of our Bible heroes praying and God answering their prayers according to His great plan.

- Joshua prayed for the sun and moon to stand still during battle (see Joshua 10:12-13).
- Sarah, Rachel, Hannah, and Elizabeth all prayed for years for a baby.
- Nehemiah turned to God often in prayer, praying for favor (see Nehemiah 1:11, 5:19, 13:14) and strength (see Nehemiah 6:9) to rebuild the wall around Jerusalem.
- David prayed and fasted for his sick infant son to be healed (2 Samuel 12:16) and for blessing for his kingdom (see 2 Samuel 7:18-29).
- King Hezekiah, when he was sick and learned he was going to die, prayed for healing and a longer life (see 2 Kings 20:1-3).
- King Asa prayed for protection from the vast army coming upon them (see 2 Chronicles 14:11).
- Samson prayed for strength (see Judges 16:28).

- Elijah prayed for a dead boy to live again (see 1 Kings 17:20-21), for fire to fall from heaven (see 1 Kings 18:36-37), and for rain after years of a famine (see 1 Kings 18:41-19:8).
- Elisha prayed for opened spiritual eyes (see 2 Kings 6:15-16).
- Jabez prayed for blessing and protection (see 1 Chronicles 4:10).
- Daniel prayed and fasted for God's favor and revelation (see Daniel 10:12).
- Jesus prayed for unity among believers (see John 17:1-26), for His cup (going to the cross) to be removed from Him, and for God's will to be done (see Matthew 26:39).
- A desperate father at Jesus' feet prayed that He would help his unbelief (see Mark 9:24).
- Paul prayed for so many things, it'd take an entire chapter to list them all! He was in constant intercession for all those he met, and he also prayed for successful ministry (see Colossians 4:3-4), for boldness in his preaching (see Ephesians 6:19-20), for a thorn in his flesh to be removed (see 2 Corinthians 12:7-8), and so much more.
- The disciples and members of the early church prayed constantly together. They asked for boldness and church growth (see Acts 4:24-30), for wisdom before selecting new church leaders (see Acts 1:24, 6:6-7, 14:23), and for more signs and wonders (see Acts 28:8).

Sometimes God answered these prayers immediately with an incredible miracle. God is, after all, able to do "immeasurably more than all we ask or imagine" (see Ephesians 3:20). Other prayers God didn't answer until His timing was right. God didn't immediately allow Sarah, Rachel, Hannah, and Elizabeth to conceive. He wanted to birth something beautiful in them before they each birthed a son who would do mighty works for God's kingdom. He knew the whole timeline of history and the entire genealogy of Christ, and He knew precisely the best time for these mighty men of God to be born. The women persevered in prayer, and when the timing was right, God gave them the desire of their hearts.

Some of these prayers God didn't grant as He was asked because He had a different plan. He didn't heal David's infant son, but in their grief over their baby's death David and Bethsheba turned to each other and conceived Solomon–who would not only be the next king but would be in the lineage of Christ.

God didn't save Jesus from having to go to the cross, but He sent an angel to strengthen Jesus while He prayed before His arrest and death. While Jesus' flesh didn't want to die and experience separation from His Father, His death made it possible for each of us to experience spiritual freedom and eternal life.

Jesus' prayer for unity among believers still hasn't happened yet, but we know it will in heaven, according to Revelation 7:9-10.

We see the fruit of many of Paul's prayers in his effective ministry, but God didn't remove the thorn in his flesh. In the process, Paul learned that our weaknesses make us strong and can bring God great glory. In Romans 8:28 Paul writes, "And we know that in all things God works for the good of those who love him, who have been called according to his purpose."

Corrie ten Boom was a Dutch Christian whose family helped hide Jews from the Nazis during World War II. Eventually they were caught hiding Jews and sent to a concentration camp. Her father and sister were killed in those camps. She is a beautiful example of holding on to hope and trusting God's plan despite the atrocities she experienced. Corrie was once speaking to a group of children where she used a tapestry in a demonstration:

> Corrie "slowly unfolded the purple cloth in her hands and revealed hundreds of strings tied in knots and pulled through the cloth. It all looked so random. She showed the children how the strings didn't seem to make sense from where they sat at her feet on the floor in the living room.

'That's the whole point,' she exclaimed. She said it was because of our limited vision, our limited perspective of what God is doing in our lives, that we question Him.

At that point, Corrie slowly turned the purple tangled mess around to reveal a beautiful tapestry: a crown of gold with multicolored jewels. 'This' she said, 'is what God sees from His perspective ... a masterpiece!'"[90]

God sees the whole story that weaves from Genesis to Revelation. He can see each of our stories and how they tie into His story. He can see inside every heart and how many tears each of His children has cried. He knows it all and He answers every single prayer according to what He knows will ultimately be best for His people.

You may feel you're in the messy, knotted-up place of the tapestry right now, but keep praying and trusting God. Eventually you'll see glimpses of the design that God is weaving together for you.

Surrendering What God Doesn't Want Us Holding Onto

In the previous chapter I mentioned my encounter with God, in which He whispered the word "embrace" to my weary and anxious heart. That encounter began a new venture: seeking to embrace all the good things God had for me in my life.

After about a year of striving to do this, I still felt like something was missing. Eventually, I found my answer in Lysa TerKeurst's book *The Best Yes*. She shares about a time she was visiting a friend after they had experienced a winter storm. Twenty inches of snow had fallen and it had led to many of the trees being broken. Lysa describes it this way:

The branches were piled everywhere. House after house. All down the street. Disastrous piles of limbs–big piles of trees–all still clinging to the leaves that hadn't dropped yet. And because the leaves hadn't dropped, the trees broke.

That's what happens when a snow comes early. The trees weren't designed to face snow before releasing their leaves. They weren't made to carry more than they should. And neither are we.[91]

I know the weight of carrying more than I should. And usually it's because I've refused to release something before taking on something else. Lysa's words reminded me that you can't open your arms to something, can't truly embrace all life has to offer and flourish, until your arms aren't holding on to sin, activities, thought patterns, and idols that bring no value to your life.

That's when I learned the value of releasing things that did not benefit me or my family. I couldn't fully embrace my children until I released my expectations and dreams I'd had for them. I couldn't embrace myself as a mother and a wife and a daughter of God until I could release my guilt and insecurities. I couldn't embrace peace and joy and thankfulness until I could release the anxiety, grief, and bitterness that had overtaken my heart. I couldn't embrace God until I had released my anger and bitterness.

In Ecclesiastes 3, it says there is a time for everything: "A time to embrace and a time to refrain from embracing, a time to search and a time to give up, a time to keep and a time to throw away" (Ecclesiastes 3:5b-6).

And so I began a new mission, one of embracing the things God had for me, while releasing those very things He wanted me to let go of. I had anger and bitterness to release. Expectations for how my childrens' lives would go. I had to release my children into His care.

As we go about our days, we find ourselves embracing more and more things in our lives and holding them close. It requires daily prayer to surrender those areas in our lives back to God. To surrender the areas we want to control into God's capable and loving hands. To surrender the objects we've found comfort in, rather than God. To surrender the things that have become such a part of us, but God never intended them to become a part of us.

As we release those things that God doesn't want us to hold onto, we find freedom. As we surrender the things that are good but that we don't have full control of–such as our children or spouse–we find peace, knowing that "He will care for everything as he sees fit."[92] The more He prunes away, the more we let go, and the more space we have for Him and His good things in our lives. In the wrestling and surrender of releasing to God what we shouldn't be holding onto, we find our arms are free to embrace God and His love and plans for us.

Surrendering Our Will

One year at Christmastime I felt God give me fresh eyes and an open heart while rereading the familiar story of the birth of Jesus. For the first time ever, I truly put myself in the young Mary's sandals and thought about what Mary must have been thinking and feeling through this journey of bringing the Savior into the world and parenting Him well. We have no idea what her thoughts and feelings were from Scripture, but since she was human, I'm sure she did have expectations about how her life would unfold.

I'm sure she daydreamed about having a loving husband, of having children (especially sons, given her cultural upbringing), and of being a good wife and mother. I doubt she had huge dreams for her life, but I'm sure she envisioned being happily married before any children arrived.

But then, an angel shows up, one that made her want to fall on her face in terror and awe, as other Bible heroes did. And this angel told her not to be afraid because she was favored. She was going to conceive and give birth to the Messiah. This was something that I'm sure all girls longed for in their culture, to bring the long-awaited Savior into the world. She must have felt both overwhelmed and honored.

She simply asked one question and was satisfied with the answer. I'm certain I would have had hundreds. Or made excuses why I wasn't qualified, like so many other Bible heroes did. Or I would have been like, "Uh, thanks for the opportunity. Let me ask Joseph about this first, and then I'll get back to you."

But not Mary. She had only one question about the logistics of a conception as an unwed woman. The angel told her, "The Holy Spirit will come on you, and the power of the Most High will overshadow you. So the holy one to be born will be called the Son of God" (Luke 1:35b).

In verse 38 we are told she responded, "I am the Lord's servant," and, "May your word to me be fulfilled." By saying "yes" to God, she got to experience the beauty of being the mother of this precious child who would change the world in ways she couldn't even imagine. It didn't all make sense, but she trusted God.

She allowed God to conceive something new and beautiful in her life. Mary received Christ into her womb, just as we now receive Him into our hearts. He grew under Mary's surrendered heart, just as He lives inside our own surrendered hearts.

Soon after this encounter with the angel, Mary goes to visit her pregnant relative Elizabeth where she sings praises of God's goodness. "And Mary said, 'My soul magnifies the Lord, and my spirit rejoices in God my Savior, for he has looked upon the humble estate of his servant'" (Luke 1:46-48a ESV). She sings ten whole verses of praise about God's goodness and sovereignty and her role in it all. She was glad to be chosen. Excited to be part of the story. Anticipating how God will use her and her Son. She had a beautiful heart of surrender, praise, and trust in God and His plan.

I personally would assume that if I was highly favored and told so by a heavenly messenger, the path forward would be clear and easy. That if I was chosen for such a divine task, the path would unfold beautifully. That there would be plenty of miracles and God-given provision and constant clarity as to next steps.

But there were plenty of challenges. Having to travel while pregnant and give birth in a new town, away from the comfort and familiarity of her home and her family. Having to live in Egypt for a while to protect the infant Jesus. Raising a son who was without sin. And witnessing Him die an excruciating and humiliating death He did not deserve.

Mary's story reminds us that we serve a God who doesn't always make following Him easy. As a parent myself, I have a tendency to want to protect my children from pain and disappointments, but they are a part of life, and God knows that. His goal is not to give us an easy-breezy life, but to nurture our growth. He knows that we learn to grow and rely on Him and trust Him when circumstances are hard, and we know we can't keep moving forward in our own strength.

It's getting through those hard and dark times in our lives that molds us the most into the man or woman we were created to be and what we are fully capable of, with God always by our side. Mary's faithful and surrendered heart convicted my own that was so resistant to the way God was working in my life.

We see the beauty of a surrendered life, despite the challenges. God enabled Moses–a man who was afraid of speaking to Pharoah –to lead His people to the Promised Land where they would experience His presence and glory. He enabled Ruth–a widowed and childless woman–to trust Him and move to a new country with a bitter mother-in-law, where He made provision for her to marry a wonderful man and have a son in the lineage of Jesus. He invited Mary–a young woman, not yet married, from a tiny town–to be the mother of our Savior and to allow the Holy Trinity into her womb.

Mary made the act of surrendering look effortless, and I'm so thankful for the example of her Son, who taught us that surrendering to God's will is hard work. There's struggle and wrestling involved. In the Garden of Gethsemane He prayed with tears and bloody sweat for hours throughout the night for there to be another way. He begged His disciples to stay awake and pray with Him.

Jesus' prayer in that vineyard–recorded in Matthew 26:39, Mark 14:36, and Luke 22:42–is what Janet Holm McHenry says is "the best human prayer we can pray. In this prayer we know that Jesus is fully

God and fully man. He prayed for his most human desire: life. And yet he prayed for God's will to be done through him ... The prayer is called a relinquishment prayer because we relinquish what we want for the better plan, God's will."[93]

Jesus struggled and prayed until He could humbly tell His Father "thy will be done" (see Luke 22:42 KJV) before going to the cross. In God's incredible provision, an angel came to strengthen Him (see Luke 22:43) and Jesus was able to stand up and face the crowd coming to arrest Him. In His free will He could have said no, and yet He chose to align His will with God's.

In prayer we wrestle our will onto the same page with God's will, giving greater weight to God's Word than to our feelings, desires, and circumstances.

Surrendering Our Desires

I read a passage in *Calm My Anxious Heart* by Linda Dillow that transformed my view of how to surrender our will, expectations, and desires and embrace God's will for us. She describes a woman named Ella, a missionary in Africa for fifty-two years, who raised her family without the modern conveniences we enjoy, such as electricity, indoor plumbing, and air conditioning. Linda Dillow writes:

In an old diary was written Ella's prescription for contentment:
- Never allow yourself to complain about anything–not even the weather.
- Never picture yourself in any other circumstance or someplace else.
- Never compare your lot with another's.
- Never allow yourself to wish this or that had been otherwise.
- Never dwell on tomorrow–remember that tomorrow is God's, not ours.[94]

Wow. I was so convicted when I read this. I am guilty of doing every single one of these. And I can see how being rooted in the present moment and in your present circumstances–rather than focusing on your desires and how you wish certain circumstances were different–can bring a lot of contentment and peace to your mind and soul. How it can encourage you to keep persevering in faith, focused on the calling God has given you. How it can help you embrace and enjoy the life you have, despite the hard circumstances.

Linda Dillow then adds that Ella's "eyes were fixed on eternity. Her tomorrows belonged to God. She had given them to Him. And because all her tomorrows were nestled in God's strong arms, she was free to live today. One day at a time she could make the right choices and grow to possess the holy habit of contentment. Ella's focus was eternal, and her focus led to an eternal contentment."[95] Ella found that contentedness was key to surrendering her will to align with God's will and to experiencing peace.

Paul learned this, too. He wrote in Philippians 4:11b-13, "For I have learned to be content whatever the circumstances. I know what it is to be in need, and I know what it is to have plenty. I have learned the secret of being content in any and every situation, whether well fed or hungry, whether living in plenty or in want. I can do all this through him who gives me strength."

Paul–who had been shipwrecked by storms, beaten, persecuted, whipped, and was in prison while writing the letter that contained these lines–decided to not focus on his circumstances. He instead focused on God, who gave him the strength to persevere and do all things. How does Paul do it? He tells us twice, "I have learned." It was a process for him. It didn't come naturally. It was something he had to be intentional about, to make a priority in his life. I'm sure not complaining about the heat didn't come naturally to Ella. That's why she had to write down her prescription for contentment. She had to remind herself whenever she felt the urge to complain or to wish that she had a washing machine or dishwasher or air conditioning. Both

Ella and Paul realized their strength to be content and to persevere came from God.

It takes prayer and effort and a change in mindset to learn to be content. To embrace the areas God wants us to embrace and to release the areas He wants us to release. To wrestle our will into alignment with His and shift to be on the same page with God. To see how God is working in our hard circumstances for our ultimate good. It takes a brave and humble heart to pray not only for the things we would like to see God do, but to invite Him to do what He wants in our lives.

Scripture Prayers of Surrender

God, help me to embrace the things You want me to embrace and to release the things You want me to release in my current season. (Based on Ecclesiastes 3:5-6.)

Help me to have a surrendered heart like Mary and to declare as she did, 'I am Your servant. May Your word to me be fulfilled.' (Based on Luke 1:38.)

Our Father in heaven, hallowed be Your name. Your kingdom come, Your will be done, on earth as it is in heaven. (Based on Luke 11:2 NKJV.)

Help me to be Your disciple and deny my own desires and will. May I take up my cross daily and follow after You. (Based on Luke 9:23.)

May I pray as Jesus did, 'Father, if it be possible, let this cup pass from me; nevertheless, not as I will, but as You will.' (Based on Matthew 26:39 ESV.)

Lord, I pray that I would not be conformed to this world, but be transformed by the renewal of my mind. May I discern Your will, which is good and pleasing and perfect. (Based on Romans 12:2.)

Lord, help me to trust in You with all my heart and lean not on my own understanding or desires. Help me to submit to You and Your will, knowing that You will make my paths straight. (Based on Proverbs 3:5-6.)

Help me to live wisely and to make the most of every opportunity. Help me to not be foolish but to understand Your will. Help me to not turn to idols in my pain, but to be filled with the Spirit. (Based on Ephesians 5:15-18.)

Lord, help me learn to be content whatever the circumstances. I know what it is to be in need, and I know what it is to have plenty. Help me to learn the secret of being content in any and every situation, whether well fed or hungry, whether living in plenty or in want. I can do everything through You who gives me strength. (Based on Philippians 4:11-13.)

Chapter 14

Praying to Fight Fear and Worry

Don't fret or worry. Instead of worrying, pray. Let petitions and praises shape your worries into prayers, letting God know your concerns. Before you know it, a sense of God's wholeness, everything coming together for good, will come and settle you down. It's wonderful what happens when Christ displaces worry at the center of your life.

–Philippians 4:6-7 MSG

I've struggled with worry and anxiety off and on for years. Certain situations will skyrocket my anxiety and I'll find my mind and heart racing. After my second son was born, I found myself unable to sleep, my mind envisioning terrible scenarios like dropping my baby down the stairs or getting into a car accident on the way to an appointment that one of my sons had scheduled for the next day. There were times I felt so anxious my heart would start pounding and my chest would feel tight.

I prayed and prayed for the anxiety to go away. The act of praying would calm my mind somewhat but it was short-lived. No matter how much I prayed for my anxiety to go away, it didn't. And so one day I found myself sitting on the crinkly sheet of my doctor's office as I poured out my slew of symptoms. The doctor was kind, asked several questions, and told me she suspected I had postpartum anxiety. She prescribed me some medication and recommended I meet with a therapist. I was hesitant at first to pursue either one but they both helped me immensely. I absolutely believe in the power of prayer and that God could have healed my anxiety, but I also believe that He gives us the wisdom and the resources to get the help we need from others. Sometimes medication can be your miracle. Sometimes having a trained professional to support and guide you can be an answer to your prayers.

My anxiety seemed to be under control, but then a few years later while on our lovely family beach vacation, I had a full-blown panic attack. My heart pounded, tears fell, and I found myself gasping for breath. Tim, understandably, was concerned about me. He told me he'd take care of the kids and sent me to the beach to go process my feelings and catch my breath. I sat on the sand and cried. I cried out to God. I ached for God to show up in that moment, and amidst the calming sound of the steadily crashing waves, He did show up for me.

This is the moment I shared about in an earlier chapter when God whispered that one word "embrace" to me that changed the trajectory of my life and my faith. But it's also when I experienced my breath slowing and deepening to match the sound of the crashing waves. It's when I watched the glorious beauty of the sun setting, a beautiful masterpiece of pinks and oranges that demonstrated the wonder of God's creation. It's when I watched the stars coming into view, twinkling in their beauty and reminding me of my smallness and God's greatness. It's a place where I found peace. And I knew Tim sent me there because being in nature has always brought me such a sense of peace and wonder.

Fear, worry, and anxiety aren't uncommon to us. There are hundreds of Bible verses–approximately one for every day of the year–to remind us to not fear or to worry, to be courageous, to trust God. Throughout Scripture, we read how fear and worry had such power over so many familiar biblical characters. Adam and Eve were afraid of God's response to their sin, so they hid. The Israelites were afraid of the giants in the Promised Land, so they refused to enter. Moses, Jeremiah, and Gideon were all afraid of their callings, so they focused on their weaknesses. The disciples feared they were going to drown in the storm, so they accused Jesus of not caring for them. And yet, in every instance, God looked out for them. He equipped them. He was with them.

Charles Spurgeon wrote, "Anything is a blessing which makes us pray. Indeed the very act of prayer is a blessing. To pray is, as it were, to bathe in a cool, swirling stream and so to escape from the heat of earth's summer sun. To pray is to mount on eagle's wings above the clouds and get into the clear heaven where God dwells. To pray is to enter the treasure-house of God and to gather riches out of an inexhaustible storehouse."[96] Both fear and anxiety have brought me to my knees in prayer so many times and God was with me every time. God has led me to some calming prayer practices that help me when my mind starts whirling with anxieties and worries, and I'll share some of my favorite fear-fighting prayer practices with you.

The Power of Praying in Nature

I believe every person is drawn to various aspects of nature because nature is a concrete way for us to grasp the character of God. Romans 1:20 tells us, "For since the creation of the world God's invisible qualities–his eternal power and divine nature–have been clearly seen, being understood from what has been made, so that people are without excuse."

When you look up at a clear night sky and see an endless array of shining stars, you catch a glimpse of His greatness and majesty, and you are reminded of your smallness in the great galaxy God has created. The stars are also a reminder of His faithful promise made to Abraham.

When you watch a thunderstorm roll in or watch a roaring river or a cascading waterfall or ocean waves crashing ashore during a storm, you see His power, as Elijah did in the earthquake and the wind.

When you see a beautiful rainbow arc across the sky, it reminds you of His faithfulness and the promise He made to Noah.

When you go to the ocean and listen to the gentle and rhythmic waves, and feel the warm sun as you dig your toes into the sand, you feel His power, peace, and comfort.

When you stroll among blooming flowers and flowering trees in a garden, you are reminded of God's ability to bring about new life, as well as His desire to connect with us. It was in a garden that the first people had complete fellowship with God, and it was in a garden that Jesus surrendered His will to that of His Father's.

When you see the kaleidoscopic display of fall colors clinging to the trees and falling to the ground below, you're reminded that letting go of things that God doesn't want us to carry can be good for us, preparing us for our next season.

J.R.R. Tolkien wrote in a letter to his son, "Certainly there was an Eden on this very unhappy earth. We all long for it, and we are constantly glimpsing it; our whole nature at its best and least corrupted, its gentlest and most humane, is still soaked with the sense of 'exile.'"[97] We are often so surrounded by the "exile" of being outside the Garden of Eden, where sin and suffering occurs, that experiencing the wonders of nature gives us a glimpse of God and His character.

I love the words of Anne of Green Gables regarding prayer. She asked, "Why must people kneel down to pray? If I really wanted to pray I'll tell you what I'd do. I'd go out into a great big field all alone or into the deep, deep woods, and I'd look up into the sky–up–up–up–into that lovely blue sky that looks as if there was no end to its blueness. And then I'd just feel a prayer."[98] Anne is right; we can pray in any posture, any place, and any time, and there is indeed something about being in nature that helps you "feel a prayer" welling up in your spirit when you experience the grandeur of creation and a longing to connect with your Creator.

Not only is nature a way for us to experience God's character and creation, but it is a way we see how God cares for us. It was in nature that God provided food for the Israelites and later for Elijah. It was in nature that God brought comfort to the grieving Hagar and to Elijah.

It was in nature that the disciples saw Jesus' authority over wind and waves and that He was with them in the storm.

Our Bible heroes prayed on mountains and in valleys. They prayed along rushing rivers and in dry deserts. They prayed in wide open fields and in cocooning caves. Jesus prayed in the wilderness, atop mountains, and in an olive grove.

Scientists have proven the benefits of nature on our bodies: "Exposure to nature not only makes you feel better emotionally, it contributes to your physical wellbeing, reducing blood pressure, heart rate, muscle tension, and the production of stress hormones. It can relieve depression symptoms. It may even reduce mortality, according to scientists Stamatakis and Mitchell. Research done in hospitals, offices, and schools has found that even a simple plant in a room can have a significant impact on stress and anxiety."[99]

Nature is a place where we can also experience spiritual health and rejuvenation. It is a healthy place to connect with friends and family. It is a sacred space where we can move our bodies and enjoy the fresh air and sunshine, or we can sit in stillness and know that He is God (see Psalm 46:10) while we marvel over His creation.

It's a place where we can listen to God's gentle whisper and marvel at His creativity and character. Perhaps it's for this reason so many people love going on prayer walks in nature. You can be in prayer, praising the Creator, while exploring the wonders of God's creation. You can listen to worship music and praise God while you walk, or you can enjoy the silence and share your heart with God as you walk.

Charles Spurgeon said, "God seems to talk to me in every primrose and daisy and smile at me from every star, and whisper to me in every breath of morning air, and call aloud to me in every storm."[100] Nature invites us to respond, communing with our Creator in His mighty creation while simultaneously eliciting peace in our hearts, minds, and spirits.

Breath Prayers to Help Battle Fear and Worry

Breath is central to life in our bodies, and unfortunately, fear and anxiety can wreak havoc on our breath. When you're feeling fearful or worried, your heart begins to pound, you take shallow breaths, or find it hard to take a breath at all.

Just as breath is central to physical life, prayer is central to our spiritual life. If you've experienced a season where you didn't pray for a while, or felt like your whole day was off because you didn't start your morning off with prayer, you know how centering prayer can be.

The practice of breath prayers is the act of taking slower, deeper, life-giving breaths while focusing on God's life-giving words.

When you say breath prayers, they are short, one sentence prayers rooted in Scripture that can be repeated several times. The first part of the sentence is prayed on the inhale, and the second half on the exhale. The goal is to meditate on and pray God's Word while releasing tension in your body and worries whirling around in your mind. Jennifer Tucker explains in her book *Breath as Prayer*:

> Breathing is the bridge between the brain and the body ... Prayer is a bridge from our heart to His. It's like our spiritual breath:
>
> - Breath has a rhythm to it, a cadence of inhales and exhales. Prayer has a rhythm too, a cadence of inhaling God's grace and exhaling our fears.
> - Breathing can reset and realign your nervous system. Prayer can help reset and realign your soul.
> - Deep breathing can calm the brain and the body. Prayer can calm the mind and the soul.
>
> When we pray, we inhale the truth of God's presence and love, breathing in His goodness and grace–and we exhale the weight of our fears and anxieties, giving God all our worries and wants.[101]

I wish I had known about breath prayers when I struggled with postpartum anxiety. It's such a beautiful practice of slowing your breath and your mind and your worries, while simultaneously turning to the comfort of God's presence and His Word.

But there are situations when I find my anxiety returning, and I'm learning to use breath prayers during that time. Some of my favorite breath prayers when I'm feeling overwhelmed or anxious are below. Do not say the Scripture reference; I simply wanted to share the reference for you to have.

> *Inhale:* I will sleep in peace
> *Exhale:* You will keep me safe. (Psalm 4:8)
> *Inhale:* You are my Shepherd
> *Exhale:* I shall not be in want. (Psalm 23:1)
> *Inhale:* I give my worries to You
> *Exhale:* You take care of me. (Psalm 55:22)
> *Inhale:* I give You my burdens
> *Exhale:* You give me rest. (Matthew 11:28)
> *Inhale:* There is no fear
> *Exhale:* In Your perfect love. (1 John 4:18)

As you inhale, breathe in the truth of the words. That God is with you. That He is good. That He will give you all you need.

As you exhale, breathe out your worries. Surrender them to God, knowing that He cares for you and He doesn't want you holding on to them. You are safe and loved.

Repeat the breath prayer as many times as you need until both your mind and your body are feeling at peace, and more centered on God's goodness, rather than your worries.

You also can make longer passages into breath prayers by dividing them into more parts. For example:

> *Inhale:* You are with me
> *Exhale:* mighty to save.
> *Inhale:* You delight in me

> *Exhale:* with great gladness.
> *Inhale:* You quiet my fears
> *Exhale:* with Your love.
> *Inhale:* You rejoice over me
> *Exhale:* with singing. (Zephaniah 3:17 NLT)

If each time you find yourself feeling anxious, worried, fearful, or overwhelmed, you turn to the practice of breath prayer, it will become more automatic and the reminders of God's goodness in your worries will be wired into your brain. Your brain is a fascinating and dynamic organ that can be reshaped as you learn, gain new experiences, and replace anxious thought patterns with God's own words.

In science, this changing, rewiring, and reshaping of your brain is called neuroplasticity. In the Bible, it's called renewing your mind: "Do not conform to the pattern of this world, but be transformed by the renewing of your mind. Then you will be able to test and approve what God's will is–his good, pleasing and perfect will" (Romans 12:2).

God created the brain and the mind, and He knew we would need to transform our minds, to rewire our thought patterns and practices. Changing our thought patterns doesn't come easily, especially when we're feeling afraid, worried, or anxious. Practicing breath prayers can help us find ourselves on the same page with God, filled with true, noble, right, pure, lovely, admirable, excellent, or praiseworthy (see Philippians 4:8) things to think about.

And it is indeed a practice. It won't come naturally to most of us. It may change as we learn more and grow in the practice of breath prayers. I encourage you to keep a list of your favorite verses that bring you peace and comfort. Find verses that are short and sweet, and divide them up, the first part said on the inhale, the second part on the exhale.

Ann Voskamp beautifully writes in the foreword of *Breath as Prayer*: "Your prayers are more than a desperate thing; they are a transporting thing, the most important thing. Your prayers immediately relocate you to the tender face of God. Your every breath –inhale, exhale–makes the sound of His name, is calling for Him– YHWH, YHWH ... When life leaves us gasping for air, prayer is how you grasp the steadying, sure hand of God."[102] When life seems overwhelming, or when circumstances leave you feeling out of control, take some time to breathe and pray. And experience God's perfect peace as you breathe and pray the very words of our faithful God.

Breath prayers can be used anytime, not just when you find yourself feeling anxious or overwhelmed. They are a beautiful way to pray God's Word and can easily be done as you go about your day.

Seeking God's Glimmers of Hope, Joy, and Peace

Recently, I learned about the term 'glimmers.' Introduced by social worker Deb Dana, a glimmer is the opposite of a trigger. Triggers activate our stress and make us feel anxious, unsafe, and/or fearful. Glimmers, on the other hand, are those moments in your day that spark feelings of joy and peace. They make you feel happy, grateful, peaceful, connected, content, and/or safe. Glimmers help calm our nervous system and are great for our mental, physical, and spiritual well-being. They are a powerful way to help us embrace this one life God has given us.

We naturally are on the lookout for danger and focus on the negative, so it takes an intentional mindset shift to be on the lookout for those glimmers, choosing to focus on the beautiful blessings present in our lives.

I find I experience glimmers most while being surrounded by nature or enjoying time with my family. And every time, it makes me feel like I'm receiving a little wink from God–a gift or a reassurance that He is with me and caring for me. It leads me to turn to God in praise and thanksgiving for His personalized gift of love to me in that current moment.

As you go about your day, look out for those God winks. He loves to pour out His love upon His children. Sometimes, these glimmers can last for a moment, or they can linger with us for a long time. One of my favorite glimmers came at a time when I was struggling with anxiety, feeling as if something was wrong with me, like maybe I was broken because I still needed to take medication for my anxiety. I worried that maybe my faith wasn't strong enough to pray the anxiety away because surely I had faith to move mountains.

It was during this time of feeling broken and discouraged that our family was invited by my aunt and uncle to stay at their cozy cabin near a lake. Trading the anxieties of our busy life for relaxation at a lake with my family sounded glorious.

One misty morning, as I began to settle down with a cup of coffee and my Bible on a porch swing by the lake, I decided to go for a little prayer walk alongside the water. Towering trees and cabins with wide windows were sprinkled all around the shoreline. I listened to the birds twittering around me, soaked in the warming sun, and circled the lake, asking God to speak to my heart.

As I was walking, I noticed a beautiful tree near the water with a hole in its trunk. It could have become a hole where rot took over, or where animals chose to build a nest. But instead, a creative gardener decided to take that broken place and plant some flourishing flowers. Gorgeous pink and purple petals and trailing green ivy were blooming from that hole.

I was enamored by this tree and snapped a picture[103] of it with the flowers bursting out of that broken place. I felt like it was God's special gift to me, and while I admired the flowers and thought about how they grew from that broken place, the verses in Jeremiah 17:7-8 came to the forefront of my mind. I practically ran back to my where my Bible sat on that beckoning porch swing, eager to find the verse in its fullness:

> "Blessed is the one who trusts in the Lord,
> whose confidence is in him.

They will be like a tree planted by the water
  that sends out its roots by the stream.
It does not fear when heat comes;
  its leaves are always green.
It has no worries in a year of drought
  and never fails to bear fruit."

Just as a creative gardener decided to take that broken place in a tree on their property and plant life and beauty in it, God–the greatest of all gardeners–can grow beautiful things from our broken places when we let Him and when we stay rooted in Him.

Seeing that tree standing strong next to the lake boasting flourishing flowers made me realize I wasn't broken because of my anxiety and struggles. It reassured me that it wasn't because my faith wasn't strong enough that I needed some medication and help in my current season of life. Instead, I was reminded that God was growing something beautiful in me as I continued to trust Him.

One of the most beautiful things our great Gardener will grow is you. And He'll faithfully provide you with glimmers of His goodness and faithfulness to remind you of that truth.

Scripture Prayers to Fight Fear and Worry

Thank You, God, that You are my Good Shepherd. I lack nothing. You make me lie down in green pastures; You lead me beside still waters; You refresh my soul. (Based on Psalm 23:1-3.)

Instead of worrying, help me turn to You in prayer. May my petitions and praises shape my worries into prayers, as I let You know my concerns. May I experience a sense of Your wholeness, of everything coming together for good to come and settle over me. May Your peace, which surpasses all understanding, guard my heart and mind in Jesus Christ. (Based on Philippians 4:6-7 MSG.)

LORD, I trust You. You keep me in perfect peace when my mind is fixed on You. May I trust in You always, for You are an everlasting rock. (Based on Isaiah 26:3-4 ESV)

May the peace of Christ rule in my heart and may I be thankful. (Based on Colossians 3:15)

God, I thank You that You did not give us a spirit of fear, but a spirit of power, of love, and of self-discipline. (Based on 2 Timothy 1:7 NLT.)

Oh Lord, help me to be still and know that You are God. (Based on Psalm 46:10.)

I thank You that I did not receive a spirit that makes me a slave to fear, but I received the Spirit of sonship and can cry out to You anytime, "Abba, Father." (Based on Romans 8:15.)

May I have no fear of bad news; may my heart be steadfast, trusting in You. (Based on Psalm 112:7.)

Help me to focus on the things that are true, noble, right, pure, lovely, admirable, excellent, and praiseworthy. Help me to put all that You have taught me into practice, and may Your peace be with me. (Based on Philippians 4:8-9.)

Help me to not worry about my life, especially about _____. Help me to seek first Your kingdom and Your righteousness, and the things I need You will give me. (Based on Matthew 6:25, 33.)

Thank You, Lord, that I can come to You worried and weary and burdened and You will give me rest. Thank You that I can come to You and learn from You, for You are gentle and humble in heart, and I can find rest for my soul. Thank You that Your yoke is easy and Your burden is light. (Based on Matthew 11:28-30.)

Chapter 15

Praying for Your Purpose

You did not choose me, but I chose you and appointed you so that you might go and bear fruit–fruit that will last–and so that whatever you ask in my name the Father will give you.

–John 15:16

When I was in high school, our church had a guest preacher share with our congregation about answering God's call for your life. He told us that a calling is when God summons you personally to a particular ministry or task He has for you to accomplish for His glory. He preached from 1 Samuel 3, reminding us it's OK if it takes a few times to make sure we clearly heard God calling us–like the young Samuel experienced. But once we do know it's Him calling, we must have a humble heart that is listening and obedient to whatever task or ministry God is calling us to do.

Fired up and passionate, he declared loudly, "Whether you're ninety years old ..." His eyes roamed around the sanctuary before settling on me. "Or nine ..."

My teenage heart bristled at the offense, but his eyes, expression, and voice all softened as he continued to look at me, saying four words that brought tears to my eyes: "You have a purpose."

We all long to know we have a purpose. That we matter. That the work we do will have eternal significance. That God has a special calling on our lives. Sometimes, we spend years struggling to find our purpose, to embrace our gifts and figure out how God wants us to use them. I think that's one of the reasons Rick Warren's book *The Purpose Driven Life* is one of the best-selling non-fiction books with over 35 million copies sold. We want to discover our purpose and make sure we're living a life of purpose.

When God created us, He knew what our gifts and talents would be; He knew the jobs we'd have, the relationships we'd be in, and how everything we'd do would fit in with His kingdom. It'd be nice if He just told us those things out loud, like He did when calling many of our favorite Bible heroes, but God will make His plans for our lives known when we seek Him. When you prayerfully discover the reason God put you on earth, it's powerful and life-changing.

Using Your Unique Gifts and Talents for His Kingdom

I'm not very good at giving gifts, but that is one of the many areas where my husband shines. Tim will prayerfully consider gift ideas and do research before selecting the perfect present for the recipient. Almost giddy with excitement, he cannot wait for the receiver to open the gift. Once opened, the recipient may often have no idea what the gift even is or may think that they don't need this particular gift, but as Tim explains the gift and how it can help them with whatever passion or interest they have, they begin to see its potential, becoming excited about using it. Tim will then take the time to help them start using their gift, answering any questions they have. Job accomplished, he settles back, content.

Tim's heart for gift giving reminds me of what it must be like for God to bestow unique talents and spiritual gifts upon each of His children. How God—the greatest of gift givers—must feel when He creates us and sees us using our gifts and talents. How He must feel when we seek Him to better understand how to use our gifts. And also, the sadness He must feel when He sees those gifts set aside or ignored.

In Exodus 31:3-5 God tells Moses, "... I have filled him [Bezalel] with the Spirit of God, with wisdom, with understanding, with knowledge and with all kinds of skills—to make artistic designs for work in gold, silver and bronze, to cut and set stones, to work in wood, and to engage in all kinds of crafts."

First of all, I find it amazing that the first person recorded in Scripture to be filled with the Holy Spirit isn't one of the biblical heroes we read about in the book of Genesis or the majority of Exodus, but rather Bezalel, a man many haven't even heard of and who God set apart to design the holy tabernacle.

Secondly, I love the sense of pride as God talks about Bezalel's gifts and talents and purpose. Bezalel was using his gifts as an artist and an entrepreneur; now God was giving him the opportunity to build Him something amazing for His glory.

In the parable of the talents in Matthew 25:14-30, the manager gave three of his servants talents of silver. A talent is a measurement of coins equivalent to several years worth of pay. Having one talent of silver (or gold) would have made the person wealthy enough to be set financially for several years, and yet the manager had multiple talents of silver to share with his servants.

The first two servants did something with the talents they were given. They invested their talents and were able to give their manager twice what they had received. The manager was pleased with them and blessed them with even more talents and opportunities.

But the third servant was afraid of losing his talent so he didn't use it. In fact, he buried it in the ground and made excuses about why he did so, saying he was afraid of the manager. And the manager was furious with him. He called him lazy, worthless, and wicked.

The parable of the talents was very convicting for me because I knew I had a gift for writing and a desire to write a book, but when God called me to write the truths I was learning about faith and parenting children with special needs into a book that would encourage other special needs moms, I had a Jonah-like reaction. I resisted it. Surely I heard God wrong. Surely I wasn't qualified enough. Surely I was too busy, taking my two young lads to a million therapy appointments. Surely someone who had been a special needs mother for longer than me was more qualified. And so I put off doing the very thing I knew God was calling me to do.

Throughout Scripture we see the excuses made by many of our Bible heroes who were convinced they were not the right one for the job God was calling them to. Sarah thought she was too old. Moses didn't think he spoke well enough. Jeremiah believed he was too young. Gideon felt too weak. Esther feared she'd be killed. Jonah felt the Ninevites didn't deserve God's forgiveness. Both Isaiah and Peter felt they were unworthy. But God still called and used them all.

Now, don't get me wrong, there are seasons of life where we may have to put some of our dreams and gifts and passions on hold. As much as I loved writing, when I had two young children with a dozen diagnoses between them, writing wasn't anywhere on my radar for a few years, and that was OK. Yet even in our busy seasons, God doesn't want us to lose ourselves and how He created us. Our gifts and passions are forms of self-care and soul-care, ways that we can reconnect with the character of God.

Many times during that overwhelming season of parenting my two little children and meeting all their unique needs, I'd write out my thoughts and questions and doubts and prayers to God in my prayer journal. I kept that gift of writing alive, and it helped me stay rooted in Him and in how He created me. When I was ready and surrendered to God's will and His calling for my life to write–with lots of prayer and trust in His plan and less focus on my own fears and insecurities and doubts–I was able to co-write that book with God, for His glory.

Jodie Berndt writes, "Our gifts should be embraced, cultivated, and handled with excellence. When we do that, giving credit to God and trusting him to help us employ our talents wisely and well-strengthening the church, meeting people's needs, pointing others to Jesus–we get to fulfill both parts of what Jesus said was the greatest commandment. We love God with all that we have, and we love others as well as we love ourselves."[104]

Johann Sebastian Bach is an excellent example of this. He added the initials S.D.G. at the bottom of his compositions for the Latin phrase *Soli Deo Gloria*, which means "glory to God alone." He embraced the idea that his gifts for music and composition were from God, desiring that each musical piece he composed would bring glory and praise to God, not to himself. He created works of art that brought people closer to God, building up God's kingdom and believers who heard his songs of worship.

Using Your Spiritual Gifts for His Kingdom

Not only are we individually handcrafted before birth with unique gifts and talents, but every single Christian is blessed with several spiritual gifts when they receive the gift of salvation. These gifts are for the purpose of ministry and are to be used within the body of Christ. These spiritual gifts can be nurtured and grown as we use them in ministry but they will not come and go.

From Romans 12:4-8, we learn several things. We all form one body of Christ. We do not all have the same function. Our gifts belong not to ourselves but to the body of Christ. Each of us have different gifts. Gifts are given to us by God's grace. We need to use our own gifts within the body. And we need to encourage others to use their gifts within the body.

There are three lists of the spiritual gifts: Romans 12:6-8; 1 Corinthians 12:4-11; and 1 Corinthians 12:28. The spiritual gifts include prophesying, serving, teaching, encouraging, giving, leadership, mercy, wisdom, faith, healing, speaking in tongues, interpreting of tongues, distinguishing between spirits, and miraculous powers.

Some believe that the last several gifts were only short-term gifts for those in the early church, as we see demonstrated by the disciples and by Peter, Paul, and Phillip throughout the book of Acts. Others believe that all of these gifts are still available to us today.

You may already have an idea of what spiritual gifts you have been given. You gravitate toward different roles in church or in your occupation based on how you are gifted, how you are uniquely wired by God. For example, my spiritual gifts are teaching and encouragement. I have taught middle school English and creative writing, and I also love to write about the truths I am learning to teach and encourage others in their faith. It's how I have been individually wired to build up the body of Christ.

If you do not know your spiritual gifts, there are many online quizzes and questionnaires that can help you determine what your spiritual gifts are. Once you have determined what your spiritual gifts are, pray about where God wants you to use them. How can you use them to bless your church family? Your workplace? Your neighborhood? Your own family? A ministry near your heart? While running errands? We're made to use our spiritual gifts, not keep them to ourselves until God calls us into a specific ministry. Every place we go and every person we come across can be a ministry. "Each of you should use whatever gift you have received to serve others, as faithful stewards of God's grace in its various forms" (1 Peter 4:10).

Romans 12:6 tells us that our gifts have been given to us by grace. When we often hear the word grace, we think of the definition of "an undeserved gift." Our spiritual gifts are definitely gifts that we don't deserve, and which bring God glory when we use them. But another definition of grace means "divine enablement." God doesn't just give us our spiritual gifts and leave us to deal with them on our own. He enables us and equips us to use those gifts. He wants to be invited alongside the journey of learning to use these gifts, and using them wisely. Like a kid receiving a gigantic LEGO® set for Christmas, he could try and build the set on his own, or he could invite his parent to join him in the creation. It requires prayer and seeking God's wisdom and direction regarding how we can best use our spiritual gifts for His glory.

While we strive to faithfully use our spiritual gifts, we also fight against the temptation to compare our gifts. I'll admit I can get jealous of leaders in ministries I serve with or other writers I follow online. I'm more of a quiet, behind-the-scenes person, and sometimes I long to have their gifts of leadership and eloquent speech and writing. But Shannon Popkin shares a beautiful illustration in her book *Comparison Girl* that I absolutely love. She shares that we are like measuring cups. Satan wants us distracted and focused on the measuring lines. We look to see how much is in our cup and how much is in other people's cups. This comparison and measuring ourselves among others only brings division and separation. Popkin writes:

> Satan points to the lines; King Jesus points to the spout ... Philippians 2:7 says Jesus 'emptied himself by taking the form of a servant, being born in the likeness of men.' From his moment of birth until his moment of death, Jesus had complete disregard for the lines on his measuring cup. He turned his measuring cup upside down ...
>
> When I tip my measuring cup, the lines become beautifully irrelevant. When I walk into a room asking, 'Who can I serve here? Whose needs can I meet? Where can I pour myself out?' I have a completely different outlook than when I measure myself against everyone I see.[105]

It is a freeing thought indeed, to focus on prayerfully pouring out the gifts and talents that God has given us to be shared with others.

Praying for Your Role in Building His Kingdom

When Nehemiah learned the walls of Jerusalem had been broken down and the people inside exposed to enemy danger, he grieved the state of Jerusalem and turned to prayer and fasting. In prayer he acknowledged God's character, confessed sin, claimed the promises of God, and then asked for God's favor. In the last verse of his prayer, he asked for the specific outcome he wanted to see, and his role in it. He knew he had a role to play in the rebuilding of the walls, and he knew God needed to be involved for it to happen. So he turned in prayer to his King of kings, before he turned to the earthly Persian king he served.

What I especially love about this prayer is that Nehemiah incorporated Scripture. In Nehemiah 1:8, he paraphrased God's promise in Deuteronomy 30:1-4, that though God's people will be scattered, God will bring them back together and restore the things they lost. Nehemiah stood on God's Word and promises, knowing what was promised to them and praying for favor so that he could help bring that promise about.

This prayer isn't just something he prayed once and then immediately went to the king. Nehemiah mentions praying and fasting for days in both Nehemiah 1:4 and 1:6, but he actually was in prayer for several months. From the month of Chislev mentioned in Nehemiah 1:1 (when Nehemiah learns of the fate of Jerusalem), to the month of Nisan mentioned in Nehemiah 2:1 (when Nehemiah has the opportunity to tell the Persian king what's going on) is a span of approximately four months. Nehemiah was persevering in prayer for God's promises and preparing his own heart for the work God was going to do.

Nehemiah's prayer life doesn't end there. There are fourteen recorded prayers in the short book of Nehemiah. He prayed for strength (see Nehemiah 6:8-9) and for favor while building the wall (see Nehemiah 5:19). When he was in trouble, he prayed (see Nehemiah 4:4-5, 6:9, 6:14). And he prayed for wisdom for the right words to say (see Nehemiah 2:4).

And while they did indeed experience opposition while building the wall, they also were able to prayerfully complete the wall in less than two months. When their enemies saw how quickly the wall had been built they "were afraid and lost their self-confidence, because they realized that this work had been done with the help of our God" (Nehemiah 6:16b). Nehemiah shows us what it looks like to be on the same page with God regarding our work. We are to prayerfully commit our work to God, then faithfully complete the task God has called us to accomplish.

Jesus also sought to be on the same page with God regarding His role in God's kingdom. From the age of twelve–when Jesus was found at the temple (see Luke 2:49)–we see He is focused on His heavenly Father's business rather than His own desires. Oswald Chambers writes, "Joy comes from seeing the complete fulfillment of the specific purpose for which I was created ... The joy our Lord experienced came from doing what the Father sent Him to do."[106]

When Jesus was ready to begin His ministry, He asked with humility to be baptized by His cousin, John. He then spent forty days in prayer and fasting before beginning His public ministry. Jesus spent frequent time in solitude with His Heavenly Father, enjoying not only His relationship with His Father but also ensuring that He was doing the very work His Father sent Him to do (see John 9:4). Joanna Weaver writes in the book *Having a Mary Heart in a Martha World*, "Jesus went from place of prayer to place of prayer and did miracles in between. How incredible to be so in tune with God that not one action, not one word falls to the ground!"[107]

The apostle Paul was also constantly in prayer, viewing himself as a humble servant of God. He was constantly humbly seeking and obediently following God's plan for him. He sought God's approval rather than man's (see Galatians 1:10) as he went on missionary trips, planted churches, discipled new believers, wrote letters, and made tents to support himself.

Paul encourages us with the truth that "he who calls you is faithful; he will surely do it" (1 Thessalonians 5:24 ESV). God doesn't leave us alone to figure out how to use our gifts or determine our calling or our role in the kingdom of God. He doesn't want us to feel overwhelmed or paralyzed by fear. He is right by our side to help us. He partners with us. Guides us. Co-creates with us. Equips us. Provides us with the help and the encouragement we need when our hearts are open to receiving it.

When we abide with Him–when we surrender our plans and our work to God–He can provide us with His wisdom, resources, encouragement, and open doors to bear fruit for His kingdom. He is able to do more than we could ever ask or imagine with our work.

As we abide and pray, we are reminded of God's love for us, and reminded of our identity, purpose, and calling. We are strengthened with His power, His wisdom, and His words so we can persevere in our work. He will enable and equip us so that we can do the work He has called us to do.

Prayer Meetings with God for Your Business/Ministry

While our hearts may be longing to serve God and do what He's called us to do for His glory, it's easy for the flesh to take over and try to do our work in our own strength. Then we find ourselves feeling overwhelmed, burned out, or like we're spinning our wheels and getting nowhere. Surrendering our work to God and asking for His wisdom and enablement to do the things He has called us to do is crucial to our well-being, and to our business or ministry as well.

Proverbs 16:3 ESV encourages us to "commit your work to the Lord, and your plans will be established." Author and entrepreneur Shae Bynes writes about a prayer practice she uses to help commit her work to the Lord. She calls them "business meetings with God," a dedicated time in which you pray over your work, business, or ministry. These business meetings with God don't have to be fancy or formal. Bynes writes about how her meetings include any number of prayer practices, such as praise and worship, asking for wisdom regarding business opportunities, journaling prayers for her ministry, and reading His Word. She writes:

Accepting the invitation to do business with the presence of God rather than simply for the glory of God is one of the most life-changing decisions you can make ... Doing business as a Kingdom-driven entrepreneur begins and thrives with intimacy with God. It is the foundation of your operations. What's amazing is that you are invited into greater intimacy with ALL of God–Abba Father, Jesus Christ, and Holy Spirit. This beautiful triune God desires to do business with you!

Doing business WITH God rather than simply FOR God is the door to experiencing more than you could ever imagine.[108]

Reading the Word, spending time in prayer for your work, and fellowshipping with other believers doing the same or similar work for God are all important in helping to make sure we're fulfilling our purpose and conducting our work in a way that honors and glorifies God.

James 1:5 reminds us that God is generous in pouring out His wisdom when we ask Him for it. As we surrender our work to God in prayer, we gain His wisdom about what our next steps should be, as well as how we should be going about our work. Jeremiah 33:3b encourages us that if we call out to God, He will "tell you great and unsearchable things you do not know." God has bigger dreams for our families, ministries, and businesses than we do. God can open doors and opportunities we couldn't on our own. God can give us greater insight into how we should run our businesses than we could ever think of on our own.

Additionally, God's Word–and His great commandment to love God and love others–should be our foundation in how we conduct ourselves as we do the work God has called us to do. As we read and pray God's Word, it will help us establish the principles and priorities we should be operating in while we do the work we are called to do and love the people God has put in our lives. Deuteronomy 28:12 encourages us that if we are listening to and following His commands, "the Lord will open the heavens, the storehouse of his bounty, to send rain on your land in season and to bless all the work of your hands." Reading and praying His living Word will help ensure we are following His commands and working for His glory, and God will bless our faithfulness.

As you find Scriptures that reflect how or why you are doing the work before you, I encourage you to write those Scriptures down so they can encourage you later. I've found many Scriptures that help me remember why I write or how I want to be loving others through the words I write. I keep those verses close by my writing desk and include them in my prayers before I start writing.

Oswald Chambers writes, "Prayer does not equip us for greater works–prayer is the greater work."[109] We can strive in our own strength, or we can seek our heavenly Father. Prayer is essential for supernatural advancement of God's kingdom and His plans and purposes.

Corrie ten Boom wrote, "What wings are to a bird and sails to a ship, so is prayer to a soul."[110] Without prayer, our business or ministry may not fly as high or may find itself stuck in the harbor. Prayer is essential to godly growth and to faithfully completing the tasks He has called you to do.

Pursuing Our Greatest Purpose

After all this talk about prayerfully serving God and others, let's end this chapter with the most freeing and greatest purpose we have. No matter what God has called you or gifted you to do, your greatest purpose of all is to have a relationship with your Heavenly Father, to seek Him and enjoy His presence.

Like Martha, it's easy to get distracted by the many things we feel called to do, choosing to focus on those tasks in our daily lives and in our prayer lives. But Jesus wants us to be like Mary and choose the better thing, sitting in and savoring His presence, where there is fullness of joy (see Luke 10:38-42 and Psalm 16:11).

Joanna Weaver writes regarding Martha, "In her effort to set a table worthy of the Son of God, she nearly missed the real banquet ...

Only one thing is needed–and that is found in true fellowship with him."[111]

God isn't demanding we do big things for Him; He desires that we delight in Him. He doesn't want us to strive; He wants us to seek Him. God doesn't want us to wear ourselves out serving Him; He wants us to rest in Him.

God isn't a slave-driver; He is our Shepherd. He isn't our CEO; He is our Wonderful Counselor. He isn't a hard master; He is our Heavenly Father.

Kelly Needham writes, "The meaning of life is not found within us. It is not found in discovering our unique purpose, calling, or dream. The meaning of life is God himself. He is the promised land. He is the goal. God himself–not what he does for us or what we do for him–is the meaning of life ... Our purpose isn't tied to our activity but to our breathing. So long as you are alive, you have a far greater purpose than you ever dared dream, namely to know and reflect the God in whose image you were made."[112]

God doesn't need anything from us, but He desires a relationship with us. He created us to seek Him and find Him (see Acts 17:24-27).

Paul was an incredible servant of God, doing incredible things for God's kingdom, but he considered them nothing in comparison to "the surpassing worth of knowing Christ Jesus my Lord," (see Philippians 3:8). Paul knew that we were created for and live for God, not for our works (see 1 Corinthians 8:6).

Moses encountered some awesome miracles and was provided for in mighty ways while leading the Israelites out of Egypt and through the wilderness, yet what he sought God in prayer for was God's wisdom, glory, and His presence (see Exodus 33:12-23). Moses wasn't seeking more miracles or miraculous provisions or the specific tasks God had for Him to do. Moses just wanted more of God. Moses established a "tent of meeting," (see Exodus 33:7-11) a sacred place where he could go to meet with God each day.

Like Mary, Paul, and Moses, let's choose the better thing. Spending time in His presence–seeking nothing from God but to experience and know our Heavenly Father–is our greatest purpose of all.

Scripture Prayers for Your Purpose

Thank You, Lord, that I am Your masterpiece. You uniquely created me so that I can do all the things You have planned for me through Your Son, Jesus. (Based on Ephesians 2:10 NLT.)

Thank You, God, that You generously provide the wisdom I need when I ask regarding my purpose. (Based on James 1:5 ESV.)

I cry out to You, God Most High, that You would fulfill Your purpose for me. (Based on Psalm 57:2 ESV.)

Thank You, God, that You use everything in my life for good, since you have called me according to Your purpose. (Based on Romans 8:28).

I commit my work to You, Father God. May You establish the work of my hands. (Based on Proverbs 16:3.)

Like Jesus, help me to follow Your will and to accomplish the work You would have me do. (Based on John 4:34.)

Help me to fan into flame the gift(s) You have given me. (Based on 2 Timothy 1:6.)

Thank You for choosing me and appointing me to go and bear fruit. May I be fruitful and bear fruit that will last. (Based on John 15:16.)

God of peace, equip me with everything good for doing Your will, and may You work in me what is pleasing to You through Jesus Christ. (Based on Hebrews 13:20-21.)

Help me to work heartily at the work You have given me to do for You and not for man. (Based on Colossians 3:23 NKJV.)

In my relationships with others, may I have the same mindset as Jesus Christ, who made Himself nothing by taking the very nature of a servant made in human likeness, who humbled Himself and became obedient, even to death. (Based on Philippians 2:5-8.)

Father, help me to not get worried and distracted by all the things I have to do like Martha, but to be like Mary and sit at Your feet enjoying Your presence. May I always remember that sitting at Your feet is the better choice. (Based on Luke 10:38-42.)

Chapter 16

Praying for Your Words

A word fitly spoken is like apples of gold in settings of silver.
–Proverbs 25:11 NKJV

I'm always on the lookout for Scriptures relating to embracing life, so I was surprised when I stumbled across a new one: "Whoever wants to embrace true life and find beauty in each day must stop speaking evil, hurtful words and never deceive in what they say. Always turn from what is wrong and cultivate what is good; eagerly pursue peace in every relationship" (1 Peter 3:10-11a TPT).

I was stunned yet again by the treasures the Bible holds. I'd been on a quest for years to find Scriptures to pray for my boys' speech, as well as verses about embracing life, and here was one that combined both.

According to Peter, we embrace a fulfilling and meaningful life when we speak kindly and honestly with one another and when we pursue peace in our relationships. I couldn't agree more. We all know words have power. When God speaks, every single word accomplishes His purpose, as we see from the creation story and as we read in Isaiah 55:11.

God's Word is so powerful that when incarnation occurred it is described in John 1:14 as the Word becoming flesh. Jesus is the living manifestation of God's message and plan for humanity. Jesus, as the Word, brings light, truth, and redemption to the world, and through Him, God communicates His love and desire for relationship with mankind.

Jesus spoke in words, parables, and sermons about God's kingdom and eternal life. He shared words of grace and truth to all those He met. In fact, when He asked if His disciples would leave Him, Peter said, "Lord, to whom should we go? You have the words of eternal life," (see John 6:67-68).

As powerful as God's words are, our words also have the ability to impact the lives and the hearts of the people around us. So it's important that we pray for our words, and that we speak words that bring life to those around us.

Speaking with Grace and Truth

In John 8 we meet a woman. We don't know her name or much about her at all, except for her sin. She was caught in adultery, so religious leaders (and probably a crowd interested in seeing a sinful woman stoned) gathered around her, rocks in their hands. The Law of Moses stated anyone caught in adultery should be stoned. So the followers of the law were ready to carry out the law.

And then Jesus came along. The Pharisees demanded He decide if Moses's law should be carried out or ignored. The Pharisees expected Jesus to back them up, and if He did, her life would end. Instead, Jesus squatted to write something in the dirt on the ground. "Let any one of you who is without sin be the first to throw a stone at her" (John 8:7b).

I wonder if she held her breath waiting for the pain of a rock, or several rocks, to be flung at her body from the religious leaders who prided themselves on following the law of Moses to the letter. But one by one, the stones dropped to the ground and the crowd dispersed.

She looked into Jesus' eyes, wondering what He would do. He was the only one qualified to throw a stone and carry out Moses's law.

"Neither do I condemn you," (John 8:11b) He said, compassion etched on His face. Relief and gratitude surely flooded through her at such amazing grace. Mercy that she didn't deserve. But that wasn't all. "Go now and leave your life of sin," (John 8:11b) He told her.

His words of truth stung a bit but reminded her that she could do better. He made it clear that her sin was forgiven and grace was given, but it didn't give her permission to continue committing sin. She could move forward in life knowing she had received undeserved grace but walk in the truth that she was called to a life of holiness.

And that right there is one example out of hundreds of how Jesus was a man of grace and truth. John 1:14 tells us, "The Word became flesh and made his dwelling among us. We have seen his glory, the glory of the one and only Son, who came from the Father, full of grace and truth." Everything Jesus did and said was a beautiful blend of sharing God's grace and truth with those around Him.

The Importance of Grace AND Truth

Grace

Grace is an undeserved gift. Favor. Love. Mercy.

What we see of both God's heart and Jesus' heart is their love toward us. Dane Ortland writes in his book *Gentle and Lowly*:

> The Holy Son of God moves toward, touches, heals, embraces, and forgives those who least deserve it yet truly desire it.
> ... The Jesus given to us in the Gospels is not simply one who loves, but one who is love; merciful affections stream from his innermost heart as rays from the sun.[113]

The way God showed us love and mercy, despite all the sin and wrongdoing in our lives, was to send His beloved son Jesus to die on the cross for our sin.

Grace is an essential part of God's nature. He loves us. It's who He is and always will be. His grace is a gift that needs to be accepted. His grace has the power to transform our lives and our identities.

Truth

Truth is revealed in the Bible as the teachings, commands, and promises of God.

Jesus prayed, "Sanctify them by the truth; your word is truth" (John 17:17).

We need to hear and apply God's truth to help us grow more into the holy men and women God has created us to be. Dr. Holly Ordway writes, "Just as yeast does not instantly make nourishing bread by itself, truth does not transform lives unless and until it is activated, given form and substance, and allowed time to develop."[114]

Truth is an essential part of God's character. He cannot lie. He does not change. He does not break His promises. God's truth keeps us on the path He has for us. God's truth can be painful to hear sometimes but, when applied, can be transformative.

Grace and Truth

In our sin and brokenness, we tend toward one side of speaking grace or truth more than the other. We may more often build up our loved ones by praising and encouraging them and neglect sharing truth with them because we don't want to discourage or hurt them, but without that truth, they are missing out on living on a strong foundation rooted in God's words and truth for their own lives.

Or we may find it easier to share God's words of truth with those around us and forget to share that God is a God of abundant grace. They might then feel worn down and weary, unable to be accepted and loved as they are, and they miss experiencing God's love and growing into all that they can be.

Sometimes we compromise God's truth by choosing to focus more on grace, God's love, and being kind and encouraging to others. Sometimes that leads us to keep silent when we should speak up. Other times it causes us to lie or to omit the truth because we want to avoid conflict and be what we perceive to be a good Christian or a nice person. I'll admit this is a struggle of mine. I have a peacekeeping nature that tends to keep things bottled up, avoiding the hard conversations. Yet somehow it ends up resulting in more conflict.

Or we choose to speak the truth, sometimes with judgment and without mention of grace and God's love. We may tell people that they are sinning and will go to hell but don't tell them that God loves them and wants a relationship with them, or that we love them, too. We aim truth at them like arrows, rather than have a conversation with them seeking truth together. This often leads individuals away from God, as they want nothing to do with a judgmental God or anyone who would follow such a God.

Jesus is our perfect example of someone who is able to balance speaking both truth and grace. He never compromised one over the other for any reason. He simply was a man full of grace and truth, and so He spoke grace and truth.

Both words of grace and of truth are good. Both are healthy. Both are needed. Both are tools toward healthy communication that helps others grow. Both truth and grace together help us love each other closer to the heart and character of God.

Truth and grace together lead to salvation, repentance, and spiritual growth. In my experience, people are more likely to accept salvation when they see God's love for them despite their sin. Then they can experience what a beautiful gift grace is. It is love, not judgment, that helps people see Christ in us and leads them toward the heart of Christ.

After about a decade of arguments and long conversations about our communication, Tim and I began to identify where a lot of the conflict in our marriage came from. I leaned toward grace and my husband leaned toward truth. But as we walked with God, as we read the Word, as we prayed, as we talked to each other and learned from each other, we both grew to be more balanced in speaking and living truth and grace. Tim taught me the value of speaking and receiving truth. And I taught Tim about the importance of giving and receiving grace.

Tim and I have journeyed together to learn how to balance speaking with both grace and truth. Our marriage is in a much healthier place because I have learned to speak and receive more truth and Tim has learned to speak and receive more grace.

As we interact with and learn from these people in our lives who exhibit more of a specific characteristic of Christ than we do, we grow more into the character of Christ. And as we read His Word and pray, we find ourselves communicating more like Christ, too.

The Power of Our Words

Scripture demonstrates time and time again that our words have the power to bring healing or to bring harm. Kathy Khang writes in her book *Raise Your Voice*, "Words can be used to free people from captivity or to sentence people into captivity."[115] Our words can encourage, teach, and bring spiritual nourishment. They have the ability to advocate for others and to build bridges. Words can also bring about discord, discouragement, and destruction.

Just as there are over two thousand Bible verses about how we use our money (our currency in life), there are many Bible verses about how we use our words (our currency of communication).

Sally and Clay Clarkson write in their book *Giving Your Words*, "Even in the godhead, there is an order of communication that is a model for us as followers of Jesus. God gave His words to Jesus; Jesus, as God, gave His words to the disciples; His disciples were given the authority to give the words to others, and on it would go. All those words are given to be received and truly understood for giving ultimate purpose and meaning in our lives because they are from God."[116]

Sharing God's words of truth, grace, and wisdom give meaning and purpose and direction to those around us. Nancy Demoss Wolgemuth writes, "Have you ever thought that each day God can work through you to give priceless gifts to your family, fellow workers, neighbors, or friends? Wise, kind words are gifts that can change lives ... When our words are sifted through God's Word, they will be cherished gifts to those we love."[117]

Paul writes to the Corinthians, "For in Him you have been enriched in every way, in all speech and all knowledge, because our testimony about Christ was confirmed in you" (1 Corinthians 1:5-6 BSB). Paul is expressing his gratitude that the Corinthians believed the words of the gospel he taught them, and that their speech and their knowledge are evidence of their salvation and their faith in Christ. It's a convicting thought for us—do the words we speak confirm that Christ is at work in us and working through us?

Jesus tells us, "For the mouth speaks out of that which fills the heart. The good man brings out of his good treasure what is good; and the evil man brings out of his evil treasure what is evil. But I tell you that every careless word that people speak, they shall give an accounting for it in the day of judgment. For by your words you will be justified, and by your words you will be condemned" (Matthew 12:34b-37 NASB).

Solomon informs us, "Words kill, words give life; they're either poison or fruit—you choose" (Proverbs 18:21 MSG). We may desire to choose to speak words of life to others, but it doesn't come naturally. It requires time in prayer and in Bible study and of staying in tune with the Holy Spirit, speaking the words He brings to our minds to share with others.

First, we need to be reading God's Word. Jesus tells us, "The words I have spoken to you—they are full of the Spirit and life" (John 6:63b). And we need to be spending time with God in prayer. As we walk in our faith, read our Bible, and pray, we store His Words in our hearts and minds so that we can remember them when needed, and so that we can share with others when needed. As Paul encourages us, "Let the word of Christ dwell in you richly, teaching and admonishing one another with all wisdom" (Colossians 3:16a ESV). Staying connected through prayer to Father, Son, and Holy Spirit is crucial if we want to share God's powerful and life-giving words with others.

When we're on the same page as God, reading and praying His words of grace and truth, we're able to share those words of grace and truth with others.

Speaking Blessings

The first time I remember blessings being spoken and prayed over someone was at an event for the middle school girls at our church. I was in college and a youth group volunteer, and we were told to think of a blessing to give each girl at this event. I researched what blessings even were, and prayed about what blessing I should give. I decided on a simple one inspired by one of my favorite verses, Zephaniah 3:17: "May you remember that you are God's beloved daughter, that He delights in you and rejoices over you with singing."

During the blessing event, the girls sat in a special chair where, hands folded and eyes closed, she received a blessing from each of the youth group leaders. Every one of those girls had tears in their eyes or broke down weeping as they received their individual blessings. I don't know about you, but I would have loved to have such beautiful blessings and words of truth spoken over me when I was an insecure middle schooler.

We can offer compliments and words of praise that can go directly to the minds and egos of the listener, but a blessing is a Scriptural truth spoken directly to the heart and the spirit of another person, based on the very word of God. Just as in Genesis 2, when God breathed life into Adam, we have the ability to breathe spiritual life, truth, and encouragement into the hearts and minds of our loved ones with God's Word. We can help our loved ones get on the same page with God as we speak and pray God's Word over them.

Throughout the book of Genesis, we see blessings spoken over the children and grandchildren of our Bible heroes. In Genesis 27 Jacob and Esau both greatly desire and seek Isaac's blessing. A generation later, in Genesis 48 and 49, Jacob bestows blessings upon each of his sons and several of his grandsons. In Hebrews 11:20-21 Isaac and Jacob are listed among our Old Testament heroes of faith for blessing their children. In Mark 10 parents brought their children to Jesus to be blessed: Jesus "took the children in his arms and placed his hands on their heads and blessed them" (Mark 10:16 NLT).

Blessings aren't just for children. Jesus' last words on earth were a blessing for His beloved friends and disciples. As we read in Luke 24:51, "while he was blessing them, he left them and was taken up into heaven." The apostles would follow Jesus' example and bless missionaries before they departed on their designated trip.

We pray blessings over a meal or pray a blessing over individuals on special occasions, but blessings can be bestowed upon anyone, anytime the Spirit prompts you to speak one. You can bless your spouse when they're feeling discouraged or before they go to work. You can bless your children or grandchildren before they go to school or as they enter a new stage of life. It doesn't need to be huge, grand, or fancy, only Spirit-led and rooted in the Word and promises of God.

God has blessed us and He wants us to operate in that identity as one who is blessed. Speaking a Scripture-based blessing over your loved ones allows both you and your loved ones' hearts to become aligned with God's heart for them. You have the power to speak that life and truth into their hearts, minds, and spirits so they can claim God's promises as their own. Speaking these words aloud has the power to break whatever strategies Satan is trying to use against them, realigning our loved ones with God's will, promises, and plan for them.

When my younger son was having night terrors and trouble sleeping, I sought and found a Scripture to pray over him while tucking him into bed. I would lay my hand over his little heart and say, based on Psalm 4:8, "May you lie down and sleep in peace, for God is with you." Not only did those truths comfort his anxious heart, but I was claiming the Word of God over my son, blessing him with peaceful sleep as promised in God's Word. Within a few nights of me speaking and claiming this Scripture over him, the night terrors stopped and he's never had another night terror since.

There's no set formula or rules for how to speak a blessing over a loved one, but I do recommend you pray first–asking God for wisdom as to which Scriptural promises you can use to bless your loved ones–before you pray a blessing over your loved one.

You can lay your hands on the person you are blessing if you wish, whether it be putting a hand on their head or their shoulder, or holding their hands. You can look into their eyes while you say it, or each have your eyes closed. No matter how you choose to do it, it's a beautiful practice to help you deeply connect with your loved ones.

Plus, no matter which love language[118] your loved ones respond to, speaking a blessing over them speaks to each love language: You are serving them through your prayers and encouragement, gifting them words of life and truth they can cling to, providing reassuring physical touch, speaking life-giving words of affirmation, and blessing them with individualized quality time and attention in a way that has eternal benefits.

Here are a few of my favorite Scripture blessings to speak life and truth to your loved ones:

Scriptural Blessings

May your love abound more and more in knowledge and depth of insight, so that you may be able to discern what is best. May you be pure and blameless for the day of Christ, filled with the fruit of righteousness that comes through Jesus Christ–to the glory and praise of God. (Based on Philippians 1:9-11.)

May God fill you with the knowledge of His will through all the wisdom and understanding that the Spirit gives, so that you may live a life worthy of the Lord and please Him in every way. May you bear fruit in every good work, grow in the knowledge of God, and be strengthened with all power according to His glorious might so that you may have great endurance and patience. May you give joyful thanks to the Father, who has qualified you to share in the inheritance of His holy people in the kingdom of light. (Based on Colossians 1:9-12.)

I have not stopped giving thanks for you, remembering you in my prayers. May the God of our Lord Jesus Christ, the glorious Father, give you the Spirit of wisdom and revelation, so that you may know Him better. May the eyes of your heart be enlightened in order that you may know the hope to which He has called you, the riches of His glorious inheritance in His holy people, and His incomparably great power for us who believe. (Based on Ephesians 1:16-19.)

May the LORD bless you and keep you; the LORD make His face shine upon you, and be gracious to you; the LORD lift up His countenance upon you, and give you peace. (Based on Numbers 6:24-26.)

May the LORD cause you to flourish. May you be blessed by the LORD, the Maker of heaven and earth. (Based on Psalm 115:14.)

Scripture Prayers for Your Words

Jesus, help me to speak to others more like You, that my words and actions may be full of truth and grace. (Based on John 1:14.)

Thank You for giving me my mouth and for helping me to speak. Teach me what to say. (Based on Exodus 4:11-12.)

Thank You, Lord, that in You I have been enriched in every way, including my speech and knowledge. May I speak words that confirm that Christ is in me. (Based on 1 Corinthians 1:5-6 BSB.)

Help me not to speak anything unwholesome, but to speak words that are helpful for building others up according to their needs, that my words may benefit those who are listening. (Based on Ephesians 4:29.)

Help me to speak beautiful, life-giving words to those around me, so my words can release sweetness to their souls and inner healing to their spirits. (Based on Proverbs 16:24 TPT.)

May all my words be fitly spoken like apples of gold in settings of silver. (Based on Proverbs 25:11 NKJV.)

Let my conversation always be full of grace, seasoned with salt. May I know how to answer everyone. (Based on Colossians 4:6.)

Keep my tongue from evil and my lips from telling lies. May I turn from evil and do good. May I seek peace and pursue it. (Based on Psalm 34:13-14.)

Help me to bless those who persecute me, to bless them rather than curse them. Give me the words to rejoice with those who rejoice and mourn with those who mourn. (Based on Romans 12:14-15.)

Help me to avoid foolish and ignorant arguments, knowing that they lead to conflict. Help me to not quarrel but be gentle to all, able to teach, and patient. Help me in humility to correct those who are in opposition, so that they may know Your truth and be led toward repentance. (Based on 2 Timothy 2:23-25 NKJV.)

May the words of my mouth and the meditations of my heart be pleasing in Your sight, oh Lord, my Rock and my Redeemer. (Based on Psalm 19:14.)

Chapter 17

Praying for Healing

I hope all is well with you and that you are as healthy in body as you are strong in spirit.

–3 John 1:2b NLT

If you could have any superpower, what would it be? Without hesitation, my answer would be the power to heal.

I have been praying for years, sometimes even decades, for loved ones with health issues, disability, or chronic pain to experience healing. I pray for their healing, believing it would be an incredible testimony we can share with others and bring glory to God.

Instead, I see loved ones continue to struggle with their health, and to be honest, it makes me doubt the power of prayer sometimes. I'll admit I've gotten jealous when I hear others share testimonies of miraculous healing.

I resonate with the words of Paul E. Miller: "Quiet cynicism and spiritual weariness develops in us when heartfelt prayer goes unanswered ... our hearts shut down."[119] Maybe for you it is similar. Maybe you or a loved one are experiencing health issues or chronic pain or a devastating diagnosis. Or maybe you've experienced the power of miracles and healing and it fuels your passion for praying for healing.

I obviously don't have the ability to heal, but what I do have is the power to approach the throne of God and pray for the bodies, hearts, and minds of my loved ones. To pray that they would be well not just physically, but emotionally, spiritually, and mentally too.

When you are struggling with physical or mental health issues, and you're persevering in prayer for healing, it can be a lonely and challenging time that can make us question the goodness of God or the strength of our faith. After all, some Bible verses (and sometimes the people around us) remind us that faith and prayer is what brings healing. We start to question if maybe our faith or our prayers aren't strong enough.

This sense of blame and shame is natural in our flesh, but these thoughts are not of God. When the disciples saw a man born blind, they wondered who was at fault–was it the man's sin, or his parents' sin? Jesus' response to their question is the same for us: "Neither this man nor his parents sinned ... but this happened so that the works of God might be displayed in him" (John 9:3).

Jesus didn't merely heal physical disorders and disabilities; He also addressed their deepest heart desires and needs. He gave them the gift of His presence and of a comforting touch when no one else did. He gave them words of truth and encouragement. He forgave them of their sin. He restored them into fellowship with others. He reminded them of their true identity.

These were the works of God that brought Him glory in the lives of others. God cares about our bodies, our minds, and our souls. Sometimes, He heals all aspects of us completely. Other times, He brings about healing in one or two of those areas.

God's Will Regarding Healing

Our family loves watching *The Chosen*, a beautiful TV series that depicts the ministry of Jesus and the people He chooses to interact with. Each episode is a beautiful journey closer to the heart of Jesus, deeper into Jewish culture and customs, and straight into the stories of Scripture.

Sure, the show's writers take several liberties. We don't know all the backstories and conversations that took place between all the characters we read about in the Bible, and so in *The Chosen* they are thoughtfully made up to create a unique story that draws you back to Scripture.

Our family especially loves the disciple Matthew, who is depicted with characteristics that would put him on the autism spectrum. Our family loves how Jesus sees Matthew's heart, not his quirks or his previous profession, and Jesus has a great love and purpose for Matthew. Because of Matthew's meticulous attention to detail, he makes an excellent candidate to record in his notebook the events that have unfolded–stories that we know will eventually make up the Gospel of Matthew.

In season 3, episode 2 there is a powerful scene regarding healing. Jesus sends His disciples out two by two, giving them permission to heal and to drive out demons. But first, Jesus' disciple Little James (not to be confused with another disciple named James who is John's brother) has a question for Jesus.

Little James doesn't say the name of his disability, but it appears he has cerebral palsy or scoliosis or maybe a combination of both (since those are the diagnoses of the actor, Jordan Walker Ross, who portrays Little James). He is not as fast as the other disciples and often uses a walking stick that is taller than him. He's indicated before to the disciples that he wants to be healed, but he's too afraid to ask Jesus for healing. Now, Little James comes before Jesus, asking how he can heal others when he himself hasn't been healed.

Jesus gently tells James that God has other plans for him. He says the stories of healing are "a good story, but there are already dozens who can tell that story. And there will be hundreds more, even thousands. But think of the story that you have, especially in this journey to come, if I don't heal you. To know how to proclaim that you still praise God in spite of this. To know how to focus on all that matters, so much more than the body. To show people that you can be patient with your suffering here on earth because you know you'll spend eternity with no suffering. Not everyone can understand that."[120]

Little James is in tears. He confesses to Jesus it's not easy, that he feels less than the other disciples. Jesus gently asks him, "Are you fast? Do you look impressive when you walk? Maybe not. But these are things the Father doesn't care about. You are going to do more for me than most people ever dream. So many people need healing in order to believe in me, or they need healing because their hearts are so sick. That doesn't apply to you."[121]

Jesus then tells Little James that he will be able to leap like a deer (Isaiah 35:6) when he meets God in heaven. "Your reward will be great. So hold on a little longer. And when you discover yourself finding true strength because of your weakness, and when you do great things in my name in spite of this, the impact will last for generations ... A man like you, healing others. Oh, what a sight! I can't wait to hear your stories when you return ... You will be healed. It's only a matter of time."[122]

It's a beautiful and touching scene that brought many people watching to tears. I loved reading Joni Earikson Tada's response to it. Joni was paralyzed in a diving accident at the age of seventeen. Despite being a quadriplegic and in chronic pain, she has started an incredible ministry called Joni and Friends that serves individuals with disabilities and their families. She shared in a Facebook post with a clip of this scene:

> I was in tears when I watched this clip from Season 3 of *The Chosen*.
>
> Like most people who live with pain, I have asked many times for Jesus to alleviate it or remove it completely. But Jesus has other plans for my pain (the same plans he shares in this imagined scene with his disciple who asks for healing).
>
> The point of the episode? Jesus doesn't always heal.
>
> It's not that the Lord isn't concerned about my physical comfort; it's just that my physical problems are not always his focus. Jesus is more concerned about the condition of my soul. He wants me to feel the sharpness of my weakness, so that I might find strength in him.

Psalm 84:11 promises me that 'no good thing will [God] withhold from those whose walk is blameless;' but the 'good thing' may not always be physical healing. Instead, he'll not withhold courage and endurance. God will not withhold patience and perseverance. He won't withhold peace and hope, making my soul brave and roomy for him. When my needs are great? His grace will be greater. That's his plan. And I think it's a good one.

So, why then did I cry over this scene between Jesus and his disciple? I wept because I identified with it. My tears overflowed at Jesus's last words: 'So hang on a little longer ... You will be healed. It's just a matter of time.' Yes, pain and disability are hard. Very hard. But what I am learning in and through it is priceless ... so, I'm happy to hang on. Healing is just over the horizon.[123]

Like Joni, when I watched this episode, my heart resonated with Little James's questions and tears. And my heart was comforted by the compassion and care the Lord has for all those He loves.

Sometimes healing comes immediately, as we see Jesus compassionately healing all the people brought to Him in Matthew 8:16-17.

Sometimes His answer is to wait, as it was for Mary, Martha, and Lazarus in John 11. Jesus raising Lazarus from the dead would bring God greater glory than rushing to heal Lazarus of his sickness.

Sometimes, His answer is no. Jesus healed one man at the pool of Bethesda in John 5, but not the others. God told Paul He wouldn't remove the thorn in Paul's side so that Paul wouldn't become prideful (see 2 Corinthians 12:7-9).

According to James 5:14, we are to pray for healing. Healing is within the heart and character of God. Whether it occurs on this side of heaven or in heaven, healing is coming. Joni Eareckson Tada writes, "I wait eagerly and excitedly for the redemption of my body–and I don't mind waiting patiently for it (Romans 8:23-25). Until such time, God is going to use my wheelchair as a convincing proof of the deeper healing He has given me–a settled soul, a hopeful spirit, and a confidence in grace that sustains me through every weakness."[124]

God's Healing Power

There is a story in Mark 5:24-34 that I love. This is the story of a woman who had been suffering a bleeding issue for twelve years and who, with great faith, reached for the hem of the garment of Jesus.

This woman was not only physically unwell (imagine the weakness that comes from a ceaseless menstrual flow for twelve years without iron supplements, as well as the continual cleansing of clothes and self), but she was also considered culturally unclean. According to the laws in Leviticus 15:19-30, she was to remain away from other people so she wouldn't make them unclean. A law meant to protect the people from unsanitary or contagious conditions became one that caused the culture to judge and isolate her from friends and family for over a decade.

For twelve years this woman does all she can to find healing. She seeks out doctors who tried many things but it only led to a dwindling of funds and her health. She had just about lost hope. But then she heard Jesus was coming to town. She heard about others who were healed. A glimmer of hope! And since she knew she couldn't be seen in public, she would have to approach Him without anyone noticing. She believed it would be enough. She had faith. And she was willing to risk everything to act on it.

She managed to make it unnoticed past the crowd to Jesus, where she reached out and touched the hem of His cloak. She immediately felt healing and strength course through her body. I can't imagine the joy and freedom she experienced as a result of that healing, realizing she was no longer unclean. She could return to her family and friends, and she could go back into the temple and pray with the other women.

She experienced physical healing, but God wasn't done with her yet. God cares about our whole being–body, mind, and spirit–

and this woman had other areas that needed healing. Jesus stopped, turned around, and asked, "Who touched me?"

I'm sure she dropped back, trying to hide, to blend in. Surely He would think someone bumped into Him. That's what His disciples told him. At least, I think that's how I would have responded. In a culture where you don't touch a man unless you are related or married to him, and you definitely don't touch anyone when you are unclean, I don't know if I would have confessed what I'd done, no matter how joyful I was to be healed.

But this woman stepped forward, "fell at his feet and, trembling with fear, told him the whole truth" (Mark 5:33). She didn't merely admit she was the one to touch Him, but she tells him her story, about her shameful disorder, about her suffering and loneliness and losing hope, about all that she'd done to find healing, and how she finally found it by touching His cloak.

And He responds to her heart and her story by calling her daughter. Daughter! How beautiful! She had come to Jesus to find healing from her physical suffering, and He knew she had some spiritual healing that needed to take place. He embraced her into His family, making her not only culturally acceptable again, but intimately connected to Him. I wonder if there was an ache in her heart from her earthly father's rejection, or maybe abandonment, or lack of love and acceptance due to her uncleanness. I don't know, but God knew what ache was in her heart and how to bring healing to it with that one beautiful word and name: daughter.

And God does the same to us. He sees the suffering and the shame we have experienced. He knows every tear we have cried. He sees the hemorrhaging in our own hearts. He can stop the bleeding with a loving touch. He can restore our identity and our relationships with a word.

And then He tells her, "Your faith has healed you. Go in peace and be freed from your suffering" (Mark 5:34). Her whole body was healed by reaching out to Him in faith. But now her heart is also healed of the wounds and shame she has carried for twelve years, and she is reminded of her spiritual identity. She sought Jesus for healing of her body. What she received was a holistic healing of her body, soul, mind, and heart.

Praying for Our Healing

This woman experienced healing of body, mind, and soul. So did the crippled beggar that Peter healed in Acts 3. The healed man was able to jump for joy and praise God. All his emotional and spiritual baggage was removed. Peter tells the amazed crowd, "By faith in the name of Jesus, this man whom you see and know was made strong. It is Jesus' name and the faith that comes through him that has completely healed him, as you can all see" (Acts 3:16).

But sometimes–like the apostle Paul–we have faith in the name of Jesus and we don't experience the physical healing we long for. Our faith is an important component to our wellness and to living the vibrant, abundant life God has called us to, but that abundant life can include God's healing touch in a variety of ways. It could include healing that comes from seeing a Christian counselor, a wise doctor, or a specialist; taking any necessary medications we need; or even from reading a book. There's no shame in getting the help our bodies and minds need to be healthy and function optimally. Or it could include God giving us the strength and joy and perseverance to keep going in our journey despite any thorns in our flesh, as Paul experienced.

When Jesus saw someone in need of healing, He was always filled with compassion and drew near to them. He didn't focus on their disabilities; He saw their hearts and their faith. He spoke to their hearts and their spirits, telling them to take heart, or that their sins were forgiven, or praising them for their faith.

God cares about our faith and our hearts, and we are invited to go before God and tell Him everything, as this woman did. We can tell Him every wound in our heart and how we've tried to heal it ourselves but can't. He wants us to approach Him and share with Him what we're feeling and thinking, even if it scares us or we're mad at Him. He can take our doubts and our emotions. In fact, He wants more of you being shared with Him, growing in relationship.

I encourage you to sit before God and be honest with Him. Pour out your words and tears. Pray Scriptures of healing and faith. Write God a letter if it's easier for you, I've done that many times. And then leave that precious time feeling relieved that He still cares for you more than you will ever grasp or understand. Being reminded that He cares about your body and soul, your heart and your mind.

Share your heart with God; He can handle it. He'll listen intently, just as Jesus did with the woman's story in Mark 5. Then it'll be your turn to listen as He whispers words of truth, encouragement, and purpose to your heart and your spirit. Keep drawing close to Him. Push through the distractions around you to be near Him and His healing presence. Reach out and touch the hem of His garment. His healing presence and power are there and are always available for you.

As you pray and surrender to God, remember that He is always after your heart. He sees the whole picture, and He is interested in your holistic healing. Our bodies, minds, and emotions are fragile and temporary, but our souls are eternal. God is after building up the things that will last forever with Him in paradise.

Scripture Prayers for Health and Healing

Thank You, Jesus, that You bore our sins in Your body so that we might die to sin and live for righteousness. It is by Your wounds we are healed. (Based on 1 Peter 2:24.)

Heal me, LORD, and I'll be healed. Save me and I'll be saved, for You are the one I praise. (Based on Jeremiah 17:14.)

I pray that _____ may enjoy good health and that all may go well with them, even as their soul is getting along well. (Based on 3 John 1:2.)

I will rejoice and be glad in Your steadfast love because You have seen my affliction. You have known the distress of my soul, and You have not delivered me into the hand of the enemy. You have set my feet in a broad place. (Based on Psalm 31:7-8 ESV.)

Equip me to praise You in my inmost being. May I remember that You forgive all my sins and heal all my diseases. Redeem my life from the pit, crown me with love and compassion, satisfy my desires with good things, and renew my youth. (Based on Psalm 103:1-5.)

When I feel brokenhearted and broken in body, may You heal me and bind up my wounds. (Based on Psalm 147:2-3.)

Lord, we do not deserve to have You near, but just say the word, and may _____ be healed. (Based on Matthew 8:8.)

May I focus on Your good news, and may others bring me good news that brings joy to my heart and health to my bones. (Based on Proverbs 15:30.)

Help me to keep Your words in my heart, for they are life and health to the whole body. (Based on Proverbs 4:21-22.)

Lord, help me to not cast blame for any illness, disorder, pain, and disease. There is no such cause-effect here. Help me to look instead for what You can do through this situation. (Based on John 9:3 MSG.)

I lift up the thorn of _____ (particular health issue) to You and plead that You would take it away. But if not, I pray that Your grace would be sufficient for me, for Your power is made perfect in my weakness. Help me to boast all the more gladly about my weaknesses so that Christ's power would rest on me. (Based on 2 Corinthians 12:7-9.)

Chapter 18

Praying for Justice

And what does the Lord require of you? To act justly and to love mercy and to walk humbly with your God.

–Micah 6:8b

When I learned about the murder of Ahmaud Arbery in February of 2020, I felt like I'd been pierced through the heart. I'd heard of other cases of racial injustice that elicited feelings of sadness or anger, but this one opened my eyes and my heart anew. I felt overwhelmed with a sense of anger and was heartbroken at such a horrific act against one of God's children.

A few months later, I learned about the death of George Floyd. I experienced a fresh wave of outrage and grief that brought me to my knees in tears. That evening I attended an online prayer meeting where we came together to grieve and to pray. I sat silent with my head bowed and eyes closed, while tears trickled down my face. I couldn't muster a single word past the lump in my throat, and to be honest, I didn't even know what words I should pray. All I could do was listen to the prayers of others and seek solace in the heart of God.

As a writer, I felt compelled to write and speak up about these acts of injustice; yet I found myself still at an absolute loss of words. I felt led to share on my Facebook page an article I had written of Scriptures to pray for America.[125] It had received a few views back when I wrote it in 2019, but the verses shared in that post seemed much more pertinent to pray at that pivotal time following George Floyd's murder in 2020.

Suddenly thousands of people were reading and sharing that list of Scriptures on my website each day. I was surprised by the overwhelming virality of an article I had written previously, yet also comforted by the fact that so many people were turning to Scripture and to prayer in response to this injustice. My weary, broken heart revived with hope, encouraged by the realization that despite all the pain and injustices in this world, despite all the differences of opinion we may have about political topics, we can find comfort and unity in the gospel message, the power of prayer, God's Word, and the blood of Jesus that covers us all.

God's Heart for Justice

In Jeremiah 9:24b God declares, "I am the LORD, who exercises kindness, justice and righteousness on earth, for in these I delight." God, in His infinite and radical love for all His beloved children, sees justice, mercy, faithfulness, love, kindness, and righteousness as concepts that belong together. In fact, I have yet to find a single verse about justice that doesn't mention at least one of those other attributes with it. For example, Psalm 89:14 praises God, declaring, "Righteousness and justice are the foundation of your throne; love and faithfulness go before you."

Dr. Tony Evans shared in a sermon:

The twin towers of God's kingdom are righteousness and justice. These two concepts are married like a husband and a wife. They are inseparable to the degree that a government establishes and operates by righteousness and justice ...

Righteousness is the standard of right and wrong. Justice is the impartial and equitable application of God's moral law in society. Justice is the standard that privileges and penalties are distributed in society.[126]

Throughout Scripture we see God's heart for all His people to be loved and cared for well. There are over two thousand Bible verses that mention poverty and justice and God's heart toward the oppressed and the vulnerable.[127]

Jesus shared the same heart toward others, spending much of His time with the marginalized: the poor, women, children, Samaritans, tax collectors, lepers, disabled, and those deemed 'unclean' and 'sinners'.

When Jesus cleared out the temple, fashioning a whip and turning over the money changers' tables, we see a side of Him that might surprise us or make us uncomfortable. Jason Porterfield explains Jesus' motivation: "When discussing the temple cleansing, we often overlook the fact that after the money changers and animal sellers went out, the blind and lame came in and were healed (Matthew 21:14). For these marginalized people, their admittance into the temple was as miraculous as the physical healing they received. Mosaic law prohibited those with physical defects from offering sacrifices (Leviticus 21:16-24) and David had banned them from ever entering the temple (2 Samuel 5:8). Matthew goes on to write that children also entered the temple courts and praised Jesus (21:15). Their presence in the temple is equally astonishing for ... children had always been excluded from the temple."[128]

Jesus' heart was that God's temple would be a "house of prayer" (see Matthew 21:13), not a place of business. He wanted it to be a place where all were welcome and invited to attend. He could not ignore the situation, leaving so many of His beloved sheep disrespected, uninvited, and unwelcome.

The day after Jesus cleared out the temple, He declared, "Woe to you, scribes and Pharisees, hypocrites! For you tithe mint and dill and cumin, and have neglected the weightier matters of the law: justice and mercy and faithfulness. These you ought to have done, without neglecting the others" (Matthew 23:23 ESV).

God hates to see any of His children marginalized or oppressed or treated unjustly. Such acts are sins, results of our fallen world. God has called us to welcome and love all of His children and to speak up for the needs of those who are being overlooked or treated unjustly.

Responding to Injustice like Esther

We'll spend the remainder of this chapter talking about Esther and how she responded to an act of injustice by progressing through four stages toward justice: listen and learn, feel and reflect, pray and fast, and take action.

Listen and Learn

Esther lived a life of privilege and safety in the palace as queen. She could have ignored the situation taking place outside the castle walls but her heart didn't operate that way. She saw that her relative Mordecai was upset and she asked him about it (see Esther 4). She listened to Mordecai's concern that her husband's right hand man, Haman, had bribed and manipulated her husband, the king, to annihilate the Jews. Now that her eyes were opened to an injustice against an entire race of people, Mordecai tells her how she can help. He tells her she is in the perfect position to speak up for them. Although she knew that going to her husband with this news would put her own life in danger, she listened to Mordecai's wise counsel.

As we listen, we learn. The best way for us to become aware of injustice happening around us is to be open to hearing other peoples' stories and perspectives, becoming aware of the situations and pain going on outside our own families and situations. As James encourages, "Be quick to listen, slow to speak, and slow to get angry" (James 1:19b NLT).

It requires humility to listen to others, especially those who are different from us. We feel more comfortable with people who are similar to us. But by doing that, we miss out on loving those who have different life experiences from us, such as those who are of a different race, religion, culture, age, lifestyle, or ability. All of us are created in the beautiful image of God and are loved by Him. Every single person has something to teach us if we're willing to learn and love others.

Bryan Stephenson, author of the bestselling book *Just Mercy*, was told by one of his mentors, "You can't understand most of the important things from a distance. You have to get close."[129] That's what Jesus did. He left the comforts of heaven to enter into our stories, our brokenness, and our pain. He spent time with people that others often overlooked. He taught all who would listen. He healed those in the temple viewed as unworthy of love and acceptance.

Imagine what our world would be like if we all took time to get close, to ask questions, to listen to each other, to learn from each other, and to show others empathy and Christ's love, even if (or maybe especially because) they are different from us? Imagine what that could do to our Christian witness to be open, teachable, and compassionate to everyone, especially those who are different from us.

Feel and Reflect

As we learn about injustices or hard situations going on around us, it often makes us feel emotions that aren't pleasant. Mordecai felt grief and mourned when he heard the news of the upcoming annihilation of the Jews. Esther felt fear, for both her life and those of the Jews. The king felt anger when he learned about the act of injustice, and at the betrayal of what his trusted man Haman was plotting against the Jews.

We see both God and Jesus experience righteous anger and grief when they witness injustice, and it's valid and healthy for us to experience our own emotions too when we witness or experience injustices. Wesley L. Deuel writes in his book *Touch the World through Prayer*, "It is spiritually criminal to pray casually, dry-eyed and burdenless, while the world is in sin and pain. It is Christlike for your heart to weep with those who weep (Rom 12:15)."[130] Emotion indicates that we care–that we are invested in something bigger than ourselves–and it often draws us to our knees in prayer, or into a time of self-reflection.

Nehemiah has several similarities to Esther in that he was also a Jew living a life of privilege and safety in the Persian palace, and he also went through similar stages of seeking justice as Esther. While Nehemiah was hard at work helping to rebuild the walls around Jerusalem, he learned about an act of injustice occurring among the poor. The wealthier nobles and officials in Jerusalem were taking advantage of the poor, helping them pay their taxes but charging such high interest that the poor were losing their land, their houses, their possessions, and sometimes even having to sell their children into slavery to help pay off their debts (see Nehemiah 5:1-5).

When Nehemiah learned of how the poor were being treated unjustly by the wealthy, he wrote, "When I heard their outcry and these charges, I was very angry. I pondered them in my mind" (Nehemiah 5:6-7a). Nehemiah's anger led him into a time of reflection, of pondering and trying to truly understand the situation and what should be done about it. After feeling his anger, and after a time of reflection where he pondered the situation, then he was able to wisely respond to the injustice (see Nehemiah 5:6-13).

To reflect on something means to seriously consider, contemplate, or think about a particular situation. When we are experiencing a strong emotion, such as anger, we want to immediately jump into action, but that isn't always wise. Reflection provides a healthy space and opportunity to examine our emotions, experiences, hearts, and God's Word. Reflection provides us opportunities to repent of and root out any sin so we can wisely discern our next steps.

Esther felt fear and it drove her toward prayer so that she could respond to the injustice in a God-honoring way. Nehemiah felt anger and it led him to wisely ponder the situation and determine what should be done to respond to the injustice in a God-honoring way.

Our emotions and our reflections can be catalysts that drive us toward God and to His Word to seek His comfort and His wisdom as to what our next steps should be.

Pray and Fast

When we learn of an act of injustice, it often sends us to our knees, to our faith communities, and to prayer vigils. Wesley Deuwel writes, "Prayer is the very business of Christ's kingdom. Prayer is joining with God the brokenhearted Father, Christ the weeping High Priest, and the tender, interceding Holy Spirit by sharing their heartbeat and bearing with them the same burdens which they carry in their loving hearts."[131]

Esther's response to the injustice being planned for the Jews–and her fear for her own life–led her to the heart of God in prayer. For three days Esther and her maids fasted and prayed. The Bible doesn't tell us what she was praying and fasting for, but I like to think she was seeking God's wisdom regarding how she should approach the king. I like to think she prayed for His favor and protection when she went to the king, and that the king would be compassionate toward her and her people.

Jesus taught his disciples that some things can only come out through prayer and fasting (see Mark 9:29). Throughout the Bible, we see fasting from food as an act of expressing grief, repentance, or a request for God to move powerfully in the person's own life or in the lives of others. Fasting has a spiritual purpose, one in which we want God to move powerfully and make our worlds right. Wesley Duewel says, "Fasting in the Biblical sense is choosing not to partake of food because your spiritual hunger is so deep, your determination in intercession so intense, or your spiritual warfare so demanding that you have temporarily set aside even fleshly needs to give yourself to prayer and meditation."[132]

Jesus and Paul both fasted and prayed before they began their own ministries. Moses fasted and prayed for forty days several times. David fasted and prayed when he was surrounded by his enemies, when he was grieved by his sin, and also for the life of his dying infant son. Daniel fasted and prayed for twenty-one days for spiritual insight and revelation. Nehemiah fasted and prayed for months–first in grief, and then for favor before he approached the king and went to work rebuilding the walls of Jerusalem. And the early church leaders fasted and prayed before sending out Barnabas and Paul as their first missionaries.

Sometimes entire groups or nations would be commanded to fast together, praying in one accord. The Ninevites all fasted in repentance of their sin after Jonah brought them God's message. The Israelites prayed and fasted together when King Jehoshaphat and King Jehoiakim called for a fast. The prophets Jeremiah and Joel and Ezra the priest also encouraged a collective fast. Esther invited her maids and all the Jews in her kingdom to join her in prayer and fasting before she went to the king.

You don't have to fast when you see injustice around you, but it is a beautiful spiritual discipline that can help you grow in your prayer life and spiritual growth when pursued with wisdom and discernment. Throughout the Bible we see fasting as giving up food for a specific period of time, but you can choose to fast from a source that is comforting or a coping mechanism for you, so that you can seek more of God and God's heart. Some people may choose to fast from TV or social media or from a particular food or drink. You can fast anytime you feel led and pray for anything that is on your heart. If you are new to the practice of fasting from food, I encourage you to read a book or articles about how to fast, especially if you have any health concerns, so that you fast with wisdom and medical guidance.

Esther chose to pray and fast, and in doing so, she was able to let go of her comfortable lifestyle and be filled with God's heart for His people, so she could move forward in faith and action. Fasting was a powerful tool in her prayer arsenal to help her defeat the enemy. We can only do so much in our own human strength, but empowered by the Holy Spirit and following the will of God, we can do mighty works for God and His people.

As we fast and pray, our hearts become aligned with God's heart not just for us, but for all His people and His purposes, and God will give us wisdom as to what to do next when we ask for it.

Take Action

After a time of humble prayer and fasting, Esther takes wise action. She invites the king and Haman to a feast she helps prepare. Full of faith, she approaches the king, humbly inviting, "If it please the king, let the king and Haman come today to a feast that I have prepared for the king" (Esther 5:4b ESV).

Esther didn't just pray for the situation to change. She didn't just hope and pray that the Jews would be saved or order her staff to make the meal themselves. She rolled up her sleeves and she got involved in the preparations for the feast. She appealed to her husband the king by first inviting him to dinner, and then, in that prepared venue, revealing to her husband what was going on. As she appealed for the lives of the Jews, she exemplified the words of Proverbs 31:8: "Speak up for those who cannot speak for themselves, for the rights of all who are destitute."

Kathy Khang shares, "We don't actually hear from Esther herself until four chapters into the book of Esther. Esther is silent for almost the entire first half of the book bearing her name."[133] But thanks to Mordecai's words, Esther is reminded that she's both in a position of power as the Persian queen and as a Jew herself with a powerful God on her side to speak up.

Kathy continues, "Speaking up is never about creating conflict or being disruptive just to shake things up and leave a mess. Speaking up is always about the gospel–speaking and painting a picture of truth, wholeness, and hope."[134]

When our thoughts and prayers align with God's heart, we are compelled toward compassion and action. We are compelled to advocate for those who may not be able to speak up for themselves. We are compelled to sit with those who are hurting and to listen and love them in their time of need. We are compelled to serve and to help those who are in need without expecting anything back in return.

Dr. Tony Evans urges us, "Injustice must be addressed, and it must be addressed by the church ... We're called not only to do justice (Micah 6:8) but we're called to love kindness."[135]

Over and over in the Gospels, we see that Jesus was moved with compassion, and it led Him to take action. He ate with people society deemed undeserving of love. He saw a hurting body and He healed. He saw crowds of physically and spiritually hungry people and he taught and fed them. Compassion prompts action. Our faith should bear fruit by being prompted toward action when we see a need: "Faith by itself, if it is not accompanied by action, is dead" (James 2:17b).

When author and activist Terence Lester was asked about his views on faith and justice after George Floyd's death, he said:

> The events in 2020 increased my desire to show up on the frontlines like Jesus. If we really think about it, Jesus was a frontline worker. He came close to lepers, healed the sick, and grieved with people who lost loved ones. He was the embodiment of what it means to show up for neighbors struggling with a crisis as it relates to injustice.
>
> Jesus addressed issues of justice not with a highlighter but with his life. In a year full of unprecedented trauma, pain, and historically significant events, the embodiment of this dedication to justice was more vital than ever. Striving for faithful justice is much more than giving talks or writing opinion pieces to highlight critical issues. Instead those striving for faithful justice must focus on real-life work on the ground where it is needed most. Faithful justice means action now.[136]

We need to humble ourselves in prayer and then take whatever action steps God places on our hearts "to act justly and to love mercy and to walk humbly with [our] God" (Micah 6:8b). That may require humbly asking those who are experiencing acts of injustice what we can do to help. Being on the same page with God includes loving the vulnerable and the oppressed, those different from us, and those He puts on our hearts and in our paths, just as Jesus humbly loved and served all those who were around Him.

Scripture Prayers for Justice

I will sing of Your love and Your justice, LORD. May I praise You and live a blameless life. (Based on Psalm 101:1-2.)

Thank You, Lord our God, that Your works of justice are throughout the earth and that You remember Your covenant promises forever. (Based on Psalm 105:7-8.)

You are our Rock, Your works are perfect, and all Your ways are just. You are a faithful God who does no wrong. You are upright and just. (Based on Deuteronomy 32:4.)

Lord, You have shown us what is good and what You require of us. Help me to act justly, to love mercy, and to walk humbly with You, God. (Based on Micah 6:8.)

Thank You, Lord, that You hear the desire of the afflicted. You encourage them and You listen to their cry. You defend the fatherless and the oppressed. (Based on Psalm 10:17-18.)

Help me to not wage war as the world does. The weapons we fight with are not the weapons of the world. On the contrary, they have divine power to demolish strongholds. I demolish arguments, acts of injustice, hatred, division, and every pretension that sets itself up against the knowledge of God. Help me to take captive every thought to make it obedient to Christ. (Based on 2 Corinthians 10:3-5.)

Help me to defend the rights of the weak and the fatherless and to uphold the cause of the poor and the oppressed. Lord, rescue them from the hand of the wicked. (Based on Psalm 82:3-4.)

Help me to do nothing out of selfish ambition or vain conceit. Help me in humility to value others above myself, looking not to my own interests, but to the interests of others. (Based on Philippians 2:3-4.)

Help me to learn to do right, to seek justice, and to defend the oppressed. Help me to take up the cause of the fatherless and to plead the case of the widow. (Based on Isaiah 1:17.)

Lord, help me to speak up for people who cannot speak for themselves and for the rights of the poor and the needy. (Based on Proverbs 31:8.)

Help me to put on righteousness as my clothing, to put on justice as a robe and turban. Help me be eyes to the blind and feet to the lame. May I help the needy and take up the case of the stranger. (Based on Job 29:14-16.)

Chapter 19

Praying for the Church

They devoted themselves to the apostles' teaching and to fellowship, to the breaking of bread and to prayer.

–Acts 2:42

I shared in a previous chapter about having my appendix removed when I was seventeen weeks pregnant with my younger son. But what I didn't share is how our beloved church family kicked into full body-of-Christ mode for our family while I was in surgery and recovery.

After signing the consent forms, I was whisked off to surgery, leaving my husband alone in the waiting room. Tim texted our pastor and our families asking for prayer. He worried and prayed alone in the hospital waiting room until a kind elder from our church came to sit and pray with him, keeping him company.

Church members were praying for us, sending texts, Facebook messages, and emails of support. Our pastor's wife set up a meal train for us so we'd have meals when we returned home, as well as for the entire time of my recovery.

When I awoke from the surgery, it was to an ultrasound technician smiling and showing me on the tiny screen that my baby was fine. Then Tim told me how our church family was rallying around us, praying for us and supporting us in ways we hadn't anticipated.

My mother didn't hesitate to help as well, flying in from another state to assist in taking care of our two-year-old son while I recovered. She got to experience the love and support of our church family when they would stop by to pray, bring meals, fellowship, and praise God right along with us that He had protected me and our baby.

The church that had loved us through every Sunday service and Bible study, who had thrown us a beautiful baby shower to celebrate our first baby's arrival, and celebrated with us the news of our second baby, was also there to love and support us through our time of need.

Praying for an Acts 2:42-47 Church

Peter's Spirit-filled sermon in Acts 2 led to 3,000 people becoming believers and building a community that would grow into the church. They were all united in their commitment to do five activities together: learn from the apostles, fellowship, eat together, pray, and meet the needs of their community (see Acts 2:42-47).

And as if this early church wasn't awesome enough, its impact surely was. They grew together, served each other, praised God, and prayed together, and they experienced favor and daily conversions (see Acts 2:47). Witnesses were "filled with awe at the many wonders and signs performed by the apostles" (Acts 2:43b).

Imagine if all of our churches were like this one in Acts 2. Imagine how it would draw others toward the church and the love of God. While we read in Acts about the beauty of a united church praying for and caring for its members, the book of Acts also demonstrates that we have an enemy at work within the church, leading church members and leaders with differing opinions, beliefs, and priorities to cause division and pain among the believers.

It's natural that a group of sinners with varying personalities, backgrounds, and opinions will find themselves in conflict. We see the disciples in conflict and competition time after time. Jesus' response is to remind His friends of the kingdom of God and to pray for them. The body of Christ is composed of beautiful yet broken people, and though we all should be striving toward wholeness and holiness together, unfortunately church hurt and even abuse can happen.

While we've had plenty of amazing church experiences, my husband and I have also had church friends or leaders who have said or done things to us that left us feeling shocked and hurt. We've watched church members and leaders we loved and respected do or say things that we believed didn't reflect the heart of Christ. We've experienced two church splits, where people we loved and respected reacted in anger and left the church. We've experienced the pain of having some church volunteers not welcoming, loving, or supporting our children due to their neurodivergent needs.

Sometimes we need time and space to heal from our church hurts and abuse that may have occurred in church, to detangle the church's teachings from Christ's, and it is OK to do that. But it's important to remember we were created for and need godly fellowship, sound biblical teaching, and a welcoming place to serve and be served within the body of Christ. In Hebrews 10:25b we are encouraged that we shouldn't give up "meeting together, as some are in the habit of doing, but encouraging one another–and all the more as you see the Day approaching."

It requires prayer and wisdom to know which you need in your current season of life, but whether you're attending a Christ-seeking church or giving yourself time and space to seek God's truth, grace, and healing, the goal is always that we end up closer to the heartbeat, the character, and the will of God.

Erica Wiggenhorn shares about struggles she had with the church and how her friend invited her to pray together for the church. She writes, "The description of the Christian church that we read about in Acts 2:42-47 is most likely a far cry from your church experience ... My friend doesn't shake her fists, upset by the fact that Christians aren't living the way they are supposed to. She bends her knees and invites others to do the same. She realizes it's not her job ... trying to convict them. It's her job–and yours and mine–to intercede for them and invite the Holy Spirit to have His way in their hearts. None of us are fully living the way the early church members did, but we can all move a step closer, and we start by praying."[137]

Praying for Unity Among Believers

Shortly before His death, Jesus prayed one of the longest recorded prayers in the Bible. In written form, He prayed a paragraph of a prayer for Himself, two paragraphs for His disciples, and three for all believers, which includes you and me. He prayed to His Father, "That all of them may be one, Father, just as you are in me and I am in you. May they also be in us so that the world may believe that you have sent me. I have given them the glory that you gave me, that they may be one as we are one–I in them and you in me–so that they may be brought to complete unity. Then the world will know that you sent me and have loved them even as you have loved me" (John 17:21-23).

Jesus' heart was that all the believers would be united in heart and mission, and that by doing so, others would see how powerful God's love truly is. This prayer is so needed today, for unfortunately we see so much division among Christians, fracturing churches, friendships, and even families. This division hurts people and pushes people away from church and Christianity. It can even sadly make people turn their backs on God.

It was during a time in which I was healing from some church hurts that I read Traci Rhoades' beautiful book *Not All Who Wander (Spiritually) are Lost*. Traci's mission is to help us see that no matter our church background or denomination, each church is full of beautiful practices and traditions that lead us closer to the heart of God. While Traci does have a home church, she loves to visit and participate in other denominations' worship services to see what she can learn about God from them. She encourages us to "attend a church expecting to find community and always, always more of Jesus ... The older I get, I realize living out one's faith is a holy marathon. That doesn't mean it has to be boring ... Exploring new spiritual practices has opened my eyes to so many beautiful things. These fresh perspectives point to Jesus. More of Jesus."[138]

Her words were a balm for my hurting and weary heart. Reading Traci's book awakened my heart to see the beauty and purpose in church again and also renewed my desire to pray for it. Traci concludes her book by sharing the prayer of Jesus over the believers from John 17:21, admitting, "I don't know if we'll ever get there, but I long for a day when we can worship with all our Christian brothers and sisters at the same table. From everything I've read, to the conversations I've had, and the various services I've attended, Christ has gotten so much bigger to me. So. Much. Bigger. Dear readers, we are missing out if we don't expand our belief system to learn from Christians who worship in other ways. Is Jesus big enough to help us look beyond our differences? I think so. Lord, help my unbelief."[139]

Praying as a Church

The book of Acts paints a picture of the creation and growth of the early church, while laying out a blueprint of church for us today. It shows us how important it is to be praying together and for each other. This early church was praying together in one accord when the Holy Spirit came on them at Pentecost, and they never stopped praying together after they were Spirit-filled. In fact, there are at least thirty mentions of the believers praying together or for each other throughout the book of Acts.

The disciples and other members of the early church "all met together and were constantly united in prayer" (Acts 1:14b NLT). These disciples, who used to bicker among themselves about who was the greatest, were now joining together to pray to the One they knew was the greatest. While they all were filled with the Holy Spirit and growing in boldness to pursue the ministry paths God had for them, they experienced the benefit of praying together. Praying together helped them grow in unity and in their purpose as they established and grew churches, shared the gospel with others, and faced great persecution.

As their church grew, so did more opportunities to pray with fellow church members. The believers declared, "We will devote ourselves to prayer and to the ministry of the word" (Acts 6:4b ESV), and the rest of the book demonstrates just how much they lived by that declaration.

Prayer precedes almost every major event of the early church—the baptism of the Holy Spirit at Pentecost, multiple healings, earthquakes that released believers from prison, bold preaching, new believers becoming saved and then baptized, and missionaries being sent out to preach the gospel. The believers prayed before making decisions; prayed over new leaders and missionaries; prayed and praised together in times of crisis and persecution; prayed prayers of both thanksgiving and repentance together; prayed forgiveness for those persecuting them; prayed for spiritual growth, miracles, protection, healing, for believers to be baptized in the Spirit, for the gospel to spread, and for their church growth.

The believers prayed fervently, frequently, and specifically for the needs of their fellow believers. They prayed in large gatherings, at prayer meetings in each other's houses, prayed with one or two other believers, in prison, and also prayed individually. They lived in communion with God and each other through prayer. Many times they fasted together while they prayed. They demonstrated their dependence on God, their desire to be united in prayer, and their love of the Lord, despite their different opinions.

God answered their fervent prayers with rapid church growth, boldness, miracles of healing, protection, miraculous releases from prison, and so much more. While God did not protect all of the believers (many of them faced brutal deaths for their faith), the fact that the early believers were willing to die for their faith is yet another testimony to the power of prayer. It does not always change our circumstances, but it does change, strengthen, and embolden the hearts of His beloved believers. God was invited to be central and foundational to every event that unfolded in the early church, and He was listening to and answering those prayers.

How I'd love to have been at one of those prayer meetings!

Meeting Together in Prayer

For many of us, our spiritual life is solitary. We may go to church and to Bible study, but often we pray alone, read our Bibles alone, and carry our burdens alone. Throughout the New Testament, the phrase "one another" is used over a hundred times. The early church did everything together and cared for each other. We are meant to be living our faith together and for each other.

Prayer and Bible reading are both spiritual practices that we can engage in together with those in our church and other faith communities. Jonathan Leeman says, "Let the words and agenda of the Bible reverberate into your individual and corporate prayer life."[140] When we're praying in community and interceding for the needs of others, God's Word gives us the confidence that we are praying in one accord, in agreement with God's Word.

Prayer in and of itself is powerful, but it multiplies in power when many people are joined together in prayer. Jesus tells us, "Truly I tell you that if two of you on earth agree about anything they ask for, it will be done for them by my Father in heaven. For where two or three gather in my name, there am I with them" (Matthew 18:19b-20).

Deuteronomy 32:30-31 adds to Jesus' words, saying, "How could one man chase a thousand, or two put ten thousand to flight, unless their Rock had sold them, unless the LORD had given them up?" I was confused by that verse until I read this explanation by Pastor Ray Stedman: "Logic would tell you that if one could chase a thousand, then two would chase two thousand–a remarkable accomplishment by any measure. But spiritual truth transcends mere logic and arithmetic! The Lord says that when two Christians get together and seek God's power, there is an exponential increase in the effect of their prayers! Two shall put not two thousand, but ten thousand to flight!"[141] When we pray with a prayer partner, we're not making our prayers twice as strong, but rather ten times stronger. Imagine what would happen when we pray as a church!

Our hearts are knit together and our prayers strengthened when we pray together and stand on God's Word together. When I pray with my local Moms in Prayer group, I feel connected not only to these other moms, but to the children and grandchildren we have been praying for in the group. Oftentimes, I haven't even met these children and grandchildren we've been praying for, but I care deeply about them and their well-being as we pray for them and plead God's promises over them, and as I keep them close in my prayers throughout the week.

Corporate prayer provides you with the encouragement and words to grow in your prayer life. It was through prayer with my Bible study ladies that I learned about the practice of praying Scripture. I find myself smiling when I hear my own kids praying using the phrases that my husband or I have prayed with them. I continue to find new topics to pray for and Scriptures to pray by listening to others when they pray. I find new ways to pray for things I've been praying for when I listen to others pray for me or my children or my other prayer requests.

In corporate prayer, we practice interceding for the needs of others. We become aware of the specific needs of others, and we are reminded of the God who holds all these needs in the palm of His hands. Paul urges us that "petitions, prayers, intercession and thanksgiving be made for all people–for kings and all those in authority, that we may live peaceful and quiet lives in all godliness and holiness" (1 Timothy 2:1b-2). Prayer meetings are great places to intercede and pray for your families, your church, your nation, for other nations, for government leaders, for ministries you serve together in, and so much more.

You don't have to attend a prayer gathering to practice praying together. You can call a friend or pray with a family member. Praying with one or two other individuals is powerful, too, and can be a lot less intimidating if praying aloud makes you nervous.

Sharing our hearts, our burdens, and our prayer requests with others can bring peace and comfort in knowing that we're not carrying our burdens alone. James 5:16b tells us to "confess your sins to each other and pray for each other so that you may be healed. The prayer of a righteous person is powerful and effective." When I confessed how much I was struggling in my faith to my Bible study group, it brought my struggles out of the darkness and into the light, and it gave me a group of women who were there to fight for me in prayer. Their prayer was indeed healing, powerful, and effective. Sometimes we find it easier to struggle alone, but there should be no shame in sharing your struggles or prayer requests with godly friends, family members, prayer partners, and church members you trust, and asking others to join you in prayer. We are meant to be encouraging one another and helping each other grow in our faith, and one of the best ways to do that is by praying for one another and with one another.

Scripture Prayers for the Church

Surround me with friends who spur each other on toward love and good deeds. Help us to get together often so we may encourage each other. (Based on Hebrews 10:24-25.)

Help me to pursue righteous living, faithfulness, love, and peace, enjoying the companionship of those who call on You with pure hearts. (Based on 2 Timothy 2:22.)

Provide me with/thank You for friends who stick closer than a brother. (Based on Proverbs 18:24.)

When I'm feeling lonely may I turn to You, remembering Jesus who often withdrew to lonely places to pray. (Based on Luke 5:16.)

I pray for those who believe in You, that all of us may be one, Father ... May we be brought into complete unity to let the world know that You sent us Jesus. (Based on John 17:20-23.)

May each member of our faith community walk in a manner worthy of the calling to which we have been called, with all humility and gentleness, with patience, bearing with one another in love, eager to maintain the unity of Your Spirit in the bond of peace. For we all are part of one body and one Spirit, one hope, one Lord, one faith, one baptism, one God and Father of all. (Based on Ephesians 4:1-6.)

Help our church leaders and pastors to shepherd the flock under their care and watch over them, to eagerly serve and to be godly examples to their flock. (Based on 1 Peter 5:2-3.)

Lord, our God, may Your favor rest upon our pastor(s) and elders. Establish the work of their hands. (Based on Psalm 90:17.)

God of hope, may You fill our church leaders with all joy and peace as they trust in You, so that they may overflow with hope by the power of the Holy Spirit. (Based on Romans 15:13.)

May our church be devoted to Your Word and to fellowship, to the breaking of bread and to prayer. (Based on Acts 2:42.)

Help our church community to tell others about Christ, warning everyone and teaching everyone with all the wisdom You have given us.

Help us to present them to You, perfect in their relationship to Christ. Help us to work hard, depending on Christ's mighty power that works powerfully within us. (Colossians 1:28-29 NLT)

Part 4

Persevering in Prayer

Chapter 20

Persevering in Prayer

Ask and keep on asking and it will be given to you; seek and keep on seeking and you will find; knock and keep on knocking and the door will be opened to you. For everyone who keeps on asking receives, and he who keeps on seeking finds, and to him who keeps on knocking, it will be opened.

–Matthew 7:7-8 AMP

One of the biggest prayer obstacles for many believers is discouragement when our prayers seem to go unanswered. We pray fervently in faith, we pray Scripture, we pray with others, we try new prayer practices, we follow God faithfully, and when the prayers seemingly go unanswered, it can cause us to wonder if our faith isn't strong enough, or if God is even listening, or if God is truly good.

R.A Torrey writes, "God does not always give us things at our first effort. He wants to train us and make us strong by compelling us to work hard for the best things. Likewise, He does not always give us what we ask in answer to the first prayer. He wants to train us and make us strong people of prayer by compelling us to pray hard for the best things." [142]

Jesus shared two different parables that emphasized the fact that we will need to persevere in prayer. In Luke 11 and in Luke 18 we find the stories of two individuals who persevered in asking, seeking, and knocking (Matthew 7:7), reminding us we can and should approach our good heavenly Father with our repeated requests.

And so, in this final chapter, we will focus on a few Bible heroes who learned to persevere in prayer. Since we see the whole picture, including how our Bible heroes stories' end, we forget that they often had to wait and persevere in prayer for a time before they saw God's promises, plan, and purpose shine through. Sometimes years or decades of prayer occurred before the empty womb contained life, the healing occurred, the battle was won, or the promised Messiah arrived. Hebrews 11–also called the Hebrews Hall of Faith–lists numerous examples of men and women of faith. Some of them received what God had promised them, and some who never did in their lifetime receive "all that God had promised. For God had something better in mind for us, so that they would not reach perfection without us" (Hebrews 11:39b-40 NLT). Yet, we see time and time again that our Bible heroes remained steadfast in faith and persevered in prayer.

Persevering in Prayer like Elijah

Sometimes called the prophet of faith and fire by Bible scholars, Elijah performed or was provided for with miracle after miracle in 1 Kings when he prayed. He was fed by both unclean ravens and holy angels, brought a dead child back to life, prayed for the rain to stop and then three years later for it to rain again, and called down God's fire from heaven to prove to the prophets of Baal that God was the one true God in one mighty spiritual showdown.

James writes of Elijah's prayer life, "Elijah was a man just like us. He prayed that it would not rain, and it did not rain for three and a half years. Again, he prayed earnestly and the heavens gave rain, and the earth yielded its crops" (James 5:17-18 BSB). While James correctly asserts that Elijah's prayers were "powerful and effective," (see James 5:16) what James doesn't mention is that Elijah had to persevere in prayer for the rain to return.

At this point, it hadn't rained in three and a half years. Elijah takes his servant up to Mount Carmel, on the same mountain where

Elijah had prayed for God to send down fire from heaven and God immediately answered. He now bends into a posture of humility and prays for God to send down rain.

After praying for rain, Elijah sends his servant to see if it's raining yet. "The servant went and looked, then returned to Elijah and said, 'I don't see anything'" (1 Kings 18:43 NLT). How I can relate to this! How often do we pray for something and don't see anything? How often do we pray and feel like nothing in our circumstances has changed?

God had promised them rain, and Elijah clings to God's promise while he continues to pray. In faith he asks his servant seven times to see if the rain is on its way. We don't know how long Elijah spent in prayer, whether it was a span of minutes, hours, or even days, but he persevered in prayer on that mountain until the sky was black with clouds, wind, and rain (1 Kings 18:45).

We've seen Elijah get discouraged before, but not this time. God had sustained him and provided for him during the famine. His prayer life and his faith had been deepened in the hard and dry season. He knew that God was in control and that the rain would come as God had promised, so he persisted in prayer and watched for rain clouds that would bring the promised rain.

Persevering in Prayer like Hannah

I find Hannah's faith and her prayer life extraordinary. She was loved by her husband and was a woman of great faith, yet she was unable to have children. I don't know how many years she prayed for a child but she didn't give up.

One day at the temple she pours out her soul and her tears before God. She didn't hide her grief or her tears as she shared her heart with God. She made a promise to the Lord that if He gave her a son, she would give that child to God's service. She prayed so passionately that Eli the priest thought she was drunk. She tells him, "I have been praying here out of my great anguish and grief" (1 Samuel 1:16b).

Eli doesn't even know what Hannah has been praying for, but he seems to admire her faith and her prayer life. He responds by telling her to "go in peace, and may the God of Israel grant you what you have asked of him" (1 Samuel 1:17).

She does. Hannah eats and sleeps and worships God, believing and trusting that He is at work. And in time, God does give her a son. She names him Samuel, which means "heard of God." In return, she faithfully honors the promise she made to God. She brings a weaned Samuel to the temple and presents him to Eli. "I prayed for this child, and the LORD has granted me what I asked of him. So now I give him to the LORD" (1 Samuel 1:27-28a).

As Hannah surrenders her child to Eli's care, she praises God in a prayer that for ten verses acknowledges God's greatness, uniqueness, steadfastness, and holiness. Her beautiful prayer of praise ends with an interesting line: that God "will give strength to his king and exalt the horn of his anointed" (1 Samuel 2:10b).

When Hannah prayed this, she lived in the time of judges, in which Israel had no king. Samuel, the son she had prayed for over many years, would become the very one who would appoint and anoint the first kings of the nation–first Saul and then David. It would be through King David's line that "the horn of his anointed"– the Savior–would come.

Perhaps this prophetic line in her prayer was a gift from God, reassuring Hannah that the child she had faithfully prayed for and now dedicated to His service would ultimately lead to the salvation of their people.

Jackie Hill Perry reminds us regarding the pain Hannah experienced while struggling with her infertility and unanswered prayers that "we have a bird's eye view of Hannah's circumstances. We know what she eventually learned–that the Lord who'd closed her womb ... wasn't causing pain aimlessly. He wanted to birth something beautiful in her heart before He allowed it to happen in her womb."[143]

Hannah experienced the pain of infertility year after year not knowing if she would ever be able to have children. If we've read her story, we see the whole picture: she experiences infertility for several years and she goes to God in prayer. God will then enable her to conceive and give birth to her son Samuel, who will do great things for God, the kingdom, and Israel. And as if the gift of Samuel isn't awesome enough, God will bless her with five more children (see 1 Samuel 2:21). God can see our whole picture–the whole timeline–while we can only see what is right in front of us. And sometimes, the whole picture is a lot more incredible than we could ever have asked for or imagined (see Ephesians 3:20).

Persevering in Prayer like Elizabeth and Zechariah

Elizabeth and Zechariah were a godly couple who loved the Lord. Zechariah was a priest and Elizabeth herself was a descendant of Aaron, Moses's brother and the first established priest. The Bible says of them, "Both of them were righteous in the sight of God, observing all the Lord's commands and decrees blamelessly. But they were childless because Elizabeth was not able to conceive, and they were both very old" (Luke 1:6-7).

They prayed for decades for a baby. Elizabeth probably experienced shame from her community and may have struggled with her identity without children to care for. But this couple still faithfully loved and served the Lord. And they continued praying. We know this because when Zechariah was in the Holy of Holies–a once-in-a-lifetime opportunity for a priest–an angel came to him and told him, "Do not be afraid, Zechariah; your prayer has been heard. Your wife Elizabeth will bear you a son and you are to call him John. He will be a joy and delight to you, and many will rejoice because of his birth, for he will be great in the sight of the Lord ... He will be filled with the Holy Spirit even before he is born. He will bring back many of the people of Israel to the Lord their God ... to make ready a people prepared for the Lord" (Luke 1:13-17).

The name John means "God is gracious," and that's what He must have seemed like to this couple who persevered in prayer and kept their faith. While Elizabeth and Zechariah fervently prayed for a baby, God was molding Elizabeth into a strong woman of faith who would be able to encourage her young relative Mary. God was molding this couple into the loving parents who would be able to teach John about self-denial, trusting in God's promises, and remaining faithful through the hard times.

God answered this couple's prayer not in their timing but His own, to show that this was no normal baby or conception. Regarding her miraculous pregnancy, Elizabeth declares, "The Lord has done this for me ... He has shown his favor and taken away my disgrace among the people" (Luke 1:25). No one would be able to doubt that this baby was a miracle, an answer to the bold and persistent prayers of a couple who faithfully served and trusted in the Lord.

As you persevere in prayer, think of the words of the angel, and replace Zechariah's name with your own. "Do not be afraid _____; your prayer has been heard" (Luke 1:13a). Trust that God is faithful, even when you don't see Him answering your prayers. He's listening and He's at work.

Persevering in Prayer like Anna

I'm grateful for Luke and his heart to include women throughout his Gospel because we learn about yet another incredible woman connected to the birth of Christ in Luke 2:36-38. We know she was widowed after only seven years of marriage. We also know she is now eighty-four, and we can assume she had no children, for a young widowed mother would not have the opportunity to worship at the temple night and day after her husband's death, as the Scriptures imply.

What we mostly learn about her is that she loves God with all her heart. In Luke 2:37b we are told, "She never left the temple but worshiped night and day, fasting and praying."

With no one else to care for or worry about, she had the time and the heart to spend the remainder of her life worshiping, serving in the temple, fasting, and praying. She didn't fit prayer into little pockets of her day; prayer was her life.

I wish I knew what she prayed about for decades at the temple. I like to imagine she clung to the Scriptures promising a Messiah and she prayed that their Savior would come soon. Maybe she prayed that she would have the honor of seeing Him in her lifetime. Regardless, after decades of prayer and worship and fasting and prophesying, God rewarded her faith and devotion by giving her the privilege of laying eyes on the Savior of the world, cradled in His young mother's arms at the temple for His dedication. I wonder if Anna got to touch His little hands or His tiny face. Or to hold Him in her arms as Simeon did in Luke 2:28. I can't imagine the joy she felt at experiencing the presence of the tiny Savior of the world–the answer to her prayers–right there within her grasp.

She recognized the Savior and had such joy at seeing Him that she began to tell everyone about Him, making her one of the first evangelists in the gospels. She had prayed and prophesied faithfully, and now she had seen the promised Christ child. Her heart was so overflowing with joy and truth that she had to share with others.

Persevering in Prayer like Paul

Paul did incredible work planting the early churches, leading thousands to Christ, and writing letters that would comprise nearly two thirds of the New Testament. His life and actions are impressive, but what I am most impressed by is his prayer life.

Every letter he wrote was filled not only with teaching, encouragement, and instruction, but also the prayers he was praying for individuals and for churches. His words indicate he didn't pray for them from time to time but continually:

- "Without ceasing, I mention you always in my prayers" (Romans 1:9b-10a ESV).
- "I give thanks to my God always for you" (1 Corinthians 1:4a ESV).
- "We have not ceased to pray for you" (Colossians 1:9a ESV)
- "I remember you constantly in my prayers night and day" (2 Timothy 1:3b ESV).

Paul's letters are filled with mentions of the prayers he was praying continually for those in his letters. Paul loved being with, investing in, and encouraging people and churches. And when he couldn't physically be with them, he was still ministering to them and encouraging them through his letters and his constant prayers. And his ministry with them didn't end when he was away from them. He was still investing in them and encouraging them through his prayers. His prayers were as important to his ministry as physically being with them.

When we consider Paul's background, Janet Holm McHenry writes, "Paul's characteristics could have been controlling and bossy. Formerly a fanatical persecutor of Christians, he could have created drama. Instead, we see that prayer was a priority for him, and the content of his prayers was focused on others' well-being ... A strong-minded personality can be competitive, but Paul's prayers show he simply wanted God's best for them. That's a mark of an intercessor, someone who is outwardly focused."[144]

Paul believed in prayer and he lived a life of prayer, exhorting those he addressed in his letters to be "praying at all times in the Spirit" (see Ephesians 6:18 ESV), to "continue steadfastly in prayer" (see Colossians 4:2 ESV), "be constant in prayer" (see Romans 12:12 ESV), and "pray without ceasing" (1 Thessalonians 5:17 ESV).

Paul knows prayer isn't always easy. He prayed in prison and during house arrest. He experienced shipwrecks, hunger, and beatings. He calls prayer "wrestling" or "laboring earnestly" (depending on the translation) in Colossians 4:12.

But he finds prayer worth the effort. Worth pursuing and persevering in. Paul could encourage others to pray without ceasing because he did the same, praying continually for those he loved.

Persevering in Prayer like Jesus

Jesus is the author, perfector, and finisher of our faith. He is the One who made it possible for us to pray, so I find looking at Him the perfect way to conclude our time together.

Jesus demonstrated how important it was to pray. He prayed in the wilderness. In the early mornings. In lonely places. He prayed for God's will to be done. For God's kingdom to come. For all believers to be united as one (see John 17). He prayed for His beloved disciple Peter, who He knew was going to deny Him soon (see Luke 22:31-32).

He prayed the most beautiful, humble prayer in an olive grove on the hardest night of His earthly life: "Father, if you are willing, take this cup from me; yet not my will, but yours be done" (Luke 22:42). He prayed in that garden, wrestling His will into alignment with God's, a process that led Him to sweat blood and confess to His sleepy disciples the deep anguish He felt.

While his disciples slept, oblivious to what was to come, Jesus persevered in prayer. But He wasn't alone. In the next verse we learn that "an angel from heaven appeared to him and strengthened him" (Luke 22:43). God's grace was with Him through an angel, comforting and strengthening Jesus so that He could get up and face the arrest and the death that He knew was coming. A death He went to willingly and obediently for our sake.

And as if Jesus didn't do enough for us on the cross (gifting us salvation and freedom from sin's entanglement, access to God through prayer, and providing us with the Holy Spirit), Romans 8:34 tells us, "Christ Jesus who died–more than that, who was raised to life–is at the right hand of God and is also interceding for us."

Jesus has been praying for us for centuries, first on earth and now in heaven, seated at the right hand of the Father (see Mark 16:19). He will continue to intercede for us until the end of the world when all Christians will be gathered and will worship around God's throne.

Now, we can pray for ourselves and others with confidence and authority in His powerful name. May we embrace a life of prayer–getting on the same page with God–as Jesus both demonstrated and made possible for us.

Scripture Prayers to Persevere in Prayer

Thank You that we can confidently approach Your throne, that if we ask anything according to Your will You hear us. (Based on 1 John 5:14.)

Lord, I am so thankful that since the first day that I set my mind to gain understanding and to humble myself before You, my words were heard by You and You have come in response to them. (Based on Daniel 10:12.)

Help me to continue steadfastly in prayer and to be watchful in prayer with thanksgiving. (Based on Colossians 4:2 ESV.)

Help me to pray in the Spirit on all occasions with all kinds of prayers and requests. Help me to be alert, to keep on praying for all the Lord's people. (Based on Ephesians 6:18.)

Jesus, help me to remember that I should pray and not lose heart. Help me to have a prayer life more like Yours. (Based on Luke 18:1, Luke 5:16.)

Thank You for bending down to listen to my prayers. May I pray as long as I have breath! (Based on Psalm 116:2 NLT).

God, our glorious Father, and our Lord Jesus Christ, may You give me the spirit of wisdom and revelation as I continue to read Your Word, and may I grow in my practice of praying Scripture so that I may know You and Your heart better. I pray that the eyes of my heart may be enlightened so that I may know the hope to which You have called me, the riches of Your glorious inheritance in the saints, and Your incomparably great power for all of us who believe. Thank You that the same power that raised Jesus from the dead is in me! May this resurrection power bring new life to my heart, my faith, and my prayers. (Based on Ephesians 1:17-20.)

Acknowledgements

Writing can be a lonely task, but this book is in your hands thanks to the encouragement and support of so many that God generously brought into my life.

First and foremost, to God who taught me everything you read within these pages and so much more. I have yet to decide if it's cheesy to mention God in the acknowledgements section or should be required of all Christian writers who co-author a book with Him, but all I know is that I must. I would have been content to not share my struggles and lessons learned onto a blank page for the world to read. But God had other plans. Thank You, Heavenly Father, for the joy, the struggle, and the journey of co-creating this book with You.

To Tim, who taught me that a changed heart is just as miraculous and just as much an answer to prayer as the miracle I was praying for. You have always supported me and my writing dreams, and I couldn't do this writing thing without you. Thank you for brainstorming ideas with me, designing my website, beautifully formatting this book, and for watching the boys while I jetted off to another writing conference. Love you always and forever.

To my amazing sons, who unknowingly started me on a new path of learning to trust God, to embrace life, and to pray Scripture. Thank you for giving up some "mom time" so I could write or go to writing conferences. You are my greatest joy, and I am so proud to be your mom.

To my parents, thank you for your unwavering love, support, and prayers. Thank you for being my first and greatest prayer warriors. With arms outstretched, your grandsons and I say, "We love you this much."

To Stephanie Buckwalter, thank you for your friendship, prayers, accountability, support, and your extraordinary editing skills. You have a gift for research, editing, and focusing on all the details, and I am blessed that you would so generously share those gifts with me.

To Rebecca Hershberger–my brilliant editor and proofreader–thank you for coming alongside me and bringing out the message of my book with polished clarity and consistency. Thank you for sharing your incredible expertise and for your focus on both the big picture and the little details throughout my manuscript. You are a gem.

To Julie Gaking, Pam Green, Debbie Hara, and Betsey Kodat–amazing prayer warriors, mentors, and beta readers–thank you for thoughtfully reading my manuscript and providing your insight, which helped me refine the message of this book. Thank you for your prayers, your friendship, and your godly example.

To all my amazing beta readers who read specific chapters of this book and shared their honest thoughts and expertise: Cheryl Balcolm, Collene Borchardt, Kristin Bryant, Fern Buszowski, Barb Creager, Darcie Fuqua, Laura Gethers, Jo Hancock, Elizabeth Harlan, Stephen Hiemstra, Elisa Johnson, Kimberly Kravolic, Lynda Lantz, Donnell Parks, Ryan Parks, Angela Prentkiewicz, Traci Rhoades, Tim Soehnlin, Nora Tatina, and Joy Yancy. Thank you for ensuring my message was clear and my theology sound.

To Stephanie Miller, I'm so thankful for your friendship, editing expertise, coaching, and encouragement. Thank you for providing your insight and helpful next steps when I felt overwhelmed or stuck in my writing journey.

To all those who said yes to endorsing this book, thank you. I am so thankful for your ministry, and I'm honored and thrilled you were willing to join me in mine. Thank you for backing this book and for your kind words.

To Angelica, Anne, Julie, Maria, and Michelle, thank you for your prayers on second Tuesdays and for your prayers on the days in between. Your intercession and friendship have meant so much to me, and I'm so thankful God brought you into my life.

To my Moms in Prayer prayer warriors, thank you for praying for my children and giving me the honor of praying for yours. I am so grateful for your friendship and for our Monday mornings in prayer as we lift each others' children and grandchildren up to the throne of God.

To my Wednesday morning Bible study ladies, thank you for your friendship, your prayers, and for sharing your lives, experiences, and wisdom. Wednesday mornings are my favorite because of you.

To all my family and friends who have loved and supported me, asked about how the book/writing thing was going, and encouraged me to keep writing, thank you. Having friends and family members like you cheering me on is such a blessing.

And to you dear reader, thank you for reading this book. I'm honored to have you join me in this journey of embracing a life of praying Scripture. I pray that you, your faith, and your prayer life will be blessed as your prayers are shaped by Scripture.

Discussion Questions

Chapter 1: The Power of Praying Scripture

1. What have been some struggles or doubts you've experienced in your own prayer life?
2. When have you experienced God answer your prayers in a powerful and/or personal way?
3. What is your experience with praying Scripture?
4. How do you feel about the idea that God moves mountains in our hearts and minds?
5. Have you experienced God move a mountain in your heart or in your mindset as your heart was aligned with His?

Chapter 2: Benefits of Praying Scripture

1. What Scripture do you find yourself praying often? How has it helped your prayer life?
2. Have you been using both of the spiritual weapons of prayer and God's Word strapped together? How do you think doing so will empower your prayer life?
3. Have you had a Scripture (or several) that has changed your heart and helped you to bear more fruit? What verses were they?
4. Have you ever had a Scripture come to mind when you really needed it? How did it help you?
5. What other benefits of praying God's Word have you experienced or hope to experience?

Chapter 3: Praying with the Father, Son, and Holy Spirit

1. How does knowing that the whole Trinity is united in your praying life encourage you to persevere in prayer?
2. How do you tend to view God when you pray? How does knowing He is a generous Heavenly Father help you pray?
3. How do you tend to view Jesus when you pray? How does knowing His various roles in your prayer life encourage you to pray?
4. How do you view the Holy Spirit? How does knowing His roles in your prayer life encourage you to pray?
5. How do you view the Holy Bible? How does its role in your prayer life encourage you to pray?

Chapter 4: The Practice of Praying Scripture

1. How did reading about George Mueller's approach to praying Scripture make you feel? Why?
2. What topic/areas of your life do you want to grow in praying Scripture? How will you find more Scriptures to pray relating to that topic/area?
3. Do you pray Scripture during your Bible reading time/practice *lectio divina*? How has it helped you, or how do you think it could help you as you engage in this spiritual practice?
4. Do you listen to God's Word being read aloud? If so, how do you/can you incorporate praying His Word while listening to it?
5. Which of the prayer practices or habits mentioned in the chapter would you like to try or continue practicing to help you pray Scripture?

Chapter 5: Prayers of Praise and Thanksgiving

1. How often do your prayers include praise and thanksgiving?
2. What are some of your favorite Scriptures that help you understand and appreciate the character of God better? How can you incorporate them into your prayer life?
3. What are you feeling thankful for today?
4. What are you feeling worried about today? How could you pray about that with thanksgiving?

5. Do you find praise, thanksgiving, and acknowledging trust of God's kingdom and character easier to include at the beginning or end of your prayers? Why?

Chapter 6: Prayers of Confession and Salvation

1. Why do you think the heart matters above all else to God?
2. How has God worked in your life to help you experience the power of salvation in your own life?
3. Do you find yourself focusing more on your guilt and shame, or do you find yourself focusing more on the grace of God and feeling like your sin isn't that bad?
4. How can you become a more healthy combination of both, feeling humbled by your sin and forgiven before God, becoming like a well-balanced frosted red velvet cupcake?
5. What is your favorite verse to pray regarding God's grace and the gift of salvation?

Chapter 7: Prayers of Petition and Intercession

1. How does knowing we have a personal God who wants to hear our prayers encourage you to pray?
2. What has been your experience with the Lord's Prayer? How has it helped you to pray?
3. What new information did you learn about the Lord's Prayer? How might that impact your prayers going forward?
4. What strategies do you use to keep track of prayers you want to pray for others? Or what strategies would you like to use?
5. Who or what do you want to be more intentional about praying for and lifting up to God's throne?

Chapter 8: Praying for Spiritual Protection

1. What spiritual battles have you experienced before? How did God help you in that battle?
2. When reading about Old Testament heroes praying during their battles, which one encouraged you the most? Why?
3. Is there a spiritual battle you are currently facing that you can share so others can join you in praying for victory?
4. What piece(s) of armor do you find the hardest to put on? What can you do to make sure you are intentional about putting on the *full* armor of God?
5. What are your favorite Scriptures to pray regarding fighting your spiritual battles?

Chapter 9: Praying for Your Family

1. Have you ever prayed over and through your home? If so, what was that experience like?
2. What practices would you like to put in place to pray more intentionally for your family and your home?
3. How does your family spend time in family worship and prayer? Or what prayer practices would you like to try with your family?
4. What Scriptures do you like to pray for your home?
5. What Scriptures do you like to pray for your family?

Chapter 10: Praying for Your Marriage

1. What has been the biggest challenge/prayer request for you in your marriage?
2. How do you think praying Scripture might help you in your marriage?
3. How have you seen God move in you, your spouse, and/or your marriage as a result of prayer?
4. What is your favorite verse you like to pray for your spouse or with your spouse?
5. What Scripture(s) do you want to claim, pray, and strive to live for your marriage?

Chapter 11: Praying for Your Children

1. When have you found yourself praying most fervently for your children? Why do you think that is?
2. What do you find you focus on the most when it comes to your children? What do you want to focus on more instead?
3. What can you do to show your children you embrace them for who they are? How can you show them you long to help nurture their hearts, their faith, and their God-given gifts and callings?
4. What specific areas would you like to see God move in your child's life and heart? Which Scriptures would you like to claim for your child in those areas?
5. What are some of your favorite Scripture(s) to pray for your children?

Chapter 12: Praying Through the Storm

1. What grief are you experiencing now, and how is that grief impacting your relationship with God?
2. Do you share how you are feeling honestly with God, like David did in the Psalms?
3. What prayer practices have helped you the most when you are struggling with grief or feeling like you are in a storm?
4. What do you feel God is wanting you to embrace in your life, even in your storms?
5. What are your favorite verses related to grief and suffering that help you feel at peace or give you hope?

Chapter 13: Praying "Thy Will Be Done"

1. What things in your heart or in your life do you think God is asking you to release or to surrender to Him?
2. What did you learn or what did you experience when you surrendered something to God in the past?
3. Does Jesus' wrestling with God's will in the Garden of Gethsemane encourage you? Why or why not?
4. How do you think experiencing contentedness despite your hard circumstances could help you embrace God's plan for your life?

5. Do you have a favorite prayer or Bible verse that helps you to surrender to God's plan and His will for your life?

Chapter 14: Praying to Fight Fear and Worry

1. What fears and worries are you struggling with? How does it impact your life?
2. What prayer practices help you when you are struggling with fear and worry?
3. Is there anything you feel God is calling you to do to get help with your worries or anxieties? (Ex: focus on His Word, talk to a friend, see a counselor, ask for help with a task that overwhelms you, etc.)
4. What is your favorite way to fix your mind on God's truths when it starts whirling with worry, fear, and/or anxiety?
5. What are your favorite verses to pray regarding worry and fear?

Chapter 15: Praying for Your Purpose

1. How do you feel about gift giving? How does the idea of gift giving change your perspective on using your gifts and talents for God's kingdom?
2. What gifts and talents do you believe God has blessed you with? How are you using them, or how would you like to use them to bless others?
3. What spiritual gifts has God blessed you with? (If you do not know, you may want to find an online spiritual gifts assessment.) How are you using them, or how would you like to use them to bless others?
4. What work has God called you to do? Do you find it easy or challenging to faithfully and obediently pursue that work?
5. Do you find yourself more like Mary or like Martha when serving and when in prayer? How can you be more intentional about spending more time in His presence?

Chapter 16: Praying for Your Words

1. Do you lean toward speaking grace, avoiding sharing the truth with people who need it? Or do you lean toward speaking truth without as much grace as you could be using?

2. In which areas do you lean toward grace or truth the most? (Ex: Do you lean more toward grace or truth in your marriage? With your children? With your other family members? With friends? With strangers? With coworkers? On social media?)

3. What do you think are your motivations for leaning toward either grace or truth more than the other? (Is it the way you were raised? Is it a defense mechanism? Do you lean toward one or the other for attention or approval?)

4. Have you ever spoken or prayed blessings over someone? Who would you like to speak blessings over?

5. What are some favorite Scriptures you can pray regarding the words you speak?

Chapter 17: Praying for Healing

1. What has been your experience with God's healing power?

2. Scripture invites us to "... pour out your hearts like water to the Lord. Lift up your hands to him in prayer ..." (Lamentations 2:19 NLT). Take some time to share your heart, your emotions, and your concerns with Him, laying them before Him.

3. What kind of healing does your heart need now? Share with God your wounds and worries. Listen for His voice as He calls you "Daughter/Son" and tells you how much He loves you.

4. Have you experienced any fruit–any spiritual growth–due to praying for healing for yourself or loved ones?

5. Which psalms have brought you the most comfort when you're struggling?

Chapter 18: Praying for Justice

1. Why do you think God's heart is so against injustice?
2. What have been your own experiences with injustice?
3. What stood out to you the most in this chapter? Why?
4. Which of Esther's steps do you need to be more intentional about practicing in your own life regarding the ideas of fighting against injustice?
5. Do you have a particular group of people that are on your heart to care for when you pray against injustice?

Chapter 19: Praying for the Church

1. Why do you think Jesus thought it so important to pray for believers to be united?
2. What have been your favorite positive church experiences?
3. What have been some negative church experiences? What did/is God teaching you about Himself as you heal from your church hurt?
4. Have you experienced celebrating other faith traditions within the Christian church? If so, what did you learn from them?
5. Do you have a group of people you pray with? What have you learned by praying with them?

Chapter 20: Persevering in Prayer

1. What are you persevering in prayer for?
2. What encourages you about knowing that our Bible heroes also persevered in prayer?
3. Which Bible hero encourages you the most to persevere in prayer? Why?
4. What are some of your favorite verses about prayer that encourage you to keep praying?
5. What is your biggest takeaway from reading this book that you want to carry with you as you continue to persevere in prayer?

References

Chapter 1

1. Berndt, J. (2021). *Praying the Scriptures for Your Life: 31 Days of Abiding in the Presence, Provision, and Power of God.* Zondervan. 15.

2. Soehnlin, J. (2018). *Embracing This Special Life: Learning to Flourish as a Mother of a Child with Special Needs.*

3. Foster, R. J. (2009). *Prayer - 10th Anniversary Edition: Finding the Heart's True Home.* Harper Collins. 15.

4. Keller, T. (2016). *Prayer: Experiencing Awe and Intimacy With God.* Penguin Books. 62.

5. Praying Christian Women [@prayingchristianwomen]. (2022, October 22). *Praying Christian Women* [Instagram profile]. Instagram. https://www.instagram.com/p/Cj8Rb6GrHmt.

Chapter 2

6. Sproul, R.C. (2018). *The Prayer of the Lord.* Ligonier Ministries. 14.

7. Whitney, D. S. (2015). *Praying the Bible.* Crossway. 37.

8. Tada, J.E. (2012). *Speaking God's Language: Using the Word of God in Your Prayers.* Rose Publishing.

9. Sorge, B. (2000). *Glory: When Heaven Invades Earth.* Oasis House. 75.

10. Shirer, P. (2015). *The Armor of God [Bible study].* Lifeway Church Resources. 35.

11. Moore, B. (2009). *Praying God's Word: Breaking Free from Spiritual Strongholds.* B&H Publishing Group. 6.

12. Bounds, E. M. (2014). *The Weapon of Prayer.* Merchant Books.

Chapter 3

13. Spurgeon, C. (1891). *"Honey in the Mouth."* Metropolitan Tabernacle Pulpit. Volume 37.

14. Keller, T. [@timkellernyc]. (2015, February 23). *The only person to wake up a king at 3:00 AM for a glass of water is a child* [Tweet]. Twitter. https://twitter.com/timkellernyc/status/569890726349307904.

15. Keller, T. (2016). *Prayer: Experiencing Awe and Intimacy With God*. Penguin Books. 79-80.

16. Miller, P. E. (2017). *A Praying Life: Connecting with God in a Distracting World*. Tyndale House Publishers, Inc. 121.

17. Miller, P. E. (2017). *A Praying Life: Connecting with God in a Distracting World*. Tyndale House Publishers, Inc. 254.

Chapter 4

18. Piper, J. (2023, October 5). *Should I Use the Bible When I Pray?* Desiring God. https://www.desiringgod.org/interviews/should-i-use-the-bible-when-i-pray.

19. Müller, G. (1871). *"How to Study the Bible."* Bethesda Chapel.

20. Torrey, R.A. (2007). *The Power of Prayer and the Prayer of Power*. Cosimo Classics. 81.

21. Müller, G. (1914). *Autobiography of George Muller; or a Million and a Half in Answer to Prayer*. J. Nisbet and Company.

22. Whitney, D. S. (2014). *Spiritual Disciplines for the Christian Life*. Tyndale House Publishers, Inc. 86.

23. *The Prayer Bible: Pray God's Word Cover to Cover*. (2023) Thomas Nelson Publishing.

24. Miller, P. E. (2017). *A Praying Life: Connecting with God in a Distracting World*. Tyndale House Publishers, Inc. 75.

25. Batterson, M. (2011). *The Circle Maker: Praying Circles Around Your Biggest Dreams and Greatest Fears*. Zondervan. 96.

26. Our Daily Bread. (2017, January 5). *Listening to God*. https://ourdailybread.org/article/listening-to-god.

Chapter 5

27. Moms In Prayer International®. https://momsinprayer.org/.

28. Foster, R. J. (2009). *Prayer - 10th Anniversary Edition: Finding the Heart's True Home.* Harper Collins. 87.

29. Ibid. 85.

30. Montgomery, E. (2017, March 24). *How to Use Music Therapy to Help in a Variety of Health Problems.* Peterson Family Foundation. https://petersonfamilyfoundation.org/music-therapy/use-music-therapy-help-variety-health-problems/.

31. Luther, M. (1872). *The Table Talk of Martin Luther.* Pantianos Classics. 340.

32. Nichols, F. (2010). *Every Child Needs a Praying Mom.* Zondervan. 52.

33. Burroughs, D. (2012). *Hunger No More: A 1-Year Devotional Journey Through the Psalms.* New Hope Publishers. 23.

34. Cypress Counseling Center, P.C. *The Link Between Practicing Gratitude and Reduced Anxiety.* (2021, April 16). https://cypresscounselingcenter.com/blog/the-link-between-practicing-gratitude-and-reduced-anxiety.

Chapter 6

35. Foster, R. J. (2009). *Prayer - 10th Anniversary Edition: Finding the Heart's True Home.* Harper Collins. 8.

36. His Vessel Ministries. *God of Order: The Blueprint for Bringing Peace to the Home.* https://www.hisvessel.org/god-of-order.

37. *Put off ... Put on - Life Action.* https://mygospelcity.org/wp-content/uploads/2019/05/PutOffPutOnRevivalWorksheet-bw.pdf. Note: This is not the exact same worksheet provided in class, but it's very similar.

38. Berndt, J. (2021). *Praying the Scriptures for Your Life: 31 Days of Abiding in the Presence, Provision, and Power of God.* Zondervan. 68.

39. Prayers That Avail Much. (2018). *Salvation Prayer.* https://prayers.org/salvation-prayer/.

Chapter 7

40. Müller, G. (1984). *The Autobiography of George Müller.* Whitaker House. 91.

41. Hutchcraft, R. (2021, October 1). *The Store Is Yours! - #9060.* Ron Hutchcraft Ministries. https://hutchcraft.com/a-word-with-you/your-personal-power/the-store-is-yours-9060.

42. Minter, K, et al. (2003). *When You Pray - Bible Study Book with Video Access: A Study of Six Prayers in the Bible.* Lifeway Press. 23.

43. Keller, T. (2016). *Prayer: Experiencing Awe and Intimacy with God.* Penguin Books. 110.

44. Tozer, A. W. (2002). *The Knowledge of the Holy: The Attributes of God: Their Meaning in the Christian Life.* Lutterworth Press. 113.

45. Ibid. 112.

46. Ibid. 113.

47. Minter, K, et al. (2003). *When You Pray - Bible Study Book with Video Access: A Study of Six Prayers in the Bible.* Lifeway Press. 26.

48. Keller, T. (2016). *Prayer: Experiencing Awe and Intimacy with God.* Penguin Books. 114.

49. Stott, J. R.W. (1985). *The Message of the Sermon on the Mount (The Bible Speaks Today Series).* InterVarsity Press. 148.

50. Minter, K, et al. (2003). *When You Pray - Bible Study Book with Video Access: A Study of Six Prayers in the Bible.* Lifeway Press. 33.

51. Keller, T. (2016). *Prayer: Experiencing Awe and Intimacy with God.* Penguin Books. 117.

52. Ibid. 118.

53. Carson, D.A. (2014). *Praying with Paul: A Call to Spiritual Reformation.* Baker Academic. 55.

54. McHenry, J.H. (2024). *Praying Personalities: Finding Your Natural Prayer Style.* Kregel Publications. 78.

55. Foster, R. J. (2009). *Prayer - 10th Anniversary Edition: Finding the Heart's True Home.* Harper Collins. 192-3.

56. Ibid. 191.

57. Miller, P. E. (2017). *A Praying Life: Connecting with God in a Distracting World.* Tyndale House Publishers, Inc. 231.

Chapter 8

58. Kendrick, A. (Director). (2015). *War Room* [Film]. Sony Pictures Home Entertainment.

59. Cowman, L. B. E. (2008). *Streams in the Desert: 366 Daily Devotional Readings.* Zondervan. 127.

60. Shirer, P. (2015). *The Armor of God* [Bible study]. Lifeway Church Resources. 35.

61. Spurgeon, C. H., & Hall, R. (1993). *The Power of Prayer in a Believer's Life.* Emerald Books. 93.

Chapter 9

62. St. Teresa of Avila. (2007). *The Way of Perfection.* Cosimo Classics. 27. Note: This quote is often attributed to Mother Teresa and quoted as, "Prayer is the mortar that holds our house together."

63. Eldredge, J. (2016). *Moving Mountains: Praying With Passion, Confidence, and Authority.* Thomas Nelson. 106.

64. Mother Teresa. (2016, September 2). *Mother Teresa's National Prayer Breakfast Message.* Crossroads Initiative. https://crossroadsinitiative.com/media/articles/mother-teresas-national-prayer-breakfast-message.

65. RK Media. *Dr. James Dobson's Family Talk.* https://rkmedia.co/family-talk?rq=family%20talk.

66. *The Chosen.* https://watch.thechosen.tv/.

Chapter 10

67. Gethers, L. [@lovehardermarriagecoaching] (2022, October 30). *Love Harder Marriage Coaching* [Instagram profile]. https://www.instagram.com/p/CkVb47YuX__/.

68. Berndt, J. (2023). *Praying the Scriptures for Your Marriage: Trusting God with Your Most Important Relationship.* Zondervan. 7-8.

69. Jackson, P. (Director). (2003). *The Lord of the Rings: The Return of the King* [Film]. New Line Cinema.

70. Gethers, L. [@lovehardermarriagecoaching] (2022, July 31). *Love Harder Marriage Coaching* [Instagram profile]. https://www.instagram.com/p/CgrRMl2OpuC/.

71. Jaynes, S. (2019). *Praying for Your Husband from Head to Toe: A Daily Guide to Scripture-Based Prayer*. Multnomah Books. 11-2.

72. Kruger, M. (2022). *5 Things to Pray for Your Spouse: Prayers That Change and Strengthen Your Marriage*. The Good Book Company. 8.

73. Kendrick, A. (Director). (2015). *War Room* [Film]. Sony Pictures Home Entertainment.

Chapter 11

74. Jakes, T. D. (2006). *Mama Made the Difference: Life Lessons My Mother Taught Me*. Penguin. 72.

75. Batterson, M. (2014, April 22). Your Greatest Legacy. *Proverbs 31 Ministries*. https://proverbs31.org/read/devotions/full-post/2014/04/22/your-greatest-legacy.

76. Omartian, S. (2005) *The Power of a Praying Parent*. Harvest House Publishers. 22.

77. Guthrie, N. (2013). *The One Year Praying through the Bible for Your Kids*. Tyndale House Publishers, Inc. xi-xii.

78. Berndt, J. (2020). *Praying the Scriptures for Your Children 20th Anniversary Edition: Discover How to Pray God's Purpose for Their Lives*. Zondervan. 39.

Chapter 12

79. Banks, J. S. (1877). *Martin Luther: The Prophet of Germany*. 123.

80. Evans, T. [drtonyevans]. (2017, March 23). *It often takes the darkness of a storm to show us the light of God's presence* [Tweet]. Twitter. https://twitter.com/drtonyevans/status/844941823441190912.

81. Warren, T. H. (2021). *Prayer in the Night: For Those Who Work or Watch or Weep*. InterVarsity Press. 47.

82. Rothschild, J., et al. (2023). *When You Pray - Bible Study Book with Video Access: A Study of Six Prayers in the Bible*. Lifeway Press. 115.

83. Whitney, D. S. (2015) *Praying the Bible*. Crossway. 54.

84. Rothschild, J., et al. (2023). *When You Pray - Bible Study Book with Video Access: A Study of Six Prayers in the Bible*. Lifeway Press. 118.

85. Ibid. 120.

86. Foster, R. J. (2009). *Prayer - 10th Anniversary Edition: Finding the Heart's True Home*. Harper Collins. 45.

87. Piper, J. (2017, March 10). *Embrace the Life God Has Given You*. Desiring God. https://www.desiringgod.org/embrace-the-life-god-has-given-you.

Chapter 13

88. Ingram, C. (2013). *True Spirituality: Becoming a Romans 12 Christian*. Simon and Schuster. 44

89. Yee, A. (2019, March 26). *God Must be the Hero*. Desiring God. https://www.desiringgod.org/articles/god-must-be-the-hero.

90. ten Boom, C. (1999). *Reflections of God's Glory*. Zondervan. 9.

91. TerKeurst, L. (2014). *The Best Yes: Making Wise Decisions in the Midst of Endless Demands*. Nelson Books. 92.

92. Foster, R. J. (2009). *Prayer - 10th Anniversary Edition: Finding the Heart's True Home*. Harper Collins. 55.

93. McHenry, J.H. (2024). *Praying Personalities: Finding Your Natural Prayer Style*. Kregel Publications. 79.

94. Dillow, L. (1998). *Calm My Anxious Heart*. Navpress Publishing Group. 12-13.

95. Ibid. 13.

96. Spurgeon, C. H. (2017). *Encouraged to Pray: Classic Sermons on Prayer*. Rich Theology Made Accessible. 69.

Chapter 14

97. Tolkien, J.R.R. (2000) *The Letters of J.R.R. Tolkien*, Carpenter H. (Ed.). Houghton Mifflin, 110.

98. Montgomery, L. M. (2008). *Anne of Green Gables*. G.P. Putnam's Sons. 51.

99. Delegran, L. (n.d.). *How Does Nature Impact Our Wellbeing?* Taking Charge of Your Wellbeing. https://www.takingcharge.csh.umn.edu/how-does-nature-impact-our-wellbeing.

100. Fullerton, W.Y. (1966). *Charles Haddon Spurgeon: London's Most Popular Preacher*. Moody Bible Institute. 197.

101. Tucker, J. (2022). *Breath as Prayer: Calm Your Anxiety, Focus Your Mind, and Renew Your Soul*. Thomas Nelson. 25, 28.

102. Tucker, J. (2022). *Breath as Prayer: Calm Your Anxiety, Focus Your Mind, and Renew Your Soul*. Thomas Nelson. 13-14.

103. Soehnlin, J. [@jennembracinglife]. (2022, July 22.) *Jenn Embracing Life* [Instagram Profile]. https://www.instagram.com/p/CgUEmyHLJXe/.

Chapter 15

104. Berndt, J. (2021). *Praying the Scriptures for Your Life: 31 Days of Abiding in the Presence, Provision, and Power of God*. Zondervan. 160.

105. Popkin, S. (2020). *Comparison Girl*. Kregel Publications. 30-31.

106. Chambers, O. & Reimann, J. (1995). *My Utmost for His Highest: The Golden Book of Oswald Chambers*. Discovery House Publishers. March 5.

107. Weaver, J. (2002). *Having a Mary Heart in a Martha World: Finding Intimacy with God in the Busyness of Life*. Waterbrook Press. 8.

108. Bynes, S. *Seek First the Kingdom*. Kingdom Driven Entrepreneur. https://kingdomdrivenentrepreneur.com/seek. Note: Quoted material is found in downloadable document.

109. Chambers, O. & Reimann, J. (1995). *My Utmost for His Highest: The Golden Book of Oswald Chambers*. Discovery House Publishers. October 17.

110. Boom, C. T. *Clippings from My Notebook*. Thomas Nelson, 1983. 64.

111. Weaver, J. (2002). *Having a Mary Heart in a Martha World: Finding Intimacy with God in the Busyness of Life*. Waterbrook Press. 63.

112. Needham, K. (2023). *Purposefooled: Why Chasing Your Dreams, Finding Your Calling, and Reaching for Greatness Will Never Be Enough*. Nelson Books. 33.

Chapter 16

113. Ortlund, D. C. (2020). *Gentle and Lowly: The Heart of Christ for Sinners and Sufferers*. Crossway. 27.

114. Ordway, Holly. (2022, 6 January). Lessons in Evangelization from the Parables. *Word on Fire*. https://www.wordonfire.org/articles/fellows/practice-patience-prayer-lessons-in-evangelization-from-the-parables/.

115. Khang, K. (2018). *Raise Your Voice: Why We Stay Silent and How to Speak Up*. InterVarsity Press. 34.

116. Clarkson, S. (2022). *Giving Your Words: The Lifegiving Power of a Verbal Home for Family Faith Formation*. Baker Books. 41.

117. Wolgemuth, N. D. (2003). *The Power of Words: A Four Week Devotional Study on Learning to Speak With Wisdom and Grace*. Revive Our Hearts Ministries. 46.

118. Chapman, G. *Discover Your Love Language® - The 5 Love Languages®*. https://5lovelanguages.com/.

Chapter 17

119. Miller, P. E. (2017). *A Praying Life: Connecting with God in a Distracting World.* Tyndale House Publishers, Inc. 2.

120. Swanson, R., Jenkins, D. & Thompson T. (Writers), & Jenkins, D. (Director). (2022, December 18). Two by Two (Season 3, Episode 2) [TV Series Episode]. In Jenkins D. (Executive Producer), *The Chosen.* Angel Studios.

121. Ibid.

122. Ibid.

123. Tada, J. E. (2022, December 18). *I was in tears when I watched this clip from Season 3 of The Chosen* [Video]. Facebook. https://www.facebook.com/ 100000915978680/videos/4751335445637000000000/.

124. Tada, J. E. (2023, October 22). *Where Is My Miracle? What to Do when God Doesn't Answer the Way We Expect.* Bible Study Fellowship Blog. https://www.bsfblog.org/where-is-my-miracle/.

Chapter 18

125. Soehnlin, J. (2019, March 29). *15 Scriptures to Pray for Our Nation.* Embracing Life. https://embracing.life/article/scriptures-to-pray-for-america.

126. Evans, T. *God and Justice and Righteousness.* Sermons.love https://sermons.love/ tony-evans/13057-tony-evans-god-and-justice-and-righteousness.html.

127. Sojourners. (n.d.). *A List of Some of the More than #2000 Verses in Scripture on Poverty and Justice.* Sojourners. https://sojo.net/list-some-more-2000verses-scripture-poverty-and-justice.

128. Porterfield, J. (2002). *Fight Like Jesus: How Jesus Waged Peace Throughout Holy Week.* MennoMedia, Inc. 59.

129. Stevenson, B. (2014). *Just Mercy: A Story of Justice and Redemption.* One World Publishing. 14.

130. Duewel, W. L. (2018). *Touch the World through Prayer.* HarperChristian. 92.

131. Ibid. 92.

132. Ibid. 96.

133. Khang, K. (2018). *Raise Your Voice: Why We Stay Silent and How to Speak Up.* InterVarsity Press. 41.

134. Ibid. 130.

135. Evans, T. (n.d.). *God and Justice and Righteousness* [Video]. Sermons.love. https://sermons.love/tony-evans/13057-tony-evans-god-and-justice-and-righteousness.html.

136. Lester, T. et al. (n.d.). *Five Authors Discuss Black History, Faithful Justice, and Hope for the Future*. InterVarsity Press. https://www.ivpress.com/pages/content/five-authors-discuss-black-history-faithful-justice-hope-for-the-future.

Chapter 19

137. Wiggenhorn, E. (2016). *An Unexplainable Life: Recovering the Wonder and Devotion of the Early Church (Acts 1-12)*. Moody Publishers. 63.

138. Rhoades, T. (2020). *Not All Who Wander (Spiritually) Are Lost: A Story of Church*. Church Publishing. 112.

139. Ibid. 128.

140. Leeman, J. (2011) *Reverberation: How God's Word Brings Light, Freedom, and Action to His People*. Moody Publishers. 170.

141. Stedman, R. C. (1997). *Talking with My Father: Jesus Teaches on Prayer*. Discovery House. 101.

Chapter 20

142. Torrey, R.A. (1983) *How to Pray*. Whitaker House. 50-51.

143. Perry, J.H. et al. (2003). *When You Pray - Bible Study Book with Video Access: A Study of Six Prayers in the Bible*. Lifeway Press. 59.

144. McHenry, J.H. (2024). *Praying Personalities: Finding Your Natural Prayer Style*. Kregel Publications. 90.

About the Author

Jenn Soehnlin (pronounced like 'not insane' + lin) is a wife, mother of two boys, and writer of hope-filled words about faith, praying Scripture, and navigating special needs parenting.

She is the author of *Embracing This Special Life* and a contributing author to the devotional collection *Life Changing Stories* and the *Prayers for Writers* handbook.

Jenn also finds joy in spending time with her family, reading several books at a time, savoring coffee shop chats with friends, and exploring nature's wonders.

To connect with Jenn–and find additional praying Scripture resources–visit www.embracing.life